Computer Fundamentals, Architecture, and Organization

Computer Fundamentals, Architecture, and Organization

Edited by

**Dr. Rahul Sharma, Dr. Manish Saxena,
Dr. Anita Soni and Dr. Urmila S. Soni**

ARCLER
PRESS

www.arclerpress.com

Computer Fundamentals, Architecture, and Organization

Edited by: Dr. Rahul Sharma, Dr. Manish Saxena, Dr. Anita Soni and Dr. Urmila S. Soni

Arcler Press
4164 Lakeshore Road
Burlington, ON L7L 1A4
Canada
www.arclerpress.com
Email: orders@arclereducation.com

ISBN: 978-1-77956-953-0 (Hardcover)

ABOUT THE AUTHOR

Dr. Rahul Sharma, working as Assistant Professor – Senior Scale in the Department of Artificial Intelligence & Machine Learning, at Manipal University, Jaipur, Rajasthan. Prior to that he has more than 8+ years of teaching experience in several universities and engineering colleges as Assistant Professor in Department of Computer Science and Engineering at Parul Institute of Technology, Parul University Vadodara, Gujarat, Chameli Devi Group of Institution, Indore and Dr. A.P.J. Abdul Kalam University, he completed B.E. (CSE) from Patel College of Science and Technology, Indore (M.P.) and M.Tech (NM&IS) from SCSIT, DAVV, Indore (M.P.), PhD degree in Computer Science and Engineering from Rabindranath Tagore University Bhopal (M.P.). His research includes Computer Network, Network Security, Cryptography, Data Mining and Web Programming's. He is having 20+ research publications in reputed international journal, International- National conferences and 6 - patents (3 published- 3 Registered). He also has qualified GATE (CSE) in 2015. He is publishing more than 30+ books in the field of computer science and Engineering.

Prof. Manish Saxena, working as Professor in Department of Computer Science and Engineering at Bansal Institute of Science and Technology Bhopal India M.P. he has more than 21+ years of teaching experience in several engineering colleges. He has completed His academic qualifications include Master in Technology (M.Tech.) from MANIT Bhopal, B.Tech. From Amravati University Maharastra. Ph.D. perusing in Electronics and Communication Engineering. His research includes Optical Communication, VLSI. He is having 21 + research publications in reputed International journal, International- National conferences and 2 - patents (1 published- 1 Registered).

Dr. Anita Soni Professor Computer Science Department, IES University, Bhopal. I am in Teaching field since more than 19 years and extensively working in Operation Research & Optimization Field, Having 6 Patents (4 Design Patent), 6 Book chapters and 11 papers in different reputed journals. Anita is a member of different Professional Society & Member of Editorial Board of many international Journals. Strong interpersonal and problem solving skills with logical reasoning.

Dr. Urmila S Soni, working as a Professor in the faculty of Engineering & technology, at the SAM Global University, Bhopal, MP, India. She is having more than 18years of teaching experience in various institutions and currently handling the position of Director-IQAC in the same organization. She is having more than 10 years of research experience. She completed B.E. from Electronics & Telecommunication Engineering from North Maharashtra University Jalgaon, & M.Tech specialization in Instrumentation & Control from Chhattishgarh Swami Vivekananda Technical University,(CSVTU)Bhilai , Chhattishgrah. She also awarded PhD in Electronics &Telecommunication Engineering from the CSVTU, Bhilai. Her research area focuses on Smart Grid, Micro Grid, Renewable Energy, Wireless Communication & Internet of Things. She has published more than 25 research papers in various journals of repute and conferences and having 6 design patents. She is having rich experience in accreditation and giving her services, guidance and support to various universities for NBA & NAAC preparation as an expert.

TABLE OF CONTENTS

LIST OF FIGURES

LIST OF TABLES

PREFACE

In today's digital age, understanding the fundamental principles of computer architecture and organization is vital. In the digital era, a solid understanding of computer fundamentals and architecture is essential for anyone pursuing a career in computer science, information technology, or electronics. This book, *Computer Fundamentals, Architecture, and Organization*, is designed to provide a balanced blend of theoretical knowledge and practical exposure for students, educators, and aspiring professionals.The book begins with the basics of computing its definition, characteristics, capabilities, and limitations. It explores the evolution of computers across different generations and describes various types such as digital, analog, micro, mini, mainframe, hybrid, and supercomputers. Current technologies like smart systems, embedded systems, GIS, and cloud computing are also introduced to help readers understand modern computing environments. The book provides a detailed understanding of input and output devices. Devices such as keyboards, scanners, webcams, monitors, printers, and touchscreens are explained along with their working principles. The memory section covers internal and external memory types, helping learners grasp how data is stored, accessed, and managed in computing systems. A strong emphasis is placed on digital electronics and binary systems. Logic gates, number systems, binary arithmetic, and digital circuits like adders, multiplexers, decoders, and flip-flops are explained in a simple and structured way. This section builds the foundation needed to understand the working of modern computing devices. The book further delves into the internal structure of a computer, including the control unit, registers, instruction formats, and instruction cycles. Concepts such as micro-operations, addressing modes, machine and assembly language are thoroughly covered to build a deep understanding of processor operations. Advanced topics like RISC vs. CISC architectures, stack organization, pipelining, and instruction execution flow are presented to prepare readers for higher-level study. It also includes memory hierarchy, I/O interfaces, DMA transfer, and interrupt systems. Practical sections on microprocessor experiments and binary programming tasks help reinforce learning through real-world application. This book is intended to serve as a complete academic guide and practical reference, equipping readers with the knowledge and skills required to understand and work with modern computer systems.

CHAPTER 1

FUNDAMENTALS OF COMPUTERS

Contents

- Bridge the fundamental concepts of computers with the present level of knowledge of the students.
- Students will be able to express basic computer hardware.
- Will be able to distinguish computer types and basic concepts.
- Identify how software and hardware work together to perform computing tasks and howsoftware is developed and upgraded

1.1. COMPUTER ESSENTIALS: DEFINITION & SCOPE

The term "computer" is derived from the Latin word '*computare*' which translates to 'to compute.' Formally it can be defined as follows:

- Computer is an electronic device that manipulates information, or data. It has the ability to store, retrieve, and process data. You probably already know that you can use a computer to type documents, send email, play games, and browse the Web. You can also use it to edit or create spreadsheets, presentations, and even videos.
- With the advancement of technology day by day, computers are now not just limited to perform calculations or play videos. They have evolved in many sectors of human life and doing all those activities that humans can do. Even faster and with zero errors.

1.1.1. Capabilities of Computer

- Computer helps in performing any task repeatedly in the easiest and most efficient way.
- Computer helps us to connect to the internet.
- Computer increases productivity.
- Computer assists us to organize and visualize vast amount of data most efficiently.
- The computer keeps us connected with all the information as well as our loved ones.

1.1.2. Characteristics of the Computer

1. **Speed:** Due to multitasking ability of computer, the speed must be also maintained. Computers can handle and process trillions of instructions sets, at a time. With this speed, tasks are completed on or before time.
2. **Time Saving:** The speed of the computer is specified in terms of Nano seconds and in Pico seconds. The functioning of computer as compared to humans is very fast in terms of speed.
3. **Accuracy:** Computers are highly reliable in terms of maintaining accuracy. Computer is that can perform not only calculations but also with accuracy. They can handle the most complex calculations easily and give an error-free solution.

4. **Multitasking:** Computers can perform various tasks at the same time. This is very advantageous feature of Computer. For example, you can work on MS word and can play songs simultaneously in the background, checking your emails on the side. Such multitasking can only be performed by a computer.

5. **Automation:** Computer is an automatic machine. There is no need to keep a constant check on computers, they are completely automated. Automation is the ability to perform a given task automatically.

6. **Data Storage Capability:** A computer can store huge amount of data. Huge storage space becomes a necessity, with the advent of large amount of digital data. Computers complete this necessity. The files can be stored and accessed quickly and efficiently.

7. **Security:** With so much information being stored digitally, the data must remain secured and out of reach from frauds. A computer provides data security by encrypting the data or key management through various applications available online.

8. **Cost-Effective:** Whatever technology is introduced it must be cost-cutting or cost-effective. Computers are one such thing that helps in reducing wastage and are cost-effective. They have replaced the use of paper on many levels this saves wastage of paper and in turn saves trees, thus beneficial to the environment. Nowadays, many businesses have also switched to online platforms. Products can be sold by creating a website and marketing could be done in the same way.

9. **Connectivity:** The internet is accessible through computers. Everything has now become digital. From online banking to online shopping, everything is now through the internet. This was all possible due to the increased usage of computers.

10. **Creating Employment:** The introduction of computers in many sectors has created job opportunities for millions of people. The IT sector is booming and recruiting people now more than ever. People who could not leave their homes can now work from their homes due to the computer and access to the internet.

11. **Reduction in Paperwork and Cost:** The use of computers for data processing in an organization leads to the reduction in paperwork and results in speeding up the process. As data in electronic files can be retrieved as and when required, the problem of maintenance of a large number of paper files gets reduced. They have replaced the use of paper on many levels this saves wastage of paper and in turn saves trees, thus beneficial to the environment.

12. **Diligence:** A computer is an electronics device. It does not suffer from the human traits of lack of concentration. So, the results will be continuously of the same standard.

13. **No Feelings:** Computers are devoid of emotions. They have no feelings and no instincts because they are machine. Although men have succeeded in building a memory for the computer, but no computer possesses the equivalent of a human heart and soul.

1.1.3. Limitations of Computer

1. **Improper Use:** Although computers were invented to ease the lives of humans, however, they are now being used for just leisure purposes. Kids these days are glued to the screen playing games or using social media platforms. This has created a negative impact on their lives.

2. **Cybercrimes:** The Internet has now become a place of conducting cybercrimes. Stealing personal information, selling illegal products on the dark web, unauthorized access to the bank accounts of people are some of the examples where computers are proving to be a curse.

3. **Unemployment:** With everything being automated computers has replaced humans on a large scale. This has created unemployment in the market.

4. **Virus Attacks and Hacking:** Hackers create viruses to steal the personal information of the user. These viruses can be found in pen drives, movie DVDs, or even mails. Such viruses can also prove to be harmful to the computer can cause a breakdown.

5. **Creating Dependency:** With our lives being dependent on computers, it becomes very difficult to complete tasks without them. If a computer breakdown or the internet server goes down for even a day, all our work will come to a halt.

6. **Impact on the Environment:** So many components are used in the making of a computer most of which cannot be recycled. If the system breaks down or gets old, it is thrown away. Such activities create a negative impact on the environment.

7. **Health Issues:** With long sitting hours, staring blankly into the screens has harmed the health of the people greatly. Spending long hours in front of the screen can cause redness in the eyes, weakening of the eyesight, backache due to a wrong sitting posture, and various such problems. Thus, long usage of computers should be avoided.

8. **Loss of Privacy:** With so much being shared online from banking information to pictures on social media platforms our lives are no longer

restricted to just us. While this can be entertaining but to the extent when it is not being invaded by online frauds, hackers, or stalkers.

9. **Lack of Learning:** With all the work being done online, from performing calculations to creating projects. The computer has limited the scope of learning in many ways. Students nowadays no more do their homework on their own, instead seek help online. This has proved harmful to their growing brain.

1.2. GENERATION OF COMPUTERS

Computer performance development and improvement are ongoing, time-bound processes. A new technical advancement has led to the creation of better, more affordable, and smaller computers that are more powerful, quick, and efficient than their predecessors. These computers' development can be divided into the following five generations:

1. First Generation Computers (1940–1956):

- The first computers used vacuum tubes for circuitry and magnetic drums for memory.
- They were often enormous and taking up entire room.
- First generation computers relied on machine language.
- They were very expensive to operate and in addition to using a great deal of electricity, generated a lot of heat, which was often the cause of malfunctions.
- The UNIVAC and ENIAC computers are examples of first-generation computing devices.

2. Second Generation Computers (1956–1963):

- Transistors replaced vacuum tubes.
- Second-generation computers moved from cryptic binary machine language to symbolic.
- High-level programming languages were also being developed at this time, such as early versions of COBOL and FORTRAN.

3. Third Generation Computers (1964–1971):

- The development of the integrated circuit was the hallmark of the third generation of computers.
- Instead of punched cards and printouts, users interacted with third generation computers through keyboards and monitors and interfaced with an operating system.
- Allowed the device to run many different applications at one time.

4. Fourth Generation Computers:
- The microprocessor ushered in the fourth generation of computers, as thousands of integrated circuits were built onto a single silicon chip.
- The technology in the first generation that filled an entire room could now fit in the palm of the hand.
- The Intel 4004 chip, developed in 1971, integrated all the components of the computer, from the central processing unit and memory to input/output controls, on a single chip.

5. Fifth Generation Computers (Present and Beyond):
- Fifth generation computing devices, based on artificial intelligence.
- Are still in development, though there are some applications, such as voice recognition. The use of parallel processing and superconductors is helping to make artificial intelligence a reality.

1.3. TYPES OF COMPUTERS

Types of computers are given in Figure 1.1.

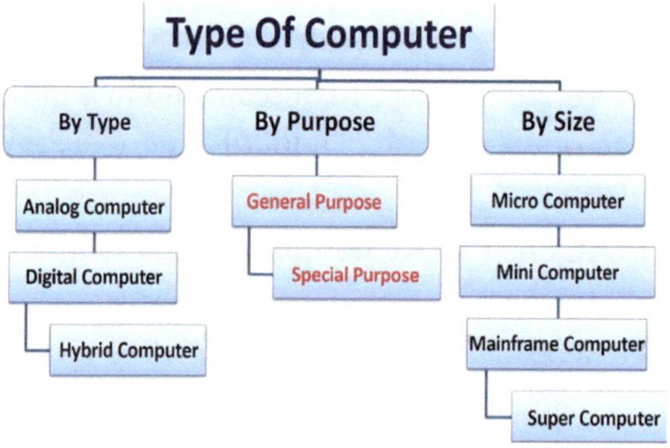

Figure 1.1. Types of computers.

1.3.1. Analog Computer

Analog data is a data that keeps varying. The computers process analog data are categorized as Analog data. It does not have any discrete value. They read the continuous change in the input, process it, and then provide the output. They are slower in comparison to digital computers and also slightly less precise.

Examples of analog computer are – speedometer, thermometer, frequency, and signal of voltage, measuring the resistance of a capacitor.

1.3.2. Digital Computer

Personal computers, laptops, mobile phones, desktops, etc. are an example of a digital computer. These computers process binary input i.e., in the form of 0s and 1s. These computers perform logical and arithmetical operations on the given input and provide output. There are classified according to requirements, size and performance.

Types of digital computers:

- According to requirements or applications:

  Special purpose – to carry out task, which are permanently stored in machine.
  - General purpose – programs are supplied at the time of execution.
- According to size and performance:
  - Embedded computer – for TV, smart watches, washing machines.
  - Microcomputer – microprocessor chip is used instead of CPU.

  Minicomputer.
  - Mainframe computer.
  - Supercomputer.

1.3.3. Microcomputer

The personal computers, laptops, tablets, and mobile phones that we use in our daily life fall under the category of microcomputers. They are single-chip systems. Such computers have the most minimalistic requirement in terms of I/O devices. And have all the circuitry mounted on a single PCB. They are less complex and comparatively inexpensive. Microcomputers are advantageous because they are flexible, portable, and loaded with features. Microcomputers require very little space and are comparatively inexpensive.

Examples: Tablets, iPads, smartwatches, lap-tops, desk-top computers.

1.3.4. Minicomputers

Minicomputer lies between micro and mainframe computers. Those who want to operate the system at the same time. Minicomputers are most popular for its feature of multiprocessing. These types of computers use multiple processors connected to a common memory and the same peripheral devices to perform different tasks simultaneously. These are also known as mid-range computer. They are generally used for applications like engineering computations, data handling, and etc. computers at the billing counters of malls or large institutions (Figure 1.2).

Figure 1.2. *Minicomputer.*

Note: A minicomputer with programmed data processor by Digital Equipment Corporation (PDP-11/40).

1.3.5. Mainframe Computers

The mainframe computers are useful when a large number of people are involved. This is a high-capacity computer. It is primarily used by large organizations where many individuals can utilize it at the same time. A mainframe computer is a large, centralized machine with a lot of memory, a lot of storage space, and many high-end processors; it has a lot of processing power compared to normal computer systems. It is used in fields like health care or the retail sector, where many users want to access data simultaneously. These computers process large amounts of data (Figure 1.3).

Figure 1.3. *Mainframe computers.*

1.3.6. Supercomputers

The biggest and fastest computers are supercomputers. This is the fastest computer category, but it is also the most expensive. A typical supercomputer is capable of performing trillions of functions within a few seconds. Supercomputers have immense RAM, high-speed interconnection among nodes, high file system speed, and more.

Among different computers, supercomputers are mostly used in computational science; supercomputers are also used for a variety of computationally intensive activities in various fields, including quantum mechanics, climate research, and weather forecasting, testing of nuclear weapons (Figure 1.4).

Figure 1.4. *PARAM – India's first supercomputer.*

1.3.7. Hybrid Computers

Hybrid computers are a blend of functionality of both analog and digital computers. These computers perform a high level of calculations. Hybrid computers are quick and efficient. A hybrid computer uses both the qualities of analog as well as digital computers and hence increases accuracy and speeds up the processing. They take input in analog form, convert it into digital form, and then process it to produce an output. They are capable to return accurate results at a fast pace.

For example, they are used in different medical equipment like CT scan, Ultrasound machine, etc., and also in the hospitals to measure the heartbeat of the patients, at research institutes to measure earthquakes and other natural calamities (Figure 1.5).

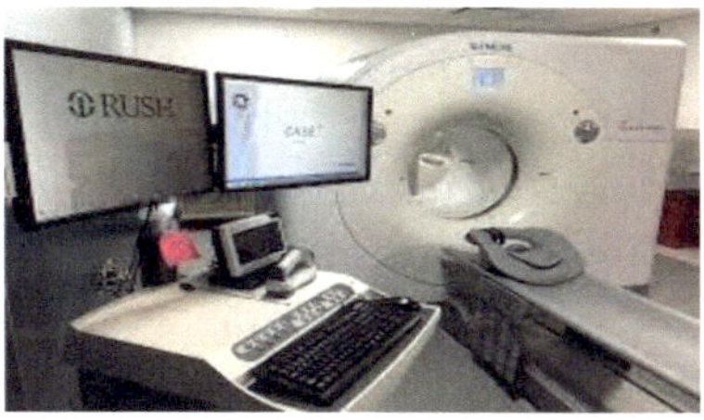

Figure 1.5. *Hybrid computers.*

1.3.8. Some Other Types of Computers

1. **Workstations:** These are one of the high-performance computer types with advanced graphics capabilities, storage space, and a powerful CPU. Workstation computers are for single usage and professional purposes. These are like our basic laptops and desktops but with added superior features.

   For example, double-processor motherboard, added graphic card, etc. The workstations are more powerful as compared to generic PCs. They can handle heavy-duty functions. Like animation, CAD, audio and video, editing, professional gaming, etc. Workstations are typically utilized for scientific and technical tasks that require a lot of computing.

2. **Servers:** These are large data storage and processing devices that exits either as hardware or as virtual storehouses located on the internet. Computers or software systems act as servers that connect to a network.

   A server can be any type of device that shares and saves information. Servers can both store and process information within their own system or request it from another.

   These are hardware components or software programs that are built to assist other computers termed as clients. Together this architecture is called the client-server model. The client sends a request to the server and the server responds in return with a result. This proves that these server computers are more powerful than standard computers.

   The main purpose of these computers is to share data and resources with other computers. Different types of servers are useful for different needs and applications.

Examples: Cloud server, application server, database server, file server. Each of these servers has a different purpose for different client needs.

1.4. SMART SYSTEMS

Now a days, the term "Smart System" means to "self-monitoring, analysis, and reporting systems. It is a technology that uses artificial intelligence, machine learning, and big data analysis to provide cognitive awareness to objects that were in the past considered inanimate.

Smart systems incorporate functions of sensing, actuation, and control in order to describe and analyze a situation and make decisions based on the available data in a predictive or adaptive manner, thereby performing smart actions.

For example, a standard switch vs. a smart switch has the same purpose of turning on and off the appliances, but the smart switch has many other advantages. It can be remotely operated; we can set a routine for it, in case of emergency, it can turn on/ off by itself, etc.

1.4.1. Characteristics of Smart Systems

- Ability to simulate and emulate in near real time;
- Automated learning and machine learning functionalities;
- Digital feedback loops that influence product development;
- Action based on sensory data and algorithms;
- Customized device experience in the cloud;
- True compute on the far edge;
- Adapting tasks based on reprogramming via cloud;
- Ability to predict stresses and failures;
- Detection and resolution of events;
- Total automation;
- Near-real-time, seamless connections across multiple ecosystems;
- Real-time collaborative workflow platform;
- Experimenting as a learning system.

1.4.2. Applications of Smart Systems

1. **Smart System for Homes (Smart Homes):** One of the best and the most practical applications of IoT, smart homes really take both,

convenience and home security, to the next level. Though there are different levels at which IoT is applied for smart homes, the best is the one that blends intelligent utility systems and entertainment together. For instance, your electricity meter with an IoT device giving you insights into your everyday water usage, your set-top box that allows you to record shows from remote, Automatic Illumination Systems, Advanced Locking Systems, Connected Surveillance Systems all fit into this concept of smart homes. As IoT evolves, we can be sure that most of the devices will become smarter, enabling enhanced home security.

2. **Smart System for City (Smart City):** Not just internet access to people in a city but to the devices in it as well – that is what smart cities are supposed to be made of. And we can proudly say that we are going towards realizing this dream. Efforts are being made to incorporate connected technology into infrastructural requirements and some vital concerns like Traffic Management, Waste Management, Water Distribution, Electricity Management, and more. All these work towards eliminating some day-to-day challenges faced by people and bring in added convenience.

3. **Smart System for Cars (Self-Driven Cars):** We have seen a lot about self-driven cars. Google tried it out, Tesla tested it, and even Uber came up with a version of self-driven cars that it later shelved. Since its human lives on the roads that we are dealing with, we need to ensure the technology has all that it takes to ensure better safety for the passenger and those on the roads.

   The cars use several sensors and embedded systems connected to the Cloud and the internet to keep generating data and sending them to the Cloud for informed decision-making through Machine Learning. Though it will take a few more years for the technology to evolve completely and for countries to amend laws and policies, what we are witnessing right now is one of the best applications of IoT.

4. **Smart System for Retail Shops:** If you have not already seen the video of Amazon Go, the concept store from the eCommerce giant, you should check it out right away. Perhaps this is the best use of the technology in bridging the gap between an online store and a retail store. The retail store allows you to go cashless by deducting money from your Amazon wallet. It also adds items to your cart in real-time when you pick products from the shelves.

   If you change your mind and pick up another article, the previous one gets deleted and replaces your cart with the new item. The best part of the concept store is that there is no cashier to bill your products. You do not have to stand in line but just step out after you pick up your products from shelves. If this technology is effective enough to fetch more patronage, this is sure to become a norm in the coming years.

5. **Smart System for Farming:** Farming is one sector that will benefit the most from the Internet of Things. With so many developments happening on tools farmers can use for agriculture, the future is sure promising. Tools are being developed for Drip Irrigation, understanding crop patterns, Water Distribution, drones for Farm Surveillance, and more. These will allow farmers to come up with a more productive yield and take care of the concerns better.

6. **Smart System for Wearables:** Wearables remain a hot topic in the market, even today. These devices serve a wide range of purposes ranging from medical, wellness to fitness. Of all the IoT startups, Jawbone, a wearables maker, is second to none in terms of funding.

7. **Smart System for Power Grids (Smart Grid):** A smart grid, is solution that applies Information Technology resources to enable existing and new gridlines to reduce electricity waste and cost. It improves the efficiency, reliability, and economics of electricity.

8. **Smart System for Industrial Internet:** The industrial IoT is mainly consists of interconnected sensors, instruments, and other devices connected with computers' industrial applications like manufacturing, energy management, etc.

9. **Smart System for Health (Tele-Health):** Telehealth/telemedicine includes the digital communication of medical imaging, remote medical diagnosis and evaluations, video consultations with specialists.

10. **Smart Supply Chain Management:** Smart supply-chains solutions supports for tracking goods while they are on the road. With the support of IoT technology, they guarantees the quality and reliability in the market for the long run.

11. **Traffic Management:** This in large cities with the Internet of Things (IoT) helps us to stay informed and suggests improvement in traffic monitoring by allowing us to use our mobile phones as sensors to collect and share data from our vehicles through apps like Google Maps. This feeds and improves the data on the various routes to the same destination, distance, and estimated arrival time.

    Analysis of traffic patterns over a long period provides an idea for improvement during peak hours. Commuters will be better prepared to avoid traffic and delays by being made aware of possible alternatives.

12. **Water and Waste Management:** For water recycling using water treatment units. Using an IoT application, you can see how much wastewater is being produced, how much is being consumed in a specific area, and how waste production is changing over time.
13. **Smart Waste Management:** We can effectively deal with this problem using internet of things applications and smart sensor technology. With a smart waste management system, authorities will be able to predict how much waste will be generated in a specific location, how to properly process it, when to clear it, and how to analyze data for future planning, among other things.

1.5. EMBEDDED SYSTEMS

These computers are mainly microcontroller-based systems. Used for processing specific tasks. The embedded computers have both a combination of software and hardware components. But are usually a part of a larger system. Each of its components is designed from scratch to serve a specific purpose or complete a specific task. Another characteristic that distinguishes them from a standard PC is that all of its components are integrated on a single PCB or motherboard. They are most helpful for industrial use. this is because of their ruggedness.

Examples: GPS systems, centralized heating systems, fitness trackers, digital watches, electronic calculators, etc.

1.5.1. GIS (Geographic Information System)

A geographic information system (GIS Software) is designed to store, retrieve, manage, display, and analyze all types of geographic and spatial data. GIS software lets you produce maps and other graphic displays of geographic information for analysis and presentation.

A geographic information system (GIS) is a computer system that analyzes and displays geographically referenced information. It uses data that is attached to a unique location.

GIS technology applies geographic science with tools for understanding and collaboration. It helps people reach a common goal: to gain actionable intelligence from all types of data.

A GIS stores data on geographical features and their characteristics. The features are typically classified as points, lines, or areas, or as raster images. On a map city data could be stored as points, road data could be stored as lines, and boundaries could be stored as areas, while aerial photos or scanned maps could be stored as raster images.

Geographic Information Systems store information using spatial indices that make it possible to identify the features located in any arbitrary region of a map. For example, a GIS can quickly identify and map all of the locations within a specified radius of a point, or all of the streets that run through a territory (Figure 1.6).

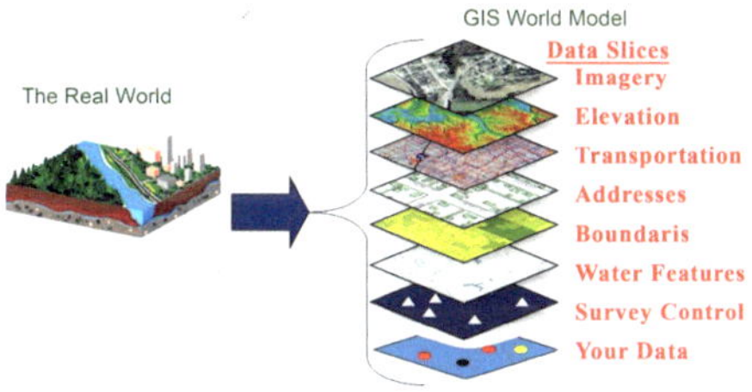

Figure 1.6. *Geographic information system.*

A GIS is used to interconnect information of location (spatial)and information stored in database. GIS provides facility of visualization of patterns, relationships and trends. This process helps analysts to analyze beyond tables and lists. Following are basic components of GIS:

Data	· One of the most important components of GIS is the data. · For GIS data must be accurate.	Types of data: · Vector data · Raster data · Image data · Attribute data
People	· People manages and uses the system, and some people develop plans for applying GIS services. · Users of GIS range from highly qualified technical professionals to planners, foresters and market analysts to those who use GIS to help with their everyday work.	Types of peoples: · Administrator · Managers · GIS technicians · Application experts · End users · Consumers

Methods	Methods of GIS are well designed plans and application-specific business rules describing how technology is applied.	Types of GIS method: · Guidelines · Specifications · Standards · Procedure
Software	· GIS software provides functions and tools to store, analyze and display geographical information.	Types of software components: · GIS software · Database software · OS software · Network software
Hardware	· GIS hardware are those peripherals on which the GIS operates. · GIS H/W could be centralized computer server running on Unix or Windows NT operating systems, a desktop PC, or an Apple Macintosh	Hardware required: · Computer · Networks · Peripheral devices · Printers · Plotters · Digitizers

1.5.2. Global Positioning System (GPS)

The "Global Positioning System" in short GPS is a satellite-based navigation system that furnishes location and time information in all climate conditions to the user. The first GPS was designed by the U. S. military, owned by the US Department of Defense. But it is available on a worldwide basis to all civil GPS users with no direct charge.

GPS is used for navigation in planes, ships, cars, and trucks also. The system gives critical abilities to military and civilian users around the globe. GPS provides continuous real-time, 3-dimensional positioning, navigation, and timing worldwide.

The global positioning system consists of a set of 24 operational satellites and land-based control stations. GPS determines distance between a GPS satellite and a GPS receiver by measuring the amount of time it takes a radio signal to travel from the satellite to the receiver. Radio waves travel at the speed of light, which is about 300,000 kilometer per second. So, if the amount of time it takes for the signal to travel from the satellite to the receiver is known, the distance from the satellite to the receiver using the formula distance = speed x time can be determined. Once the exact time when the signal was transmitted and the exact time when it was received are known, the signal's travel time can be determined.

1.5.2.1. GPS System Segments

The GPS consists of three major segments: space, control and user (Figure 1.7(a) and (b)).

1. **The Space Segment:** It consists of 24 satellites, each in its own orbit 20,200 kilometers above the Earth. The nominal GPS Operational Constellation consists of 24 satellites that orbit the earth in 12 hours. There are often more than 24 operational satellites as new ones are launched to replace older satellites. The satellite orbits repeat almost the same ground track once each day. The orbit altitude is such that the satellites repeat the same track and configuration over any point approximately each 24 hours (4 minutes earlier each day). There are six orbital planes with nominally four satellites in each, equally spaced (60 degrees apart). This constellation provides the user with between five and eight satellites visible from any point on the earth.
2. **The Control Segment:** It consists of a system of tracking stations located around the world, the GPS Master Control Station, and several monitor stations.

   It measure signals from the NAVSTAR satellites, and it calculates any position or clock errors for each individual satellite based on information received from the monitor stations. The "new" corrected data are uploaded by the Master Control station. And at least the NAVSTAR satellites send the new data over radio signals to the GPS receiver back to earth.

   The four monitor stations are unmanned stations located around the world (Hawaii and Kwajalein in the Pacific Ocean; Diego Garcia in the Indian Ocean; Ascension Island in the Atlantic Ocean. They track up to 11 satellites twice a day.
3. **User Segment:** It consists of GPS-receivers, located in cars, planes or even in GPS collars for wildlife. They can be as small as a mobile phone.

(a)

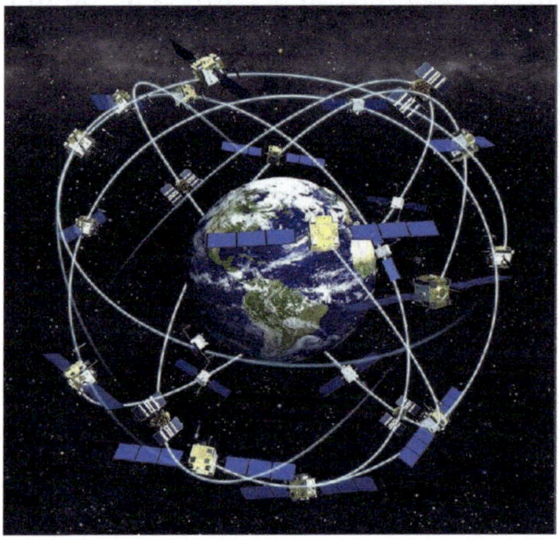

(b)

Figure 1.7. *GPS system.*

1.5.3. Cloud Computing

Cloud computing is on-demand access, via the internet, to computing resources— applications, servers (physical servers and virtual servers), data storage, development tools, networking capabilities, and more—hosted at a remote data center managed by a cloud services provider (or CSP). The CSP makes these resources available for a monthly subscription fee or bills them according to usage.

Compared to traditional on-premises IT, and depending on the cloud services you select, cloud computing helps do the following:

1. **Lower IT Costs:** Cloud lets you offload some or most of the costs and effort of purchasing, installing, configuring, and managing your

own on-premises infrastructure.

2. **Improve Agility and Time-to-Value:** With cloud, your organization can start using enterprise applications in minutes, instead of waiting weeks or months for IT to respond to a request, purchase and configure supporting hardware, and install software. Cloud also lets you empower certain users—specifically developers and data scientists—to help themselves to software and support infrastructure.
3. **Scale More Easily and Cost-Effectively:** Cloud provides elasticity—instead of purchasing excess capacity that sits unused during slow periods, you can scale capacity up and down in response to spikes and dips in traffic. You can also take advantage of your cloud provider's global network to spread your applications closer to users around the world.

The term 'cloud computing' also refers to the technology that makes cloud work. This includes some form of *virtualized IT infrastructure*—servers, operating system software, networking, and other infrastructure that has abstracted, using special software, so that it can be pooled and divided irrespective of physical hardware boundaries. For example, a single hardware server can be divided into multiple virtual servers.

Virtualization enables cloud providers to make maximum use of their data center resources. Not surprisingly, many corporations have adopted the cloud delivery model for their on-premises infrastructure so they can realize maximum utilization and cost savings vs. traditional IT infrastructure and offer the same self-service and agility to their end-users (Figure 1.8).

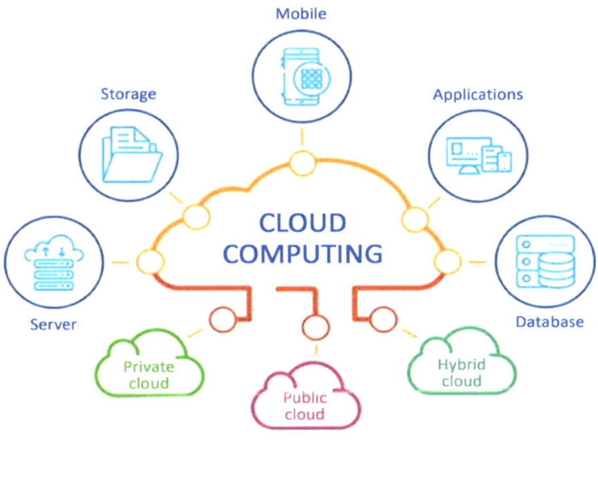

Figure 1.8. Cloud computing.

1.5.4. Cloud Computing Services

SaaS (software-as-a-service), PaaS (platform-as-a-service) and IaaS (infrastructure-as-a-service) are the three most common models of cloud services, and it is not uncommon for an organization to use all three. However, there is often confusion among the three and what is included with each:

1. **SaaS (Software-as-a-Service):** Also known as cloud-based software or cloud applications—is application software that is hosted in the cloud and that you access and use via a web browser, a dedicated desktop client, or an API that integrates with your desktop or mobile operating system. In most cases, SaaS users pay a monthly or annual subscription fee; some may offer 'pay-as- you-go' pricing based on your actual usage.

   In addition to the cost savings, time-to-value, and scalability benefits of cloud, SaaS offers the following:

   i. **Automatic Upgrades:** With SaaS, you take advantage of new features as soon as the provider adds them, without having to orchestrate an on-premises upgrade.

   ii. **Protection from Data Loss:** Because your application data is in the cloud, with the application, you do not lose data if your device crashes or breaks.

   SaaS is the primary delivery model for most commercial software today—there are hundreds of thousands of SaaS solutions available, from the most focused industry and departmental applications to powerful enterprise software database and AI (artificial intelligence) software.

2. **PaaS (Platform-as-a-Service):** This provides software developers with on-demand platform—hardware, complete software stack, infrastructure, and even development tools—for running, developing, and managing applications without the cost, complexity, and inflexibility of maintaining that platform on-premises.

   With PaaS, the cloud provider hosts everything—servers, networks, storage, operating system software, middleware, databases—at their data center. Developers simply pick from a menu to 'spin up' servers and environments they need to run, build, test, deploy, maintain, update, and scale applications.

   Today, PaaS is often built around *containers*, a virtualized compute model one step removed from virtual servers. Containers virtualize the operating system, enabling developers to package the application with only the operating system services it needs to run on any platform, without modification and without need for middleware.

3. **IaaS (Infrastructure-as-a-Service):** This provides on-demand access to fundamental computing resources–physical and virtual servers, networking, and storage—over the internet on a pay-as-you-go basis. IaaS enables end users to scale and shrink resources on an as-needed basis, reducing the need for high, up-front capital expenditures or unnecessary on-premises or 'owned' infrastructure and for overbuying resources to accommodate periodic spikes in usage.

In contrast to SaaS and PaaS (and even newer PaaS computing models such as containers and serverless), IaaS provides the users with the lowest-level control of computing resources in the cloud.

Cloud Computing Services	**Examples**
SaaS	Google Docs, Office-365
PaaS	Google App Engine, Microsoft Azure
IaaS	Amazon Web Services

1.6. CONCEPT OF HARDWARE, FIRMWARE, SOFTWARE, AND LIVEWARE

1. **Hardware:** These are physical components of computer system, they are mainly consists of electronic devices, designed to work together as a single unit. **Users** can physically interact with. Examples include PCBs like motherboard, RAM, Integrated Circuits, Processor, Microcontroller, etc.

   Hardware is the hardest part to change in a given product's life cycle. If you need to change it, you need to design the PCB, manufacture it, assemble components on it, do the necessary tests to ensure everything is connected in the way it is supposed to be, and all the components are working as they should. After all of this is done the hardware is said to be "ready" for software development.

2. **Firmware:** It is a program that is specifically designed to work with particular hardware, and it lives in non-volatile memory (ROM or a flash drive), and it is executed directly from there.

   Originally Firmware is written on Masked ROMs, on which the data cannot be changed once written. The products were shipped with these unchangeable programs called firmware and they run for ages till the device goes out of use. Nowadays these kinds of firmware can be found in devices like TVs, washing machines and microwaves. On your computer, it can be found in the BIOS of your motherboard.

3. **Software:** These are group of interrelated programs that can work for or satisfy user's need. They interact with a wide variety of hardware, and they are usually copied from non-volatile memory (Hard-disk or SSD) onto volatile memory (RAM) before execution.

   Software is very easy to change (soft) with no trouble at all. The software comes in the form of setup files on removable media like CDs, DVDs, flash drives, or downloaded from the internet straight onto your local machine. They are then installed onto the hard disk. Once invoked, the code to be executed is transferred to the RAM and run from there.

Examples: Operating systems (System Software), Microsoft Office / Open Office (Application Software) that run on them, drivers and middleware (Utility Software)

4. **Liveware:** This is a term that typically refers to human beings in the context of computer systems. It encompasses individuals who interact with and operate technology, making them an essential component of the system's functionality alongside hardware and software.

   In the realm of technology, liveware is indispensable as it provides the cognitive abilities, decision-making capabilities, and physical actions necessary for systems to achieve their intended purposes. Unlike hardware, which consists of physical components like computers and peripherals, and software, which includes programs and instructions, liveware introduces variability, creativity, and adaptability into technological ecosystems.

   Liveware's role extends beyond mere operation; it includes system design, maintenance, and improvement through feedback and innovation. Human factors such as usability, ergonomics, and user experience heavily influence the design of interfaces and interactions, ensuring that technology serves human needs effectively.

1.7. E-GOVERNANCE

E-Governance promotes the use of computers in e-governance and various public domains and services: It has supported and developed the efficiency of governance with the application of ICT in the processes of governing called Electronic-Governance or e- Governance.

E-governance empowered the transparency, accountability, efficiency, effectiveness and inclusiveness in the governing process in terms of reliable access to the information within government, between government, national, state, municipal, and local level governments, citizens, and businesses. The main focus of the e-Governance is to provide transparent, equitable, and accountable service delivery to the citizens. The aim of the e-governance facilitates and improves the quality of governance and ensures people's participation in the governing process through electronic means like e-mail, websites, SMS connectivity, and others.

1.7.1. Features of E-Governance (e-GOV)

It has been proven from the concept of e-governance that it is a powerful means of public service in the present era. Some of its features can be found by observing the functioning of e-governance.

1. **De-Bureaucratization:** Due to e-governance, the gap between the people and the government in all the services of the government is narrowing and the dependence of the people on the bureaucracy is also greatly reduced.
2. **E-Services:** Its main feature is the provision of services through the Internet. As a result, we get G2C, G2B, G2E, etc. services. This is already discussed in the section of 'types of governance.'
3. **International Services:** Through e-governance, all the essential services can be delivered to the citizens who are living outside of their country for job purposes or any other reasons.
4. **Citizen Engagement:** It enhances the right to express to the citizens. Using the means of e-governance anyone can share their views with the government on any bill or act, or decision taken by the government.
5. **Economic Development:** With the introduction of e-governance, various information like import-export, registration of companies, investment situations, etc. are available through the internet. As a result, time is saved, procrastination decreases, and economic dynamism increases.
6. **Reduce Inequality:** Using e-governance tools everyone can gather information and empower themselves. In this globalized world, knowledge is power and means of e- governance empower us by providing relevant information at minimal cost, effort, and time.

1.7.2. Types of E-Governance

1. **Government-to-Citizen (G2C):** This refers to the government services that are accessed by the familiar people. And Most of the government services fall under G2C. Likewise, the primary goal

of Government-to-citizen is to provide facilities to the citizen. It helps the ordinary people to reduce the time and cost to conduct a transaction. A citizen can have access to the services anytime from anywhere.

Furthermore, many services like license renewals, and paying tax are essential in G2C. Likewise, spending the administrative fee online is also possible due to G2C. The facility of Government-to-Citizen enables the ordinary citizen to overcome time limitation. It also focuses on geographic land barriers.

2. **Government-to-Business (G2B):** This is the exchange of services between Government and Business organizations. It is efficient for both government and business organizations. G2B provides access to relevant forms needed to comply. The G2B also consists of many services exchanged between business sectors and government.

   Similarly, the Government to business provides Timely business information. And A business organization can have easy and convenient online access to government agencies. G2B plays a crucial role in business development. It enhances the efficiency and quality of communication and transparency of government projects.

3. **Government-to-Government (G2G):** This refers to the interaction between different government department, organizations, and agencies. This increases the efficiency of government processes. In G2G, government agencies can share the same database using online communication. The government departments can work together. This service can increase international diplomacy and relations.

   In conclusion, G2G services can be at the local level or the international level. It can communicate with global government and local government as well. Likewise, it provides safe and secure inter-relationship between domestic or foreign government. G2G constructs a universal database for all member states to enhance service.

4. **Government-to-Employee (G2E):** This is the internal part of G2G sector. Furthermore, G2E aims to bring employees together and improvise knowledge sharing.

   Similarly, G2E provides online facilities to the employees. Likewise, applying for leave, reviewing salary payment record. And checking the balance of holiday. The G2E sector provides human resource training and development. So, G2E is also the relationship between employees, government institutions, and their management.

1.8. COMPUTER BLOCK DIAGRAM SYSTEM

Mainly computer system consists of three parts, which are central processing unit (CPU)Input devices, and Output devices.

The central processing unit (CPU) is divided into two parts again: arithmetic logic unit (ALU) and the control unit (CU). The set of instruction is in the form of raw data.

A large amount of data is stored in the computer memory with the help of primary and secondary storage devices. The CPU is like the heart/brain of the computer. The user does not get the desired output, without the necessary option taken by the CPU. The Central processing unit (CPU) is responsible for the processing of all the instructions which are given by the user to the computer system (Figure 1.9).

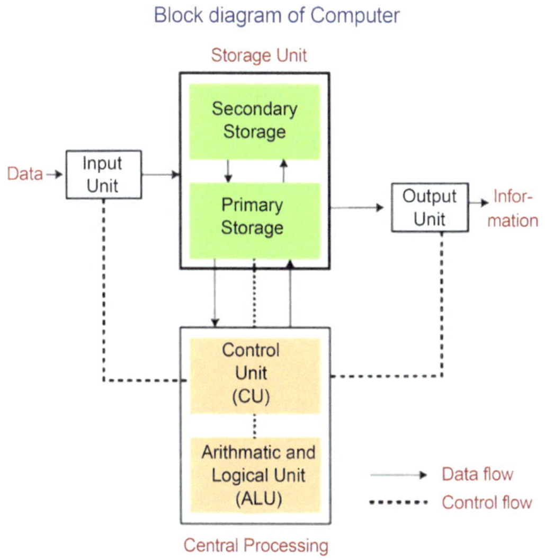

Figure 1.9. Block diagram of the computer.

1. **Input Unit:** It is a unit that accepts any input device. The input device is used to input data into the computer system.

   Functions of input unit:

- It converts inputted data into binary codes.
- It sends data to main memory of computer.

2. **Central Processing Unit (CUP):** It is called the brain of a computer. An electronic circuitry that carries out the instruction given by a computer program. CPU can be sub classified into three parts:

i. **Control Unit (CU):** This manages the various components of the computer. It reads instructions from memory and interpretation and changes in a series of signals to activate other parts of the computer. It controls and co-ordinate is input output memory and all other units.

ii. **Arithmetic and Logic Unit (ALU):** This, which performs:

- Simple arithmetic operation such as +, –, *, /;
- Logical operation such as >, <, =<, <=;
- Controlling operations Print, Halt, Wait.

iii. **Memory Unit (MU):** Memory is used to store data and instructions before and after processing. Memory is also called Primary memory or internal memory. It is used to store data temporary or permanently.

Functions of CPU:

- It controls all the parts and software and data flow of computer.
- It performs all operations.
- It accepts data from input device.
- It sends information to output device.
- Executing programs stored in memory.
- It stores data either temporarily or permanent basis.
- It performs arithmetical and logical operations.

3. **Output Unit:** This is a unit that constituents a number of output device. An output device is used to show the result of processing.

Functions of output unit:

- It accepts data, or information sends from main memory of computer;
- It converts binary coded information into HLL or inputted languages.

Memory Aid

- A computer is a multipurpose electronic machine that can be programmed to carry out sequences of arithmetic or logical operations (a program) automatically.
- The sets of operations (instructions) to accomplish a task are known as programs. The group of programs (software) enables a computer to perform a wide range of tasks.
- The physical components of a computer are called hardware and peripherals.

- "Peripheral devices" are used for taking input and providing output of computation. Sometimes removable memory devices (like floppy disks, hard disks, and optical disks) are also considered peripheral devices because they are used for both input and output.
- "The complete computer" includes the hardware, operating system (main software), and peripheral equipment for "full" operation, which are commonly known as a "computer system."
- The term computing system sometimes also refers to a group of computers linked and functioning together as a computer network or computer cluster.

CHAPTER 2

INPUT DEVICES, OUTPUT DEVICES, AND MEMORY

Contents

2.1. INPUT DEVICES

Input devices are devices that are designed to enter data into a system. Input devices allow the users to send signals to the computer to perform a certain task. The receiver at this end is the Central Processing Unit (CPU) which then sends the signal to the output devices. Input devices further classify according to modality like visual or audio, discrete or continuous, and is it direct or indirect.

Following are some input devicсs:

- Keyboard;
- Mouse;
- Trackball;

- Joystick;
- MICR;
- OMR;
- OCR;
- Light Pen;
- Digitizer;
- Scanner;
- Microphone;
- Barcode reader.

2.1.1. Keyboards

The keyboard one of the most prominent input devices of the computer, looks similar to typewriters. The keyboard is designed to input data in the format of the *text, numbers, and special characters*. The computer keyboard is one of the actual examples of input devices in computing.

Keyboards are of two sizes 84 keys or 101/102 keys but now keyboards with 104 keys or 108 keys are also available for Windows and Internet.

Computer keyboard has following types of keys:

1. **Typing Keys:** A keyboard has many types of keys such as numeric, alphabetic and special purpose keys. Numeric keys includes the digit keys (0–9), and alphabetic keys includes letter keys (A–Z). Computer keyboard generally have same layout as that of typewriters.
2. **Numeric Keyboard:** It is used to enter numeric data or cursor movement. Generally, it consists of a set of 17 keys that are laid out in the same configuration used by most adding machines and calculators.
3. **Function Keys:** The twelve function keys are present on the keyboard which are arranged in a row at the top of the keyboard. Each function key has unique meaning and is used for some specific purpose.
4. **Control Keys:** These keys provide cursor and screen control. It includes four directional arrow keys. Control keys also include Home, End, Insert, Delete, Page Up, Page Down, Control(Ctrl), Alternate(Alt),Escape(Esc).
5. **Special Purpose Keys:** Keyboard also contains some special purpose keys such as Enter, Shift, Caps Lock, Num Lock, Space bar, Tab, and Print Screen.

2.1.2. Scanner

Scanner is an input device, which works more like a photocopy machine. It is used when some information is available on paper, and it is to be transferred to the hard disk of the computer for further manipulation.

Scanner captures images from the source which are then converted into a digital form that can be stored on the disk. These images can be edited before they are printed.

2.1.3. Mouse

Mouse is the most popular pointing device. It is a very famous cursor-control device, having a small palm-sized box with a round ball at its base, which senses the movement of the mouse and sends corresponding signals to the CPU when the mouse buttons are pressed.

Generally, it has two buttons called the left and the right button and a wheel is present between the buttons. A mouse can be used to control the position of the cursor on the screen, but it cannot be used to enter text into the computer.

There are three types of mouse:

1. **Mechanical Mouse:** This has a trackball at its bottom. It can be rolled across a flat and smooth surface to control the position of the cursor on the screen. By pointing and clicking on icons and menu options displayed on the screen, it is easy for the user to control the computer with a mouse. Mechanical sensors within the mouse detect the direction the ball is rolling and move the screen pointer accordingly.
2. **Optomechanical Mouse:** It is more or less the same as the mechanical mouse, but it uses optical sensors to detect motion of the ball.
3. **Optical Mouse:** This uses a laser to detect the mouse movement. The mouse requires to be moved along a special mat with a grid so that the optical mechanism has a frame of reference. It has no mechanical moving parts. It responds more quickly and precisely than mechanical or opt mechanical mouse. Optical mouse is more expensive than the other two.

2.1.4. Light Pen

Light pen is a pointing device similar to a pen. It is used to select a displayed menu item or draw pictures on the monitor screen. It consists of a photocell and an optical system placed in a small tube. When the tip of a light pen is moved over the monitor screen and the pen button is pressed, its photocell sensing element detects the screen location and sends the corresponding signal to the CPU.

A light pen utilizes a light-sensitive detector to select objects on a display screen. A light pen is similar to a mouse, except that with a light pen you can move the pointer and select objects on the display screen by directly pointing to the objects with the pen.

2.1.5. Barcode Reader

A barcode reader is a hand-held or stationary input device used to capture and read information contained in a barcode. A bar-code reader consists of a lens, light source and a light sensor which translates optical impulses into electrical ones. A barcode scanner works by directing a beam of light across the barcode and measuring the amount of light that is reflected. The dark bars on the barcode reflect less light than the white spaces between them. The scanner then converts the light energy into electrical energy, which the decoder then converts into data and forwards to a computer.

2.1.6. OMR (Optical Mark Reader)

An optical mark reader (OMR) is a device used to detect marks made by a human on a specially designed document, often in the form of checkboxes or filled circles. It operates by illuminating the document and detecting the reflected light from the marked areas. OMR technology is widely used in assessments, surveys, and multiple-choice examinations due to its efficiency in processing large volumes of data quickly and accurately.

The key components of an OMR system include a light source, sensors to detect reflected light, and software to interpret the data. The marks made by users are translated into digital data which can then be processed and analyzed electronically. OMR systems are known for their reliability and speed in capturing data, making them valuable in educational institutions, government agencies, and market research firms where processing large amounts of data accurately and efficiently is essential.

2.1.7. OCR (Optical Character Recognition)

OCR stands for "Optical Character Recognition." It is a technology that recognizes text within a digital image. It is commonly used to recognize text in scanned documents and images.

OCR software can be used to convert a physical paper document, or an image into an accessible electronic version with text. For example, if you scan a paper document or photograph with a printer, the printer will most likely create a file with a digital image in it. The file could be a JPG/TIFF or PDF, but the new electronic file may still be only an image of the original document. You can then load this scanned electronic document it created, which contains the image, into an OCR program. The OCR program which will recognize the text and convert the document to an editable text file.

2.1.8. Magnetic Ink Character Recognition (MICR)

The full form of MICR is Magnetic Ink Character Recognition. It is a system that is used for the recognition of characters with the help of a special ink as well as characters or in other words. It can be understood as a technology that is used to verify the originality and authenticity of physical documents (especially cheque) and is mostly used by banking institutions. MICR is a device commonly present in banks as they deal with many cheques every day. The bank's code number and cheque number have magnetic ink present in them allowing machines to read the letters. This process is Magnetic Ink Character Recognition that has fewer errors and is very fast. This technology is used in cheques to make it safer and secured. MICR characters are printed information on documents so that the code line information can be captured by magnetic recognition.

Special ink, which is sensitive to magnetic fields, is used in the printing of certain characters on the original documents.

- Quick processing and reduced cheque clearing time;
- Reduced cheque related fraudulent activities.

2.1.9. Track Ball

Track ball is an input device that is mostly used in notebook or laptop computer, instead of a mouse. This is a ball which is half inserted and by moving fingers on the ball, the pointer can be moved. Since the whole device is not moved, a track ball requires less space than a mouse. A track ball comes in various shapes like a ball, a button, or a square. The advantage of trackballs over mouse is that the trackball is stationary, so it does not require much space to use it. In addition, you can place a trackball on any type of surface, including your lap. For both these reasons, trackballs are popular pointing devices for portable computers.

2.1.10. Joystick

A joystick is an input device used primarily in gaming and computer systems to control movement or actions. It consists of a stick that pivots on a base and typically has buttons on the stick or base for additional functions. The movement of the stick in various directions translates into corresponding actions on the screen, such as character movement in games or cursor control in graphical interfaces. Joysticks can be digital or analog, with analog joysticks offering finer control by detecting varying degrees of movement. They are also used in flight simulators, industrial control systems, and assistive technologies. Joysticks provide users with intuitive and precise control over digital environments, enhancing interaction and gameplay experiences.

2.1.11. Touch Screen

A touch screen is a display device that allows users to interact with a computer or device by touching areas on the screen directly with their fingers or a stylus. It incorporates sensors that detect the touch and translate it into input signals, enabling users to navigate menus, input data, and execute commands without the need for external peripherals like keyboards or mice. Touch screens can be found in smartphones, tablets, laptops, kiosks, and interactive displays. They offer intuitive and user-friendly interfaces, supporting gestures like tapping, swiping, pinching, and rotating. Touch screens have revolutionized user interaction by providing a more direct and responsive way to engage with digital content and applications, enhancing productivity and user experience in various industries.

2.1.12. Webcam

A webcam is a digital video camera that captures real-time video or images and transmits them over a computer network. It is commonly used for video conferencing, online streaming, and recording videos. Webcams are typically integrated into laptops, tablets, or external devices that connect via USB. They capture video at various resolutions and frame rates, allowing for clear and smooth visuals during communication or recording sessions. Webcams often include built-in microphones for capturing audio alongside video, enhancing their utility in virtual meetings and content creation. With the rise of remote work and online education, webcams have become indispensable tools for connecting people across distances and facilitating face-to-face interactions in digital environments. Their ease of use and versatility make webcams essential for both personal and professional applications in today's interconnected world.

2.1.13. Microphone

A microphone is a device that converts sound waves into electrical signals, allowing for the capture and transmission of audio. It consists of a diaphragm or membrane that vibrates in response to sound waves, which in turn moves a coil or capacitor to generate an electrical signal proportional to the sound waves. Microphones are used in various applications, from recording studios and live performances to telecommunication devices and voice recognition systems. They come in different types such as dynamic, condenser, and ribbon microphones, each suited to different environments and purposes. Microphones play a critical role in enabling clear communication and high-quality audio recording, enhancing the effectiveness of multimedia content, teleconferencing, and voice-based applications in both professional and personal settings.

2.1.14. Digitizer

Responsible for converting analog information into digital form, a digitizer converts signals into numeric values stored in a computer. The computer can now do anything with it as long as the camera is pointing out the image. A graphic tablet is also a digitizer converting graphics into binary data. It is ideal for drawing and image manipulation applications.

Digitizer tablets offer a variety of special features and can be used in numerous applications. Some devices are backlit in order to highlight details without distorting colors. Others feature selectable output resolutions or non-volatile memory. Digitizer tablets with integral tables and stands do not require mounting. Devices with a flexible surface can be rolled up and are designed to be portable.

Digitizer tablets are also used in (Figure 2.1):

1. **Construction Estimating:** It is the process of calculating the costs involved in a construction project. It includes assessing materials, labor, equipment, and other expenses to provide accurate estimates for budgeting and bidding purposes. Estimators use historical data, blueprints, and industry knowledge to create comprehensive cost projections.
2. **Cartography:** It is the art and science of creating maps. It involves compiling geographic data, interpreting aerial photographs, and employing specialized software to design accurate representations of landscapes, regions, and spatial relationships. Cartographers use symbols, scales, and projections to convey spatial information effectively for navigation, analysis, and planning purposes.
3. **Soil Conservation:** This aims to prevent soil degradation and erosion by implementing practices like terracing, contour plowing, and planting cover crops. It preserves soil fertility, structure, and biodiversity, crucial for sustainable agriculture and ecosystem health. Conservation efforts also include watershed management, erosion control structures, and promoting sustainable land use practices to maintain soil quality.

4. **Civil and Architectural Engineering:** This involves designing and constructing infrastructure and buildings. Civil engineering focuses on large-scale projects like bridges, roads, and water systems, ensuring structural integrity and functionality. Architectural engineering combines architecture and engineering principles to design aesthetically pleasing and efficient buildings, integrating systems for lighting, heating, and ventilation.
5. **Aerial Photo Interpretation:** This is the analysis of photographs taken from aircraft or satellites to gather information about the Earth's surface features. It involves identifying and mapping terrain, vegetation, land use patterns, and environmental changes. This data aids in urban planning, agriculture, disaster response, and natural resource management.
6. **Property Appraisal:** It is the process of determining the market value of real estate. Appraisers assess factors like location, size, condition, and comparable sales to provide an unbiased valuation. Their reports are crucial for mortgage lending, property taxation, insurance purposes, and transactions, ensuring fair pricing and informed decision-making in the real estate market.
7. **Real Estate Development:** This involves acquiring, financing, planning, designing, constructing, and managing property projects. Developers identify opportunities, secure funding, navigate regulatory approvals, and oversee construction to create residential, commercial, or mixed-use developments. The goal is to enhance property value and meet market demands while considering sustainability, economic feasibility, and community impact.

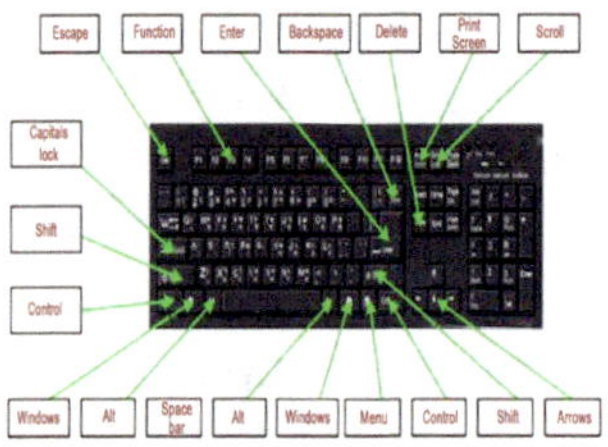

Keyboard

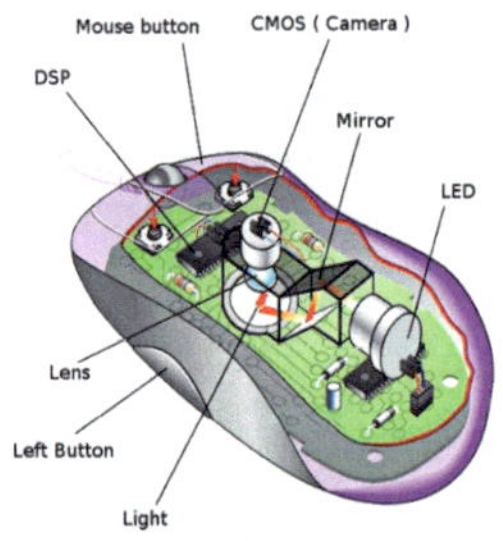

Mouse

Figure 2.1. *Input devices.*

2.2. OUTPUT DEVICES

An output device is a piece of computer hardware that receives data from a computer and then translates that data into another form. That form may be audio, visual, textual, or hard copy such as a printed document. The key distinction between an input device and an output device is that an input device sends data to the computer, whereas an output device receives data from the computer. For example, using a microphone to record a podcast is an example of using an input device. Listening to the recorded podcast through a connected speaker is an example of using an output device. Both output and input devices are examples of *auxiliary* or peripheral devices (Figure 2.3).

2.2.1. Monitor

The monitor is an output device that displays the output in the form of images on a digital screen. The images formed are made up of millions of tiny dots called pixels. The more pixels, the better the resolution of the image is. Earlier monitors had screens made of CRT, but they are now replaced by flat panel displays.

2.2.1.1. Types of Monitors

There are nine different types of monitors:

1. **LCD Monitor:** An LCD (liquid crystal display) monitor uses liquid crystal cells and backlighting to display images. It offers sharp resolution, vibrant colors, and energy efficiency compared to CRT monitors. LCDs are standard for computer displays, TVs, and devices due to their slim profile, light weight, and ability to display high-definition content with low power consumption.
2. **LED Monitor:** An LED (light emitting diode) monitor utilizes LED backlighting to illuminate an LCD panel, enhancing brightness and color accuracy while reducing energy consumption. LED monitors offer sharper images, deeper blacks, and thinner profiles compared to traditional LCDs. They are widely used in displays for computers, TVs, and digital signage due to their efficiency and visual quality.
3. **Curved Monitor:** This features a gently arched screen designed to wrap around the viewer's field of vision, offering a more immersive viewing experience. It reduces distortion at the edges and enhances depth perception, making it popular for gaming, multimedia, and professional applications where wide viewing angles and enhanced visual engagement are desired.

4. **CRT Monitor:** A CRT (cathode ray tube) monitor uses a vacuum tube to display images by directing electron beams onto a phosphorescent screen. It was once ubiquitous but has been largely replaced by flat panel displays due to its bulky size, heavy weight, and higher power consumption. CRTs offered good color fidelity and refresh rates for their time.
5. **Flat Panel Monitors:** These refer to display screens that use LCD (Liquid Crystal Display) or LED (Light Emitting Diode) technology, offering slim profiles and lightweight designs. They provide sharp images, vibrant colors, and energy efficiency compared to CRT monitors. Flat panels are standard in modern computers, TVs, and digital devices for their compactness and visual clarity.
6. **Touch Screen Monitors:** These integrate a touch-sensitive layer that allows users to interact directly with the display by tapping, swiping, or pinching. They are used in interactive kiosks, retail POS systems, and digital signage for intuitive navigation and user engagement. Touch screen monitors facilitate ease of use and enhance interactive experiences in various applications.
7. **OLED Monitors:** OLED (organic light emitting diode) monitors use self-emitting organic compounds to produce light and color directly on a display panel. They offer superior contrast ratios, faster response times, and thinner profiles compared to LCD or LED monitors. OLED monitors deliver vibrant colors, deep blacks, and energy efficiency, ideal for high-quality visual applications.
8. **DLP Monitors:** DLP (digital light processing) monitors use a technology where microscopic mirrors reflect light to create images. They offer high contrast ratios, sharp details, and fast response times. DLP monitors are used in projectors for home theaters, classrooms, and large venues due to their ability to produce bright, detailed images with smooth motion.
9. **TFT Monitors:** TFT (thin film transistor) monitors utilize active-matrix LCD technology to display images with improved brightness, contrast, and color accuracy. Each pixel is controlled by a transistor, allowing for faster response times and clearer visuals. TFT monitors are widely used in computers, laptops, and multimedia devices for their high-quality display capabilities.

2.2.2. Printers

Printers are another peripheral device used as output devices. The output from the computer is achieved on paper from the printer. The data gets printed on paper which can be both colored and black and white, an image, text, or even both.

The printer can be majorly divided into two types:

1. **Impact Printers:** These printers work by having direct contact with the ink ribbon and paper. Due to this, the noise produced by these printers resembles that of a typewriter.
2. **Non-Impact Printers:** These printers work with technologies like inkjet, laser, electrostatic, xerographic, etc. These printers work silently and are much faster than the impact ones.

2.2.2.1. Impact Printer

Impact printer strikes a head or a needle against an ink ribbon to make a mark on the paper. Impact printer may be three types:

i. **Daisy Wheel Printers:** It is used to print one character at a time. The head of this printer resembles a daisy flower, with the printing arms that appear like the petals of a flower, and thus it is named a daisy printer. It can be used to print professional letter-quality documents. It is also known as a letter-quality printer, as the print quality is better than that of a high-quality typewriter. It gives high-resolution output. Its reliability is higher than that of a dot matrix printer. It can have a speed of up to 90 cps. The time required to rotate the print wheel for each desired character is a reason it is slow in use. Therefore, these printers are slower and more expensive than dot matrix printers.

ii. **Drum Printers:** This prints a single line at a time. Its printing speed varies from 150 lines to 2500 lines in a minute with 96 to 106 characters on a 15-inch line. Line printers are designed for heavy printing applications. These printers are faster than character type printers. These types of printers produce a lot of noise.

iii. **Dot Matrix Printers:** This printing technology is very old. It can print one character at a time. It can print any shapes of character, special characters, graphs and charts which the user wishes to print.

This printer's speed can be measured by character per second (cps). The speed can vary from about 200 to 500 cps.

The print quality is determined by the number of pins, which can be varying from 9 to 24. For the higher print resolution, more pins per inch are given.

2.2.2.2. Non-Impact Printer

Non-impact printers does not use striking device to produce characters on the paper. These types of printers' spray ink on papers through nozzles to form characters and patterns.

Non-impact printer may be of two types:

1. **Inkjet Printers:** These are generally used for home purposes. It is a printer that places extremely small droplets of ink onto paper to create an image.

Its cost is relatively higher than dot matrix printers, but the quality is better. These kinds of printers produce high quality prints and graphics due to its high-resolution feature.

2. **Laser Printers:** This produces high quality text and images for personal computers. Laser printers are also known as page printers. Reason being they process and store the entire page before printing it. They do not produce noise and print faster. Thus, they are also preferred to print large amounts of content on large volumes of papers.

2.2.2.3. 3D Printer

3D printing is the process of creating a physical object from a digital model. 3D printing is an additive process. Layers of plastic are built up one after the other to create an object.

There are a variety of 3D printing materials, including thermoplastics such as acrylonitrile butadiene styrene (ABS), metals (including powders), resins and ceramics (Figure 2.2).

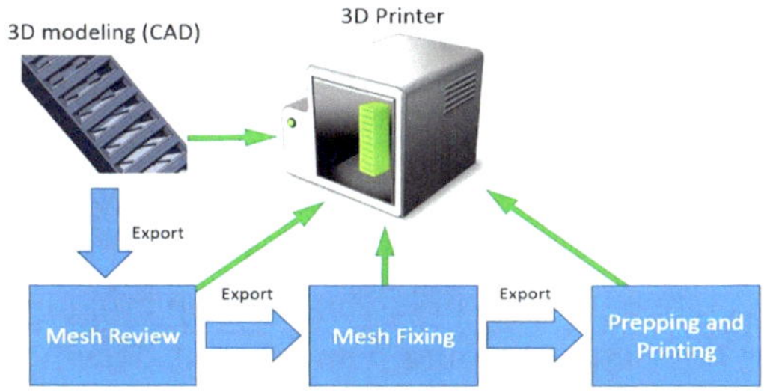

Figure 2.2. 3D printing technologies.

There are three broad types of 3D printing technology – sintering, melting, and stereolithographic:

1. **Sintering:** This is a technology where the material is heated, but not to the point of melting, to create high resolution items. Metal powder is used for direct metal laser sintering while thermoplastic powders are used for selective laser sintering.
2. **Melting:** These methods of 3D printing include powder bed fusion, electron beam melting and direct energy deposition, these use lasers, electric arcs or electron beams to print objects by melting the materials together at high temperatures.
3. **Stereolithography:** These utilizes photopolymerization to create parts. This technology uses the correct light source to interact with the material in a selective manner to cure and solidify a cross section of the object in thin layers.

2.2.2.4. Wi-Fi Printers

The simple definition of a Wi-Fi printer is a printer that does not require any cables to be connected between the printer and your computer, tablet, mobile or device. Wi-Fi printers in reality are not 100% wireless since they still need to be plugged into a power socket, but other than that there are no wires involved. Wireless printers can also be considered as Wi-Fi printers.

2.2.2.4.1. Benefits of Wi-Fi Printing

There are many benefits to Wi-Fi printing which may not always be obvious:

1. **Clutter Free:** Never have to worry about keeping all of those cables tidy again, simply remove the cables from the equation.
2. **Share Printers and Lower Printing Costs:** In office environments where multiple people need to be able to access a printer the old solution is to simply buy each person their own printer which can be quite costly. With a Wi-Fi enabled printer, it is now possible for multiple people to use the same printer with minimal setup required.
3. **Print from Anywhere:** Wireless technology in printers enables you to easily send documents to your printer from anywhere within wireless range. Instead of having to keep bringing your laptop back to your desk and plugging it in to print documents, you can send documents to the printer while you are in a meeting room or while having lunch in the cafeteria, so your printouts will be ready for you to pick up by the time you have walked to the printer.
4. **Independent of Computers:** Wireless printers are totally independent of any computers that are connected to it. What this

means is that your computer, or anyone else's computer does not need to be turned on for someone to send a document or photograph to the printer. This type of setup can be ideal when some people may be taking their laptops out of the office on a regular basis.

5. **Save Money on Cables:** While this is admittedly a small benefit, but the cost of installing cables between the printers and peoples' computers can be completely removed. This is both a cost saving on the actual cables but also on the staff time that is required to physically plug in the cables.

2.2.3. Audio Output Devices

2.2.3.1. Headphone

The audio or the sound produced by the computer is in the form of electric signals. These are perceived by us in the form of sound using the output device, headphones. The headphones are transducers that convert electrical energy into mechanical energy and thus help us in listening to songs and recordings on the computer. The best thing is that they are light and thus portable, unlike heavy computer speakers.

2.2.3.2. Computer Speaker

The computer speakers are an output device that works the same way as a headphone does. They make our entertainment experience easier. We can watch movies, listen to music, recordings, or any audio with the help of speakers. They can be used instead of headphones when multiple people want to listen to the audio (Figure 2.3).

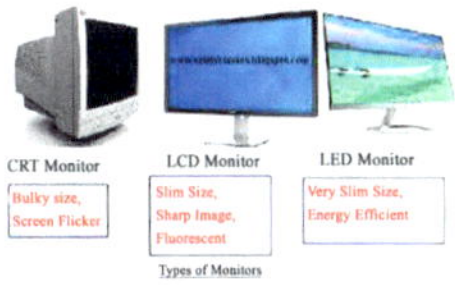

Touch Screen

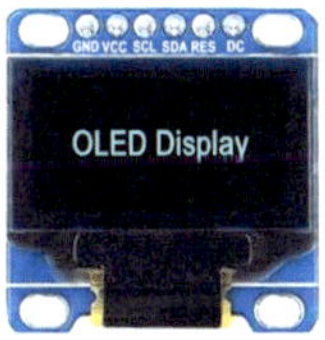

OLED Monitor

DLP Monitor

Impact Printers	
 **Drum Printer**	 **Daisy Wheel Printer**
 **Dot Matrix**	
Non-Impact Printers	
 **Inkjet Printer**	 **Laser Printer**
 **Headphone**	 **Speakers**

Figure 2.3. *Output devices.*

2.2.4. Projector

The projector is an output device that is used to project the image displayed on the computer monitor on a large wall or screen. This is a good option when the output is to be shown to a large number of people. It can be used to watch movies with friends or show a presentation in a group meeting.

The projector is connected to the computer using HDMI cables or VGA cables. The output from the computer is taken as input by the projector. Nowadays, the traditional blackboards are also getting replaced by smart screens, which use projectors to display images and videos to the students for better understanding.

2.2.5. Sound Card

The sound card is an expansion card used in computers to connect input-output devices. It is either integrated. The sound card audio ports are visible on the side or back of the computer, where you can connect any device like a keyboard, headphones, speakers, microphones. Each sport is specifically designed for each type of device. The main function of the soundcard is used to play any audio, record audio, connect joysticks or controllers for gaming purposes, and speakers to listen to music or any sound.

2.2.6. Plotter

A plotter is an output device that works similarly to a printer, but for large vector graphics. The lines are made on the paper using a pen or any other such tool mechanically by the plotter. These devices are used to print large high resolution, vector-based graphics, such as those used in architectural firms. They also prove advantageous as they can draw not only paper but on varied types of surfaces like plywood, aluminum sheet, plastic, etc. The only drawback is that they are quite expensive and require much larger space than normal printers.

2.2.6.1. Different Types of Plotters

There are six different types of plotters which are discussed and explained below:

1. **Drum Plotter:** These are also pen plotters. These drum plotters were used as the output devices to print graphics, engineering drawings, diagrams, construction maps, architectural plans, engineering drawings, business charts, etc. (Figure 2.4).

Figure 2.4. *Drum plotter.*

2. **Flatbed Plotter:** It is used in complex design, engineering drawing, construction maps, and architectural plans (Figure 2.5).

Figure 2.5. *Flatbed plotter.*

3. **Inkjet Plotter:** The advertising agencies and printing press uses inkjet plotters where images are created and developed with the help of ink droplets which are sprayed on the paper to derive clean and proper output.

   These inkjet plotters are used in printing large images and documents like billboards, hoardings, large designs, massive banners, etc. (Figure 2.6).

Figure 2.6. *Inkjet plotter.*

4. **Cutting Plotter:** This is a large cutting device that helps in producing vinyl lettering and huge graphic designs.

These plotters are attached to a computer system that helps develop designs, and also these plotters are equipped with automatic plotter knives that cut the sheet when kept on a flat surface.

These plotters are well-known for developing and creating high-quality graphics, banners, designs of vehicles, billboards, sign making, etc.

They generally work with almost 100% accuracy as they possess some of the excellent features and have easily replaced old-fashioned plotters (Figure 2.7).

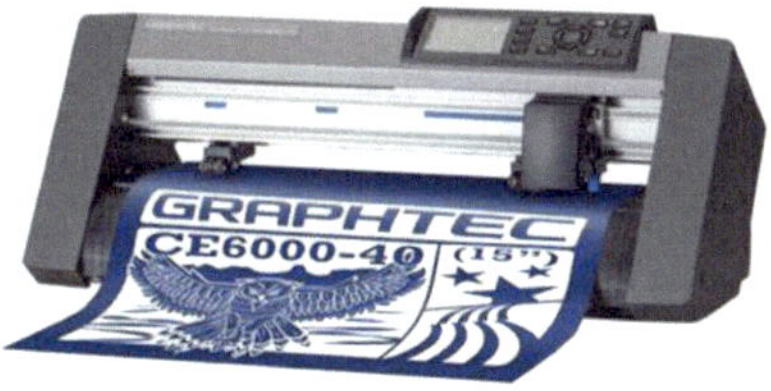

Figure 2.7. Cutting plotter.

5. **Pen Plotters:** These are commonly found working with color pens where several colored inks are filled in them. This ink, when used with pen and holder, produces high-quality multicolor graphics and design.

   These drawings produced by pen with various colors can be printed on paper sheets, plastic sheets, or any other conductive material (Figure 2.8).

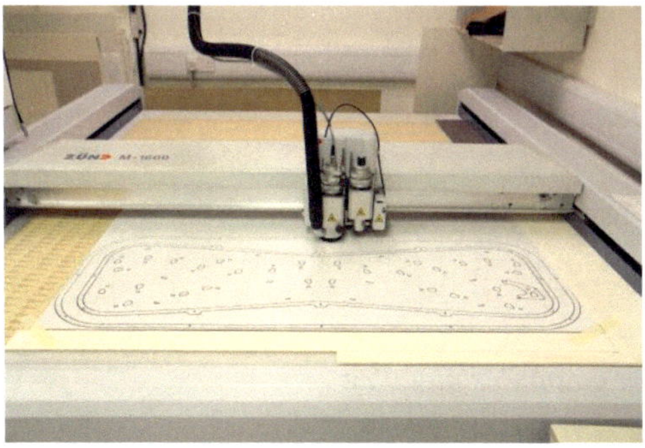

Figure 2.8. Pen plotters.

6. **Thermal Plotter:** It is a well-known plotter used in all sectors where high-quality designs and products are required.

To produce output, it takes the help of an electronic pin which is developed by heat that assists in building images and design as output (Figure 2.9).

Figure 2.9. Thermal plotter.

2.3. COMPUTER MEMORY AND ITS TYPES

- What is computer memory?

  Computer memory is a data storage technology that is capable of storing or saving data, temporarily or permanently. The data stored are in a binary form such as 0 and 1 as well, allowing the user to save and retrieve the information anytime they require it (Figure 2.10).

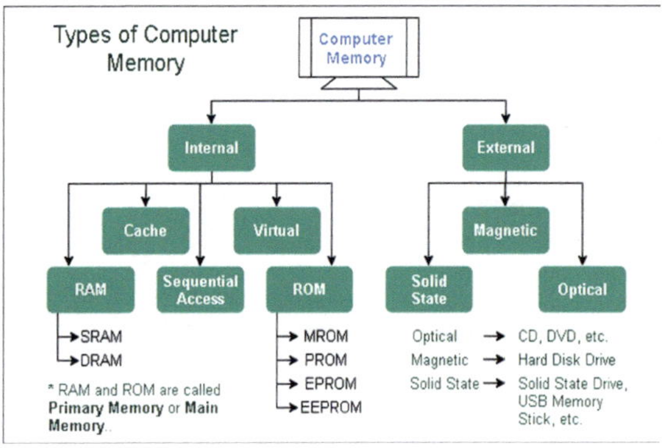

Figure 2.10. *Types of computer memory.*

Group of Bits	Notations	Unit Name
1 bit	Binary digit (0 or 1)	Bit

4 bits	1 nibble	Nibble
8 bits	2 nibble = 1 bytes	Byte
1024 bytes	1 KB	Kilobyte
1024 kilo bytes (KB)	1 MB	Megabyte
1024 MB	1 GB	Gigabyte
1024 GB	1 TB	Terabyte
1024 TB	1 PB	Petabyte
1024 PB	1 EB	Exabyte
1024 EB	1 ZB	Zettabyte
1024 ZB	1 YB	Yottabyte
1024 YB	1 BB	Brontobyte
1024 BB	1 Geopbyte	Geopbyte

2.3.1. Internal Memory

Internal memory, also known as primary memory, stores small amounts of data that the computer can access while you are actively using it. Internal memory consists of chips connected to the motherboard and needs to be connected directly to the device in order to use it. There are two basic types of internal memory called RAM and ROM, and those have their own subsets of memories.

2.3.1.1. RAM

Random access memory (RAM) is the primary internal memory of the central processing unit (CPU). Your electronic device uses it for storing temporary data. It does this by providing applications with a place to store data you are actively using so that it can quickly access the data. The amount of RAM on your device controls its performance and speed. If you do not have enough RAM, it may process programs slowly which can affect the output and speed with which you can use the computer.

RAM also has "volatile memory" because it loses the data it was storing if you turn off the device. For example, if you are on your laptop using the internet browser and your computer gets turned off, it may not have saved the web pages you were previously using because RAM only stores that information temporarily (Figure 2.11).

Figure 2.11. *RAM.*

- **Types of RAM:**

1. **DRAM:** Dynamic random-access memory (DRAM) is one of the two specific types of RAM seen in modern devices, such as laptops, desktops, portable devices and gaming systems. It's the more affordable of the two types of RAM and produces high-capacity memory. It is made of two components, transistors and capacitors, which require a recharge every few seconds to retain its data. Like RAM, it also loses data when it loses power and has volatile memory (Figure 2.12).

Figure 2.12. *DRAM.*

2. **SRAM:** Static random-access memory (SRAM) is the second type of RAM and stores data as long as there is power in the system, unlike DRAM which is refreshed much more frequently. Because it holds power longer, it is more expensive than DRAM, which typically makes it not as widely used. Users generally use SRAM for cache memory, which makes it a faster form of memory than DRAM (Figure 2.13).

Figure 2.13. *SRAM.*

2.3.1.2. ROM

Read-only memory (ROM) is another type of primary internal memory, but unlike RAM, ROM is non-volatile and stores data permanently. It does not depend on the device to be turned on in order to save data. Instead, a programmer writes the data into individual cells using binary code, which represents text using the "1" and "0" two-symbol system. Because you cannot alter the data on ROM, you can use this type of memory for aspects that do not change, such as the boot-up of software or firmware instructions, which help a device function properly (Figure 2.14).

Figure 2.14. *ROM.*

- **Types of ROM:**

1. **PROM:** Programmable read-only memory (PROM) is a type of ROM that begins as memory with no data on it. A user can write data onto the chip using a special device called a PROM programmer. Like ROM, data is permanent once a user has written it onto the chip. This type of memory may be useful to programmers who would like to create specific firmware for a chip and use it to alter the typical function of a system (Figure 2.15).

Figure 2.15. *PROM.*

2. **EPROM:** Erasable programmable read-only memory (EPROM) is another type of ROM chip that users can write data on as well as erase old data and reprogram it. You can erase the current data by using ultraviolet (UV) light in the form of a quartz crystal window at the top of the chip. After you have erased the data, you can use the PROM programmer to reprogram it. You can only erase data from an EPROM chip a certain number of times because excessive erasing can damage the chip and make it unreliable for future use (Figure 2.16).

Figure 2.16. *EPROM.*

3. **EEPROM:** Electrically erasable programmable read-only memory (EEPROM) is the final type of non-volatile ROM chip that usually replaces the need for PROM or EPROM chips. This type of memory also allows users to erase and reprogram data onto the chip but does so using an electric field and is much quicker at erasing data than the EPROM. In addition, you can conveniently erase data while the chip is still inside the computer, whereas EPROM chips need to be taken out of the computer to erase it (Figure 2.17).

Figure 2.17. *EEPROM.*

2.3.1.3. Cache

Cache memory is an internal high-speed semiconductor memory that stores instances of data frequently used by the CPU. It provides access to the CPU, so when the CPU requests data or programs the cache memory can transfer them to the CPU almost instantly. Cache memory usually sits between the CPU and RAM serves as a buffer between the two (Figure 2.18).

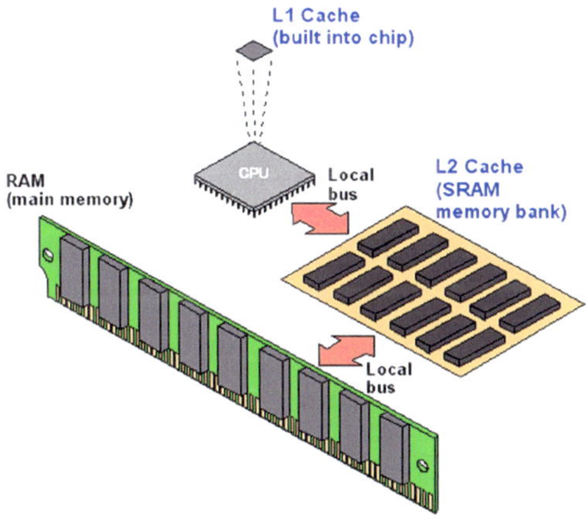

Figure 2.18. *Cache memory.*

2.3.2. External Memory

External memory, also known as secondary memory, is memory not directly connected to the CPU that you can attach or remove as needed. There are many types of external memory that individuals use in their devices. Examples include external hard drives, flash drives, memory cards and compact discs (CDs). You can store data from a computer onto external memory, remove it from the device and connect it with another compatible device to transfer data (Figure 2.19).

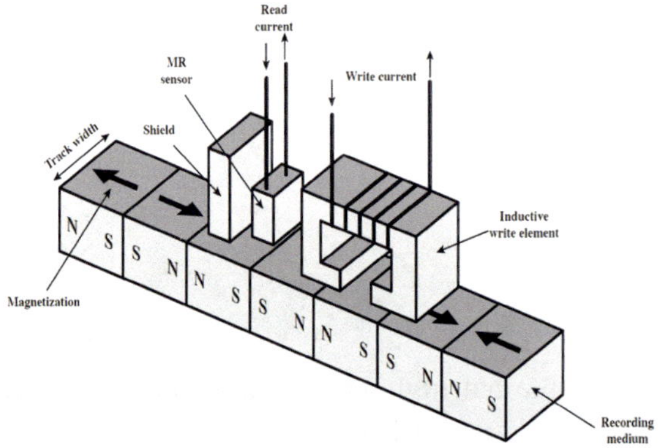

Figure 2.19. External memory.

2.3.2.1. Optical Drive

Optical drive memory is an external memory that can both store and read data using light. The most common types are CDs, DVDs and Blu-ray discs. To access the contents on an optical drive, you place the disc inside the computer and the computer spins the disc. A laser beam inside the system scans it, receives the data on the optical drive and uploads it onto the computer. This type of memory can be useful because it is generally inexpensive, easily accessible and stores a lot of data (Figure 2.20).

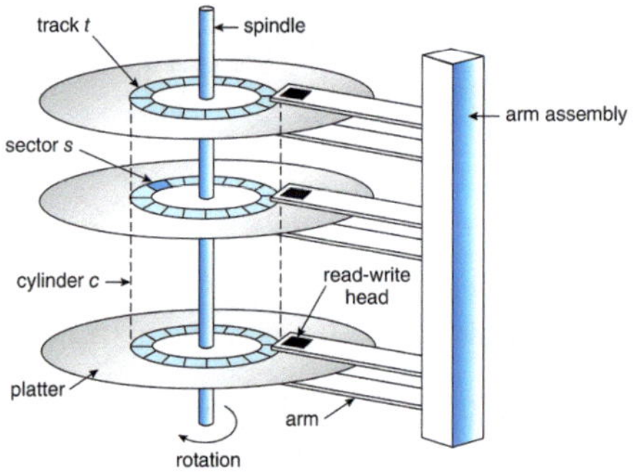

Figure 2.20. *Optical drive.*

2.3.2.2. Magnetic Storage

Magnetic storage devices have a coating of magnetic material where it encodes data as an electric current. This type of memory uses magnetic fields to magnetize small sections of a metal spinning disk. Each section represents a "1" or a "0" and contains an extensive amount of data, often many terabytes. Users like this type of memory because it is affordable, durable and can store a lot of data. Common forms of magnetic storage devices are magnetic tape, hard disk drives and floppy disks.

2.3.2.3. Solid-State Drives

Solid-state drives are a form of external memory made up of silicon microchips. They are similar to magnetic storage devices because you can remove them from the device you are storing or extracting data from, but solid-state drives are more modern. They are also faster because the memory keeps the binary data stored electronically in silicon chips known as cells. RAM uses a similar technique, but solid-state drives can keep memory stored even when you turn off a device because they use flash memory. Common types are the universal serial bus (USB) memory stick or USB flash drive (Figure 2.21).

Figure 2.21. *Solid-state drives.*

2.3.2.4. Magnetic Tapes

Magnetic tape is most commonly used to record and to store computer and video data. Before the CD and DVD came along, the magnetic tape was widely used by consumers. Magnetic tape is most commonly used by large companies and organizations that require massive data stores. Here this pose gives information about the advantages and disadvantages of magnetic tape to better understand this topic (Figure 2.22).

Figure 2.22. *Magnetic tapes.*

- **Advantages of Magnetic Tape:**
  - Magnetic tape can are recorded over and reused repeatedly.

  Magnetic tape is inexpensive and budget friendly.
  - Can storage large amount of data unto 1 terabyte per tape cartridge.
  - Data collection can go without interruption overnight or for an entire weekend.
- It can be set up to do the back up overnight or over the weekend.
  - It is probably the cheapest form of storage per megabyte of storage.
- **Limitations of Magnetic Tape:**
  - This tape is necessary to keep older tape equipment just to be able to read the stored data.
- If the data is stored near a strong magnetic field or large speaker, the tape can be damaged.
- Magnetic tape is in physical contact with the recording heads, causing friction and wear.
- It is slow compared to the magnetic disks.
- It is not flexible, updating the records is difficult.

2.3.2.5. Floppy Disk

A floppy disk drive (FDD) is a small disk drive used in computers for data transfer, storage and backup of small amounts of data, as well as installation of programs and driver updates. A floppy disk drive accesses data recorded on small, removable diskettes known as floppy disks. Floppy disk drives were widely used throughout the '90s but has since become obsolete in favor of other removable storage media such as CDs, DVDs and compact flash drives (Figure 2.23).

Figure 2.23. Floppy disk.

- **Characteristics of Floppy Disk:**

1. **Portability:** Floppy disks are small, and light weighted. Hence, they are easy to carry to the places the user wants.
2. **Compatibility:** Floppy disks are still compatible with the older systems. Particularly, computers made before the 2000s do not include a CD/DVD drive.
3. **Cost:** In terms of pricing too, floppy disks are relatively inexpensive. But since the production of floppy disks stopped a long time back, the prices of them cannot be compared to the storage mediums today.
4. **Write Protection:** In addition to the plastic casing, floppy disks also include a small notch which provides a function known as Write Protection.
5. **Booting Disks:** Floppy disks can also be used as a boot disk where it saves the appropriate boot programs for it to load.

2.3.2.6. Hard Disks

Hard disks are also called HDD; FIXED DISK they are considered to be the most reliable and popular secondary storage medium where users can store their important information permanently. The Hard drives are made up of rigid materials, it has a disk-shaped platter made up of aluminum or glass and is coated with a thin layer of magnetic material the platters are hard and cannot be bent, therefore, are called a fixed disk. The Sizes of disk platters vary from 1 to 14 inches in diameter.

HDD records data by magnetizing ferromagnetic material directionally to represent either 0 or 1 in a binary form (Figure 2.24).

Figure 2.24. Hard disks.

- **Characteristics of HDD:**

1. **Storage Capacity:** The modern computer hard disk drive [HDD] has an enormous capacity to store a huge amount of data/information. This is the major advantage of HDD as it is capable of handling such huge data almost permanently.
2. **Volatile:** The computer hard disk drive [HDD] is non-volatile in nature; it does not tend to lose data when there is no power supply.
3. **Cost:** The cost of an HDD depends particularly on the capacity and size. It is obvious that the bigger the size the more the price.
4. **Easy Availability:** Due to the heavy demand in the IT sector especially in the computer peripherals division, the requirement for computer products increased dramatically, therefore, manufacturers around the globe have increased their production immensely.

2.3.2.7. Compact Discs (CDs)

CDR or compact disc recordable is a type of CD that is made with reflective metal on the bottom side and dye on the top. They are used to store data for a long time and have a storage of 700–800 MB.

They are read-only disks. The data that is once stored in the disc cannot be removed or replaced. In other terms, the data stored in a CDR cannot be re-written or erased. So, it is a multisession disk on which different data types like audio, video, etc. can be written.

Once the data is stored, it is then converted to CD-ROM so that the stored data can be viewed. This is usually done by a CD player that can read and play the data stored in CDs. Almost all the CDRs are compatible with all types of CD players (Figure 2.25).

Figure 2.25. CD-ROM.

CD RW or compact disk rewritable is another type of CD that can store and view data. It stores up to 700–800 MB of data. On a CD-RW, the data once stored can be re-written if the already existing data is erased. So, a CD-RW can be used multiple times.

The disadvantage of CD-RW is that it is not compatible with all the CD players. The old CD players cannot read CDRW. CDRW also costs more than CDR. This owes to the fact that they can be used multiple times as the data in a CD RW can be re-written.

2.3.2.8. Video Compact Disks (VCDs)

VCD is short for "Video Compact Disc". A VCD is basically a CD that contains digital video and audio files on it. Both the video file and audio track are in MPEG-1 quality.

VCD software typically refers to any type of computer program that can be used to read, convert, or burn data onto a CD in order to create or read from a VCD. This software can be fairly simple and may be available as freeware or it may be more complicated professional software. VCD software is typically used by home computer users, as digital versatile discs (DVDs) have become increasingly popular and replaced VCDs for most professional uses (Figure 2.26).

Figure 2.26. VCD.

2.3.2.9. Digital Versatile Discs (DVDs)

A DVD (Digital Versatile Disc or Digital Video Disc) is an optical disc capable of storing up to 4.7 GB of data, more than six times what a CD can hold.

DVDs are often used to store movies at a better quality. Like CDs, DVDs are read with a laser. The disc can have one or two sides, and one or two layers of data per side; the number of sides and layers determines how much it can hold. A 12 cm diameter disc with single sided, single layer has 4.7 GB capacity, whereas the single sided, double layer has 8.5 GB capacity. The 8 cm DVD has 1.5 GB capacity.

The capacity of a DVD-ROM can be visually determined by noting the number of data sides of the disc. Double-layered sides are usually gold-colored, while single layered sides are usually silver-colored, like a CD.

2.3.2.9.1. DVD-R

Digital versatile disk rewritable (DVD-R) is a write-once (read only) digital versatile disc used to permanently store data files. It is an optical disc that generally has a storage capacity of 4.71 gigabytes (GB/s), seven times larger than a compact disc rewritable (CD-R) that holds around 700 megabytes (MB/s). When both sides of a DVD-R are writable, it can store up to 17 GB/s of data.

The DVD-R is one of the three industry standards for DVD recordable formats; the other two are DVD–Random Access Memory (DVD-RAM) and DVD+Recordable (DVD+R). DVD-RAM can be continuously erased and recorded. It is only compatible with devices that support the DVD-RAM format.

A DVD+R can record data once; the data on the disc is permanent. The DVD-R is similar to the DVD+R but has two additional standards.

2.3.2.10. USB Drive

A USB drive, also referred to as a flash drive or memory stick, is a small, portable device that plugs into the USB port on your computer. USB drives are commonly used for storage, data backup, and transferring files between devices. USB drives come in multiple storage capacities and different ports, each having a unique shape.

Using a USB drive can differ depending on the type of computer to which you want to connect. A USB flash drive can be used in place of a compact disc. When a user plugs the flash memory device into the USB port, the computer's operating system (OS) recognizes the device as a removable drive and assigns it a drive letter.

2.3.2.11. Blu Ray Disc

Blu-ray disc is a high-density optical disc format similar to DVD. Blue ray is the type of disc used for Play station games and for playing High definition (HD) movies. In the past, there were other standards for such movies, such as the HD DVD format (Figure 2.27).

Figure 2.27. Blu ray disc.

A dual-layer Blu-ray disc can store up to 50 GB of data. This is over five times the capacity of a DVD, and over 70 times more than a CD or VCD.

The disc was developed by the Blu-ray Disc Association (BDA). a group of consumer electronics, personal computer and media manufacturers. The format was developed to enable recording, rewriting and playback of high-definition video (HD), as well as storing large amounts of data.

2.3.2.12. SD/MMC Memory Cards

SD is also known as Secure Digital. It is a memory card used in portable devices such as digital cameras and MP3 players. It was developed by SanDisk, Panasonic and Toshiba. Most standard SD cards have a wide range of storage capacities (ranging from 152 MB to 2 GB). High-capacity SD cards or SDHC can hold a very large amount of data, ranging from 4 GB to 32 GB (Figure 2.28).

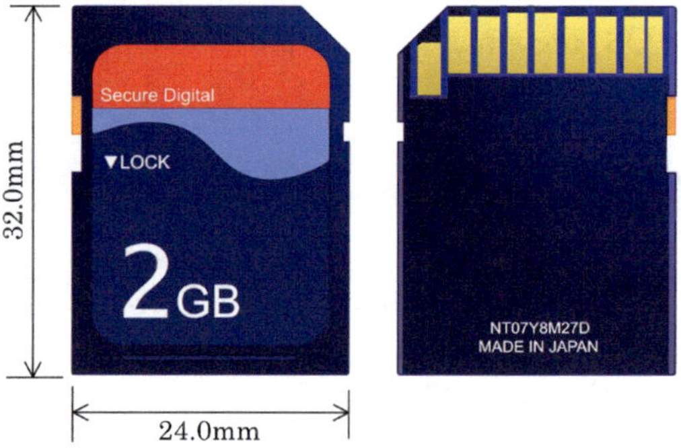

Figure 2.28. SD/MMC memory cards.

2.3.2.13. MMC

Multi-Media Card (MMC) is a standard flash memory card. Typically, an MMC is used as storage media for a portable device, in a form that can easily be removed for access by a PC. Secure Digital (SD) is a flash (non-volatile) memory card format and is used for storage. MMC and SD cards differ in their physical size, capacity, and usage. Both come in different memory sizes as well. While MMCs can be used in a standard SD card slot, the latter cannot be used in an MMC slot.

CHAPTER 3

FUNDAMENTALS OF DIGITAL ELECTRONICS

Contents

Digital electronics or the digital circuit makes components of digital computers. These components perform specific functions. These components are divided into two categories:

i. **Active Components** – Diodes and transistors; and

ii. **Passive Components** – Capacitors, resistors, inductors.

The active components (deliver power/ energy to circuits) are the transistors and diodes while the passive components are the capacitors, resistors, inductors, etc. (Figure 3.1).

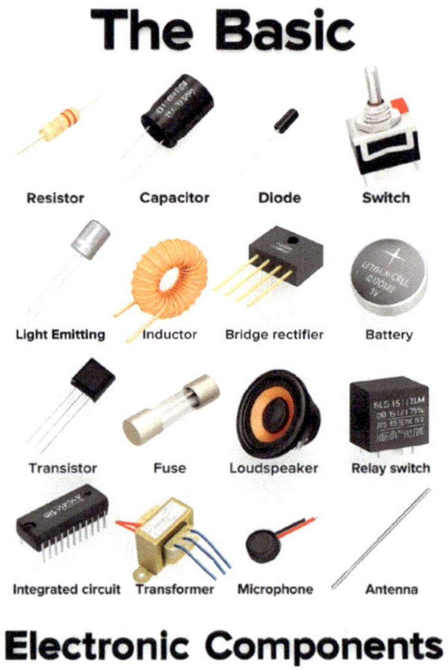

Figure 3.1. Electronic components.

3.1. ELECTRONIC COMPONENTS

1. **Diodes:** Diodes are 2-terminal semiconductor materials. They are used as a switch to allow the flow of current in a particular direction. Different types of diodes are used in the construction of the digital circuit.
2. **Transistors:** These are 3-terminal semiconductor devices the main function of the transistor is to amplify the signal. In digital electronics they are used as a switching device.
3. **Capacitors and Inductors:** They are used to store electrical energy. A capacitor is made using two conducting plates and between these plates, an insulator is placed. They store electrical energy in the form of charge. The change in the current is resisted with the help of an inductor. They are used for storing electric energy in the form of magnetic field.

3.2. LOGIC GATES

These are basic building blocks of digital logic circuits / digital computers. Logic gate performs the logical operations. Gates are blocks of hardware that produce a logic-1 or logic-0 output signal if the input logic requirements are satisfied. Each logic gate has associated a mathematical /logic function, which are Boolean Function. Some of the logic gates are shown below:

<table>
<tr><th>Logic Gate</th><th>Symbol and Boolean Function</th><th>Truth Table</th></tr>
<tr><td>AND Gate</td><td>Symbol:
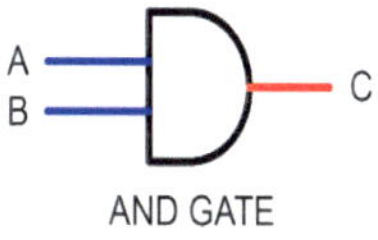
</td><td>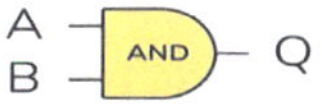

<table>
<tr><th>A</th><th>B</th><th>Q</th></tr>
<tr><td>0</td><td>0</td><td>0</td></tr>
<tr><td>0</td><td>1</td><td>0</td></tr>
<tr><td>1</td><td>0</td><td>0</td></tr>
<tr><td>1</td><td>1</td><td>1</td></tr>
</table></td></tr>
<tr><td>OR Gate: It is one of the basic logics gates whose output is high when any one of its inputs is high and output is low when all inputs are low.</td><td>Symbol:
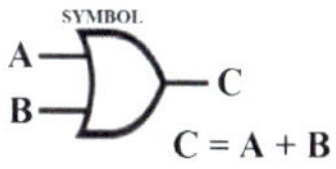

Boolean Function: Y = A OR B
Y = A + B
OR gate</td><td>Truth Table
<table>
<tr><th>Input A</th><th>Input B</th><th>Output</th></tr>
<tr><td>0</td><td>0</td><td>0</td></tr>
<tr><td>0</td><td>1</td><td>1</td></tr>
<tr><td>1</td><td>0</td><td>1</td></tr>
<tr><td>1</td><td>1</td><td>1</td></tr>
</table>
2 Input OR Gate</td></tr>
<tr><td>NOT Gate: (Inverter): It is one of the basic logics gates whose output is high when input is low and output is low when input is high.</td><td colspan="2">Symbol:
NOT Gate
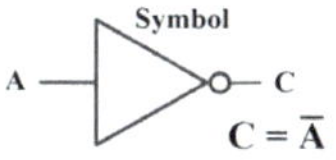

Truth Table
<table>
<tr><th>INPUT</th><th>OUTPUT</th></tr>
<tr><td>A</td><td>NOT A</td></tr>
<tr><td>0</td><td>1</td></tr>
<tr><td>1</td><td>0</td></tr>
</table>
Projectiot123.com</td></tr>
<tr><td>NAND Gate: It is made up of two types of logic gates i.e., a combination of AND and NOT gate. Its output is high when any of its input is low and output is low when all inputs are high.</td><td colspan="2">Symbol:
NAND GATE
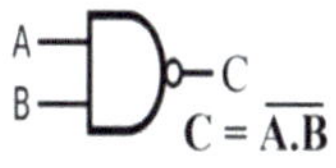

Truth Table
<table>
<tr><th colspan="2">INPUT</th><th>OUTPUT</th></tr>
<tr><td>A</td><td>B</td><td>A NAND B</td></tr>
<tr><td>0</td><td>0</td><td>1</td></tr>
<tr><td>0</td><td>1</td><td>1</td></tr>
<tr><td>1</td><td>0</td><td>1</td></tr>
<tr><td>1</td><td>1</td><td>0</td></tr>
</table>
ProjectIoT123.com</td></tr>
</table>

NOR Gate: It is made up of two types of logic gates i.e., a combination of OR and NOT gate. Its output is high when all its inputs are low and output is low when any one of its inputs is high.	Symbol: 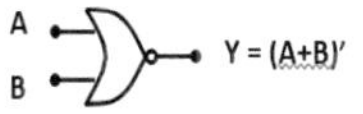 **Boolean Function :** Y = NOT(A OR B) Y= (A+B)'	
EX-OR Gate: It has a graphical symbol similar to that of the OR gate, except for the additional curved line on the input side. Its output is low when all its inputs are high and for other input cases the outputs of EX-OR and OR gate are exactly the same.	Symbol: 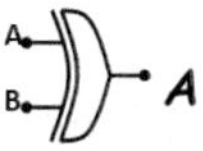 **Boolean Function :** Y = A ⊕ B	
EX-NOR Gate: It is made up of two types of logic gates i.e., a combination of EX-OR and NOT gate. Its output is high when all its inputs are high and for other input cases the outputs of EX-NOR and NOR gate are exactly the same.	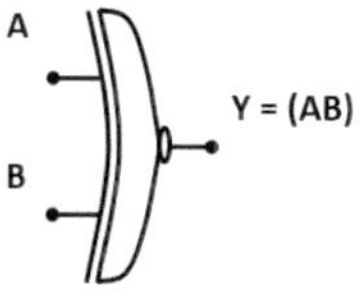 **EX- NOR gate**	

3.3. UNIVERSAL GATES

NAND and NOR gates are called universal gates because any digital circuit, combinational and sequential circuits, can be implemented with it.

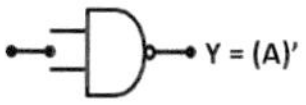 NAND gate as NOT gate	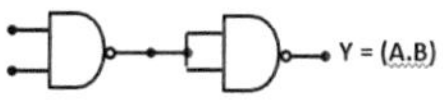 NAND gate as AND gate

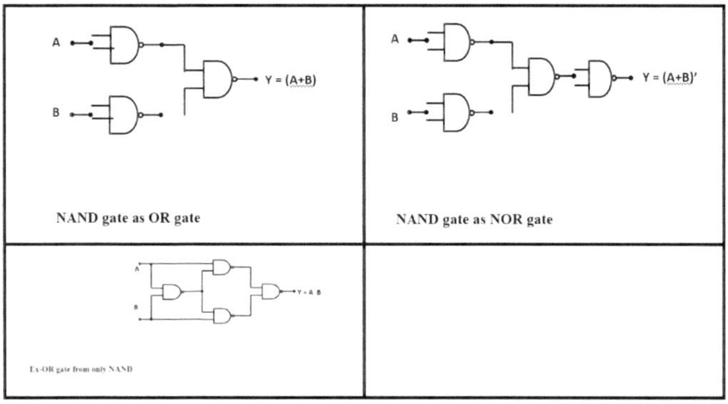

NAND gate as OR gate

NAND gate as NOR gate

Ex-OR gate from only NAND

3.4. ADVANTAGES OF DIGITAL SYSTEM

- The transmission of data in digital systems takes place without degradation due to noise when compared to an analog system.
- The digital system comes with noise-immunity, which makes the storage of data easier. Whereas the analog system undergoes wear and tear, which degrades the information in storage.
- The digital system comes with an interface with computers which makes it easy to control the data. The system can be kept bug free by updating the software. This feature is not available in the analog system.

3.5. LIMITATIONS OF DIGITAL SYSTEM

Though the digital system has noise-immunity and better storage it does have disadvantages too:

- The energy consumed by the digital system is more compared to the analog system. This energy is consumed in calculations and signal processing which results in the generation of heat.
- These systems are expensive.
- The digital systems are fragile, that is if one of the digital data is misinterpreted, the final data will change completely.
- Taking care of analog issues in digital systems could be demanding as analog components are used in designing the digital system.

3.6. APPLICATIONS OF DIGITAL CIRCUITS

Digital electronics or digital circuits are an integral part of electronic devices and here are the uses of digital circuits:

- The display of digital watches is designed based on digital circuits.
- Rocket science and quantum computing use digital electronics.

3.7. REPRESENTATION OF REAL NUMBERS USING FLOATING-POINT REPRESENTATION

Digital Computers use a Binary number system to represent all types of information inside the computers. Alphanumeric characters are represented using binary bits (i.e., 0 and 1). Digital representations are easier to design, storage is easy, and accuracy and precision are greater. There are various types of number representation techniques for integers in digital number representation, for example: Binary number system, octal number system, decimal number system, and hexadecimal number system etc. But Binary number system is most relevant and popular for representing numbers in digital computer system.

3.7.1. Storing Real Number

There are two major approaches to store real numbers (i.e., numbers with fractional components) in modern computing. These are (i) Fixed Point Notation and (ii) Floating Point Notation. In fixed point notation, there is a fixed number of digits after the decimal point, whereas floating point number allows for a varying number of digits after the decimal point.

3.7.2. Fixed-Point Representation

This representation has a fixed number of bits for the integer part and for the fractional part. For example, if the given fixed-point representation is IIII.FFFF, then you can store the minimum value as 0000.0001 and the maximum value as 9999.9999. There are three parts of a fixed-point number representation: the sign field, integer field, and fractional field.

- **Signed Fixed Point Real Number:** (for Decimal Values)

Sign (+ or –)	Integer part (4 digit)	Decimal point	Fractional part (4 digit)

- **Maximum Value:** +9999.9999
- **Minimum Value:** = –9999.9999

We can represent these numbers using (for binary values of k bits):

- Signed representation: range from $-(2^{(k-1)}-1)$ to $(2^{(k-1)}-1)$, for k bits.
- 1's complement representation: range from $-(2^{(k-1)}-1)$ to $(2^{(k-1)}-1)$, for k bits.

- 2's complementation representation: range from $-(2^{(k-1)})$ to $(2^{(k-1)}-1)$, for k bits.

  2's complementation representation is preferred in computer systems because of its unambiguous property and easier for arithmetic operations.
- ***Example:*** Assume number is using a 32-bit format which reserves 1 bit for the sign, 15 bits for the integer part and 16 bits for the fractional part.

Then, –43.625 is represented as following:

1	000000000101011	1010000000000000
Sign bit	Integer part	Fractional part

Where, 0 is used to represent '+' and 1 is used to represent '–'. 000000000101011 is 15-bit binary value for decimal 43 and 1010000000000000 is 16-bit binary value for fractional 0.625.

The advantage of using a fixed-point representation is performance and disadvantage is the relatively limited range of values that they can represent. So, it is usually inadequate for numerical analysis as it does not allow enough numbers and accuracy. A number whose representation exceeds 32 bits would have to be stored in exactly.

Smallest	0	000000000000000	0000000000000001
	Sign bit	Integer part	Fractional part

Largest	0	111111111111111	1111111111111111
	Sign bit	Integer part	Fractional part

These are above smallest positive number and largest positive number which can be stored in 32- bit representation as given above format. Therefore, the smallest positive number is $2^{-16} \approx 0.000015$ Approximate and the largest positive number is $(215-1) + (1-2^{-16}) = 2^{15}(1-2^{-16}) = 32768$, and gap between these numbers is 2^{-16}. We can move the radix point either left or right with the help of only one integer field is 1.

3.7.3. Floating-Point Representation

This representation does not reserve a specific number of bits for the integer part or the fractional part. Instead, it reserves a certain number of bits for the number (called the mantissa or significand) and a certain number of bits to say where within that number the decimal place sits (called the exponent). The floating number representation of a number has two parts: the first part represents a signed fixed-point number called mantissa. The second part designates the position of the decimal (or binary) point and is called the exponent. The fixed-point mantissa may be a fraction or an integer. Floating-point is always interpreted to represent a number in the following form: $M \times r^e$. Only the mantissa m and the exponent e are physically represented in the register (including their sign). A floating-point binary number is represented in a similar manner except that it uses base 2 for the exponent. A floating-point number is said to be normalized if the most significant digit of the mantissa is 1.

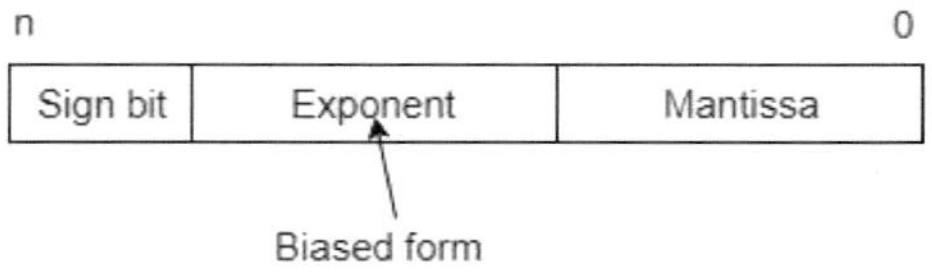

3.7.3.1. IEEE Floating Point Number Representation

IEEE (Institute of Electrical and Electronics Engineers) has provided a standard for Floating-Point Representation and their arithmetic. This standard specifies how single precision (32 bit) and double precision (64-bits) floating point numbers are to be represented.

1. **Single Precision:** The IEEE single floating point standard representation requires a 32-bit word. The first bit to the left is the sign bit, the next 8 bit are the exponent bit, and the final 23 bits form the fractional part.

- The value of normalized number= $(-1)^s(1 + m) \times 2^{(e-127)}$,
- where; $s = 1$ for negative numbers; $s = 0$ for positive number; *m* is the mantissa; *e* is the exponent value; and *Bias* is the –127.

31	30	29	28	27	26	25	24	23	22	21	20	19	18	17	16	15	14	13	12	11	10	9	8	7	6	5	4	3	2	1	0
1-bit sign	8-bits exponent								23 Bits mantissa																						
32 bits single precision IEEE standard																															

2. **Double Precision:** The IEEE double precision floating point standard representation requires a 64-bit word. The first bit is the sign bit, next 11-bit are the exponent bits and the final 52-bits form the fractional part.

63	62	61	60	59	58	57	56	55	54	53	52	51	50	…	7	6	5	4	3	2	1	0
1-bit sign	11-bits exponent											52 bits (20 bit+ 32 bits) Mantissa										
64 bits single precision IEEE standard																						

3.8. BINARY CODES

Numbers, letters or words are represented by a specific group of symbols, called code (Figure 3.2).

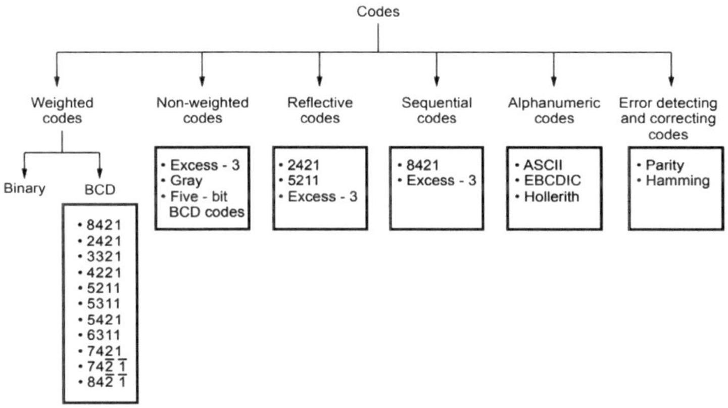

Figure 3.2. *Binary codes.*

3.8.1. Weighted Code

Weighted binary codes are those binary codes which obey the positional weight principle. Each position of the number represents a specific weight.

Example: Straight bit binary code, BCD code, 2421 code, biquinary (5043210) code.

1. Straight Bit Binary Code:

Decimal Number	2			
Positional Weights	$2^3 = 8$	$2^2 = 4$	$2^1 = 2$	$2^0 = 1$
Binary Code	0	0	1	0

2. **Binary Coded Decimal (BCD) code or (8421) Code:** In this code each decimal digit (0 to 9) is represented by a 4-bit binary number. BCD is a way to express each of the decimal digits with a binary code. In the Binary, with four bits we can represent sixteen numbers (0000 to 1111). But in BCD code only the first ten of these are used (0000 to 1001). The remaining six code combinations i.e., 1010 to 1111 are invalid in BCD.

Decimal	0	1	2	3	4	5	6	7	8	9
BCD	0000	0001	0010	0011	0100	0101	0110	0111	1000	1001

Advantages of BCD Codes:

- It is very similar to the decimal system.
- We need to remember the binary equivalent of decimal numbers 0 to 9 only.
- **Disadvantages of BCD Codes:**
- The addition and subtraction of BCD have different rules.
- The BCD arithmetic is a little more complicated.
- BCD needs more bits than binary to represent the decimal number. So, BCD is less efficient than binary.

Example: Representation of decimal number in different weighted codes:

Decimal No.	Straight Bit Binary Code	BCD Code	2421 Code	Biquinary (5043210) Code
0	0000	0000	0000	0100001
2	0010	0010	0010	0100100
6	0110	0110	1100	1000010

8	1000	1000	1110	1001000
9	1001	1001	1111	1010000

3.8.2. Non-Weighted Code

In this type of binary code, the positional weights are not assigned. The examples of non-weighted codes are Excess-3 code and gray code or reflected code.

1. **Excess-3 Code:** The Excess-3 code is also called XS-3 code. It is a non-weighted code used to express decimal numbers. The Excess-3 code words are derived from the 8421 BCD code words adding $(0011)_2$ or (3)10 to each code word in 8421.
2. **Reflected Code or Gray Code:** It is the non-weighted code and it is not an arithmetic code. That means there are no specific weights assigned to the bit position. It has a very special feature that only one bit will change each time the decimal number is incremented. As only one-bit changes at a time, the gray code is called a unit distance code or reflected code. Gray code cannot be used for arithmetic operation.

Decimal	Binary	Excess-3	Gray Code
0	0000	0011	0000
1	0001	0100	0001
2	0010	0101	0011
3	0011	0110	0010
4	0100	0111	0110
5	0101	1000	0111

3.8.3. Alphanumeric Codes

The alphanumeric codes are the codes that represent numbers and alphabetic characters. Mostly such codes also represent other characters such as symbols and various instructions necessary for conveying information. An alphanumeric code should at least represent 10 digits and 26 letters of alphabet i.e., total 36 items. The following alphanumeric codes are very commonly used for the data representation:

- American Standard Code for Information Interchange (ASCII);
- Extended Binary Coded Decimal Interchange Code (EBCDIC);
- Unicode;
- Indian Standard Code for Information Interchange (ISCII).

ASCII code is a 7-bit code whereas EBCDIC is an 8-bit code. ASCII code is more commonly used worldwide while EBCDIC is used primarily in large IBM computers.

3.8.4. Error-Detection Codes

If any external noise is introduced into the radio wave (pulse modulated signal) during transmission, it may change the bit values from 0 to 1 or vice versa. So, an error detection code can be used to detect errors during transmission. Hence, a parity bit (an extra bit) is added to the message to make the total number of 1's either odd or even. Table of parity bit generation:

(a) Message	Parity(ODD)	(b) Message	Parity(EVEN)
0000	1	0000	1
0010	0	0010	0
1010	0	1010	0
0110	0	0110	0
0111	0	0111	0
1111	1	1111	1

3.9. BINARY ARITHMETIC

3.9.1. Unsigned Binary Numbers

In unsigned binary numbers all the bits are used for representing only the magnitude of the corresponding decimal number. For example, the smallest 8-bit binary number is 0000 0000 and the largest 8-bit binary number is 1111 1111. Hence the total range of unsigned 8-bit binary numbers is from (00)H to (FF)H or from (00)10 to (255)10. With 16- bit binary numbers, the total range is from (0000)H to (FFFF)H

1	0	1	1	0	1	0	0

All the bits are used for representing only the magnitude.

3.9.2. Sign-Magnitude Numbers

Binary numbers which contain a sign bit followed by magnitude bits are called Sign- Magnitude Numbers. 0 is used to represent the (+) sign and 1 is used to represent a (-) sign. The MSB of the binary number is used to represent the sign and the remaining bit is used to represent the magnitude. MSB represents the sign and the rest of bits represent the magnitude.

1/0	0	1	1	0	1	0	0
MSB	**Magnitude**						

For an 8-bit sign-magnitude number, the largest negative number is $(-127)_{10}$ and positive number is $(+127)_{10}$.

3.9.3. Binary Addition

1. 0 + 0 = Sum 0 with carry of 0.
2. 0 + 1 = Sum 1 with carry of 0.
3. 1 + 0 = Sum 1 with carry of 0.
4. 1 + 1 = Sum 0 with a carry of 1.
5. 1 + 1 + 1 = Sum 1 with carry of 1.

Example: Add $(111011.1101)_2$ with $(011111.0110)_2$

	1	1	1	1	1	1		1				**carry**
	1 1 1 0 1 1 .							1	1	0	1	**Augend**
+	0	1	1	1	1	1	.	0	1	1	0	**Addend**
1	0	1	1	0	1	1	.	0	0	1	1	**sum**

3.9.4. Binary Subtraction

The basic principles of binary subtraction include the following:

(A) 0 − 0 = 0; (B) 1 − 0 = 1; (C) 1 − 1 = 0; (D) 10 − 1 = 1 with a borrow of 1 from the next more significant bit.

Example: Subtract $(11111.011)_2$ from $(111011.1101)_2$

	1	1	1	0	1	1	.	1	1	0	1	**Minuend**
–	0	1	1	1	1	1	.	0	1	1	0	**Subtrahend**
	0	1	1	1	0	0	.	0	1	1	1	**Difference**

3.9.5. Binary Subtraction Using 1's Complement Method

1's complement of any binary number is obtained by subtracting each binary bit by 1. For example: $(1110011)_2$ 1's complement (1111111 – 1110011) = $(0001100)_2$

Example:

a. Subtract (5–3) Using 1's Complement Method:

(5)10 = $(0\ 1\ 0\ 1)_2$ and $(3)_{10}$ = $(0\ 0\ 1\ 1)_2$

First, obtain the 1's complement of the negative number, i.e., the 1's complement of 3 = 1 1 0 0. Second, add the result to the positive number, i.e.:

	0	1	0	1
+	1	1	0	0
End Around Carry 1	0	0	0	1

Now in the result we can see that there is an overflowing bit/end around carry which we have to add with the remaining result.

	0	0	0	1
+				1
	0	0	1	0

$(0010)_2$ = $(2)_{10}$ is the desired result.

b. Subtract (3–5) Using 1's Complement Method:

$(5)_{10}$ = $(0\ 1\ 0\ 1)_2$ and $(3)_{10}$ = $(0\ 0\ 1\ 1)_2$

First, obtain the 1's complement of the negative number, i.e., the 1's complement of 5 = 1 0 1 0. Second, add the result to the positive number, i.e.,

	0	0	1	1
+	1	0	1	0
No carry bit generated	1	1	0	1

From the result, we can see that no carry bit/end around carry bit is generated. So, to get the desired result, take the 1's complement of the result and attach a negative sign i.e.

1's complement of $(1101)_2$ is $-(0010)_2$

$-(0010)_2 = -(2)_{10}$ is the desired result.

3.9.6. Binary Subtraction Using 2's Complement Method

2's complement is obtained by adding 1 to the 1's complement. For example, we have to find out 2's complement of 0100.

We have to subtract 0100 from 1111 since it is the highest four-digit number to find out 1's complement i.e., 1111 — 0100 = 1011. Hence, 2's complement will be 1011 + 1 = 1100.

Example:

a. Subtract (65–63) Using 2's Complement Method:

- Find the 2's complement of the negative number, i.e., the 2's complement of 63 = 1000001.
- Add the positive number to the 2's complement of the negative number, i.e.

	1	0	0	0	0	0	1
+	1	0	0	0	0	0	1
1 Carry generated	0	0	0	0	0	1	0

- Discard the carry generated.
- After discarding the carry, keep the result, which is the result of subtraction, i.e., Final answer is (0000010)

b. Subtract (63 – 65) Using 2's Complement Method:

- Find 2's complement of the negative number, i.e., 2's complement of 65 = 0111111
- Add the positive number and 2's complement of the negative number, i.e.,

	0	1	1	1	1	1	1
+	0	1	1	1	1	1	1
No carry generated	1	1	1	1	1	1	0

From the result, we can see that no carry bit/end around carry bit is generated. So, to get the desired result, take the 2's complement of the result and attach a negative sign i.e.

2's complement of $(1111110)_2$ is $-(0000010)_2$ i.e., Final answer is $-(0000010)$.

3.9.7. Binary Multiplication

The basic rules of multiplication are listed as follows:

- $0 \times 0 = 0$.
- $0 \times 1 = 0$.
- $1 \times 0 = 0$.
- $1 \times 1 = 1$.

Example: Multiply $(10.11)_2$ by $(11)_2$

		1	0	.	1	1	**Multiplicand**
			X		1	1	**Multiplier**
		1	0	.	1	1	
+	1	0	1	.	1	0	
1	0	0	0	.	0	1	**Product**

3.9.8. Binary Division

Example: Divide $(110001)_2$ by $(111)_2$

Divisor 111	110001-Dividend –0111	111 Quotient
	01010 –111	
	0111 –111	
	0000-Remainder	

3.10. DIGITAL CIRCUITS

3.10.1. Combinational Circuits: Adder, Subtractor, Multiplexer, Demultiplexer, Decoders, Encoders

A combinational circuit is a logic circuit whose output at any instant of time depends only on the present input. It contains no memory element (Figure 3.3).

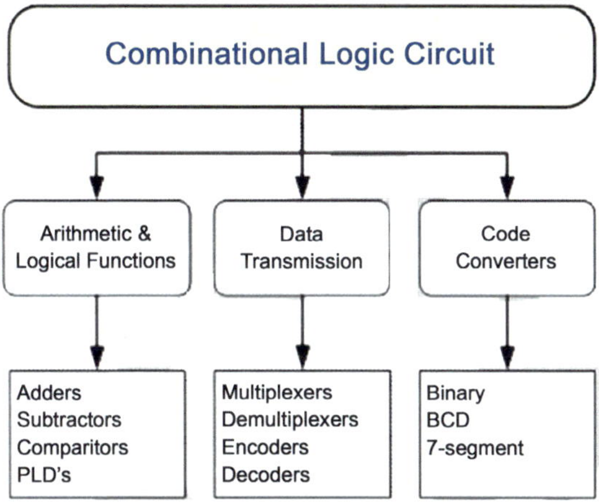

Figure 3.3. Combinational logic circuit.

A combinational logic circuit consists of logic gates whose outputs at any time are determined directly from the present combination of inputs without regard to previous inputs. It consists of input variables, logic gates and output variables. The design of combinational circuits starts from the verbal outline of the problem and ends in a logic circuit diagram, or asset of Boolean functions from which the logic diagram can be easily obtained. The design steps are:

- The problem is stated;
- The number of input and required output variables is determined;
- Truth table is derived;
- Simplified Boolean function for each output is obtained;
- Logic diagram is drawn.

Some examples of combinational circuits are: Half adder, full adder, half subtractor, full subtractor, BCD adder, Series and parallel adder, BCD adders, Look-ahead carry generator.

3.10.2. Half Adder

A combinational circuit that performs the addition of two bits is called half adder. This circuit needs two binary inputs and two binary outputs. The input variables, augend (X) and addend (Y) bits; the output variables SUM (S) and CARRY (C).

Truth Table:

Input s		**Outputs**	
X	**Y**	**SUM (S)**	**CARRY(C)**
0	0	0	0
0	1	1	0
1	0	1	0
1	1	0	1

The simplified output Boolean function: SUM (S) = X'.Y + X.Y' and CARRY (C) = X.Y

The logic diagram of Half Adder:

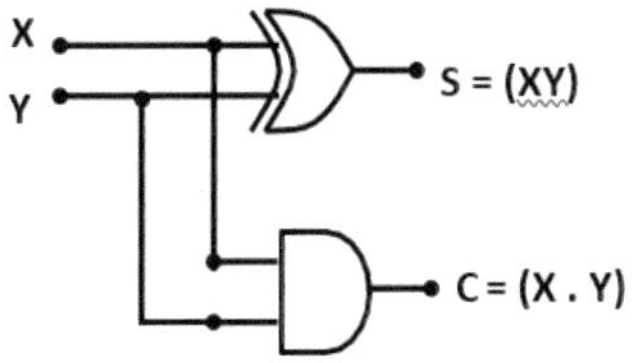

3.10.3. Full Adder

When the augend and addend numbers contain more significant digits, the carry obtained from the addition of two bits is added to the next higher order pair of significant bits. The combinational circuit that performs the addition of three bits (two significant bits and a previous carry) is a full adder. It consists of three inputs (X and Y are actual 2-inputs and the third input represents the CARRYING (CIN) generated from the previous lower significant bit position) and two outputs, SUM (S) and CARRYOUT (COUT).

Truth Table:

Inputs			**Outputs**	
X	**Y**	**CIN**	**SUM (S)**	**CARRY(COUT)**

0	0	0	0	0
0	0	1	1	0
0	1	0	1	0
0	1	1	0	1
1	0	0	1	0
1	0	1	0	1
1	1	0	0	1
1	1	1	1	1

Boolean expression shown from the truth table which is shown:

SUM = X.' Y.' CIN + X.' Y. CIN' + X. Y.' CIN' + X. Y. CIN SUM = (X ⊕ Y ⊕ CIN)

CARRY = X.' Y. CIN + X. Y. CIN' + X. Y.' CIN + X. Y. CIN

= Y.CIN(X + X') + X. Y. CIN' + X. Y.' CIN

= Y.CIN + X. Y. CIN' + X. Y.' CIN

= Y(CIN + CIN.'X) + X. Y.' CIN

= Y(CIN + X) + X. Y.' CIN

= Y.CIN + Y.X + X. Y.' CIN

= CIN (Y + X. Y') + Y.X

= CIN (Y + X) + Y.X

CARRY = CIN.Y + CIN.X + Y.X

Logic diagram of full adder using 2-half adder and OR gate:

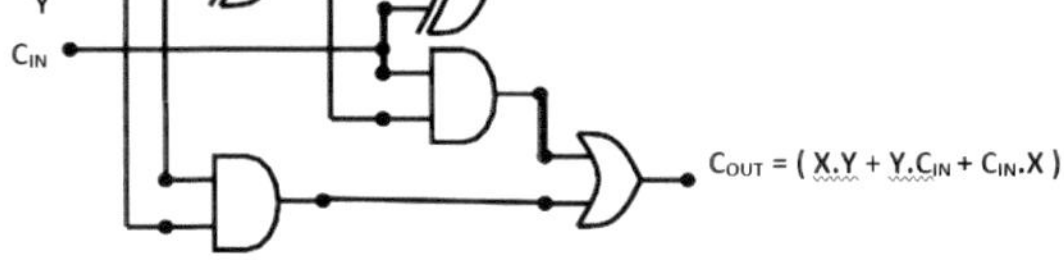

3.10.4. Half Subtractor

A logic circuit which is used for subtracting one single bit binary number from another single bit binary number is called half subtractor. It has two inputs,

A(minuend) and B (subtrahend) and two outputs D (difference) and Bo (borrow). D indicates the difference and Bo is the output signal generated that informs the next stage, that a 1 has been borrowed.

Truth Table of Half Subtractor:

Inputs		Outputs	
A	B	Difference (D)	Borrow (B)
0	0	0	0
0	1	1	1
1	0	1	0
1	1	0	0

Simplified Boolean expression for DIFFERENCE (D) = A'.B + A.B' BORROW (Bo) = A'.B

Logic Diagram of Half Subtractor:

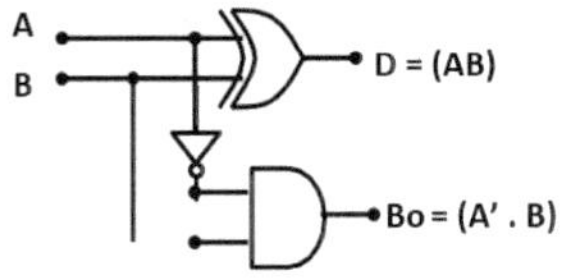

3.10.5. Full Subtractor

The half-subtractor can be used for LSB (Least Significant Bit) subtraction. If there is a borrow during the subtraction of the LSBs, it affects the subtraction in the next higher column; the subtrahend bit is subtracted from the minuend bit, considering the borrow from that column used for the subtraction in the preceding column. Such a subtraction is performed by a full-subtractor.

The Full-subtractor is a combinational circuit which is used to perform subtraction between two bits, taking into account that a 1 may have been borrowed by a lower significant stage. It has three inputs, A(minuend) and B (subtrahend) and BORROW IN (BORIN) and two outputs D (difference) and BOROUT (borrow out)

Truth Table for Full Subtractor:

Input			Output	
A	B	BO-RIN	Difference (D)	Borrow (BOROUT)

0	0	0	0	0
0	0	1	1	1
0	1	0	1	1
0	1	1	0	1
1	0	0	1	0
1	0	1	0	0
1	1	0	0	0
1	1	1	1	1

Logic Diagram of Full Subtractor:

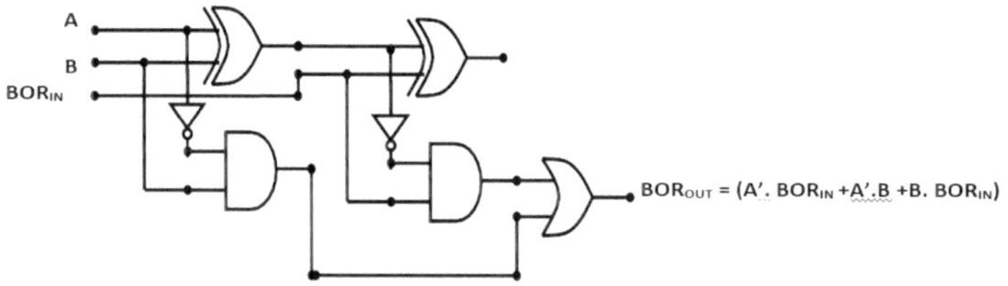

3.10.6. Decoders

A decoder is a combinational logic circuit that converts binary information from n-input lines to a maximum of 2^n unique output lines. If the n-bit decided information has unused or do not care combinations, the decoder output will have less than 2^n outputs.

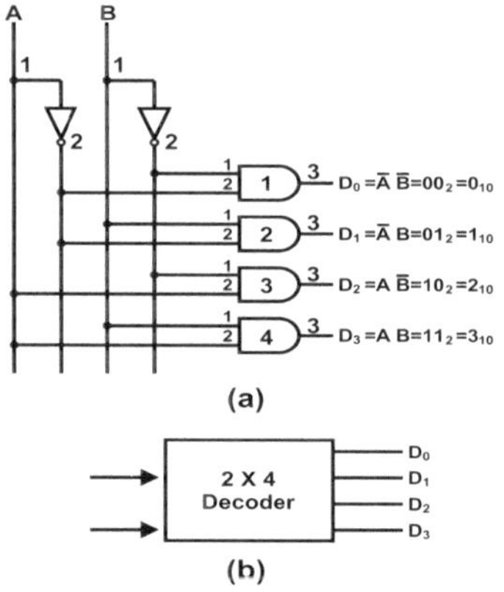

(a)
(b)

‘m’$\leq$ 2

3 to 8 Line Decoder: Block diagram of decoder:

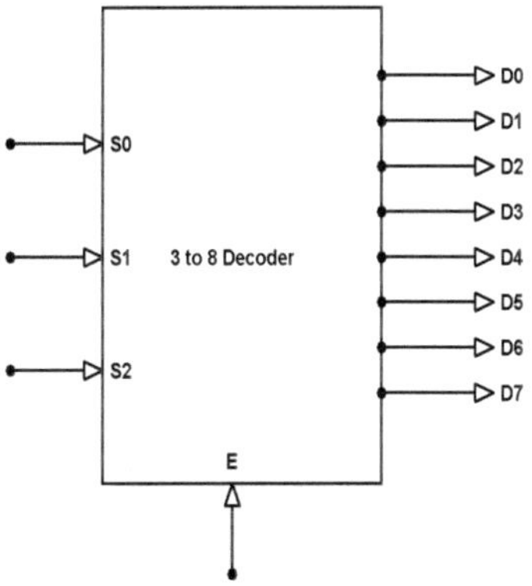

Three inputs are decoded into eight outputs, each output representing one of the minterms of the three input variables.

Truth Table of 3 to 8-Line Decoder:

Inputs			Outputs							
X	Y	Z	D_0	D_1	D_2	D_3	D_4	D_5	D_6	D_7
0	0	0	1	0	0	0	0	0	0	0
0	0	1	0	1	0	0	0	0	0	0
0	1	0	0	0	1	0	0	0	0	0
0	1	1	0	0	0	1	0	0	0	0
1	0	0	0	0	0	0	1	0	0	0
1	0	1	0	0	0	0	0	1	0	0
1	1	0	0	0	0	0	0	0	1	0
1	1	1	0	0	0	0	0	0	0	1

3.10.7. Encoders

A combinational logic circuit that produces the reverse operation of a decoder. Encoder has 2^n(or less) input lines and 'n' output lines. The output lines generate the binary code for 2^n input lines.

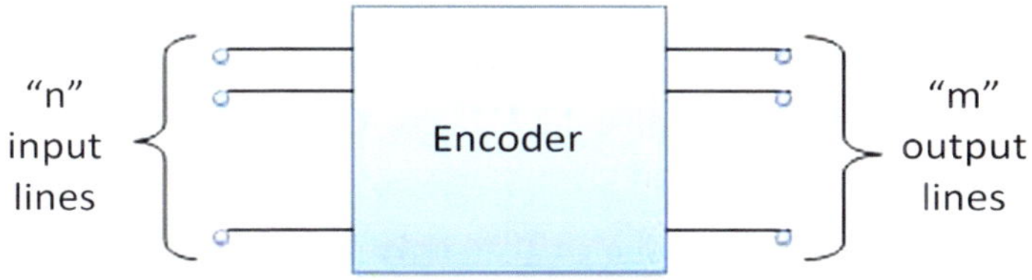

Block Diagram of m: n Encoder

- **8 to 3 Line Encoder (Octal to Binary Encoder):** Octal to binary encoder consists of eight inputs, one for each of the eight digits, and 3-outputs that generate the corresponding binary number.

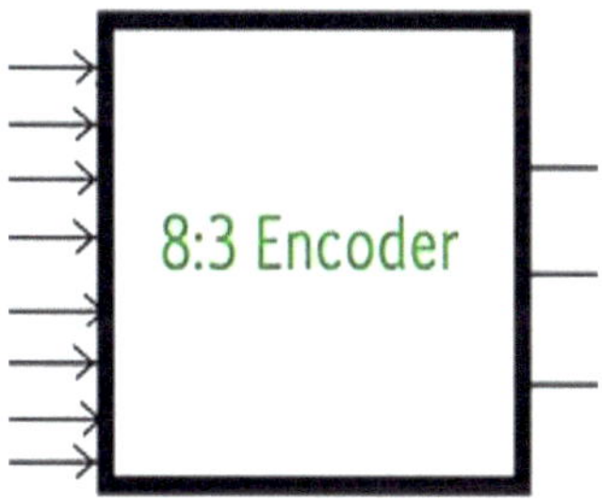

Truth Table:

Inputs								Outputs		
D_0	D_1	D_2	D_3	D_4	D_5	D_6	D_7	X	Y	Z
1	0	0	0	0	0	0	0	0	0	0
0	1	0	0	0	0	0	0	0	0	1
0	0	1	0	0	0	0	0	0	1	0
0	0	0	1	0	0	0	0	0	1	1
0	0	0	0	1	0	0	0	1	0	0
0	0	0	0	0	1	0	0	1	0	1
0	0	0	0	0	0	1	0	1	1	0
0	0	0	0	0	0	0	1	1	1	1

Output:

- "X" is 1 for octal digits: 4,5,6,7. So, $X = D_4 + D_5 + D_6 + D_7$
- "Y" is 1 for octal digits: 2,3,6,7. So, $Y = D_2 + D_3 + D_6 + D_7$
- "Z" is 1 for octal digits: 1,3,5,7. So, $Z = D_1 + D_5 + D_3 + D_7$

The encoder in the figure, assumes that only one input line can be equal to 1 at any time. Note that, circuit has 8-inputs i.e., $2^8 = 256$ possible input combinations and only 8 of these combinations have any meaning. The other input combinations do not care. The output V in figure is to indicate the fact that all inputs are not 0's. Similarly, we can design priority encoder, decimal to BCD encoder, hexadecimal to binary encoder.

3.10.8. Multiplexers (MUX)

Multiplexing means transforming a large number of information over a smaller number of channels or lines. A multiplexer is a combinational logic circuit that selects binary information from one of the input lines and directs it to a single output line. That is why a multiplexer is also called a data selector. Selection of a particular line is controlled by a set of selection input lines.

A Multiplexer has 2^n input lines and "n" selection lines, whose bit combination determines which input is selected.

- **Block Diagram of Multiplexer: 4 × 1 Multiplexer:** A 4x 1 Multiplexer has 4-input lines, 1-output line and 2-selection lines.

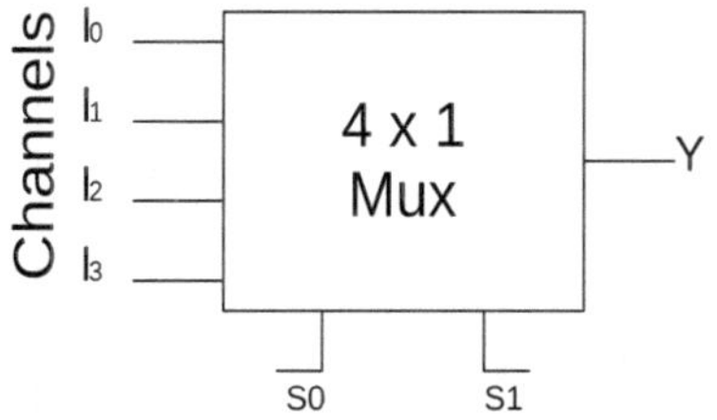

- **3.4 Block Diagram of 4×1 Multiplexer:** From the block diagram of 4×1 multiplexer, there are 4- input lines (A_0, A_1, A_2, A_3), 2-selection lines (S_0 and S_1) and 1-output line (Y).

Truth Table:

Input Selection Lines		**Output Line**
S_1	S_0	Y
0	0	A_0

0	1	A_1
1	0	A_2
1	1	A_3

According to the truth table:

1. When selection line $S_0 = S_1 = 0$; input line A_0 is connected with output Y.
2. When selection line $S_0 = 1$ and $S_1 = 0$; input line A_1 is connected with output Y.
3. When selection line $S_0 = 0$ and $S_1 = 1$; input line A_2 is connected with output Y.
4. When selection line $S_0 = S_1 = 1$; input line A_3 is connected with output Y.

Output Expression: $Y = A_0.S_0'.S_1' + A_1.S_0.S_1' + A_2.S_0'.S_1 + A_3.S_0.S_1$

Similarly, multiplexers 2×1, 8×1, 16×1, 32×1 and so on can be designed.

3.10.9. Demultiplexers (DEMUX)

A demultiplexer is a combinational logic circuit that receives information on a single input line and transmits this information on one of 2^n possible output lines. The selection of a specific output line is controlled by the bit values of "*n*" selection lines.

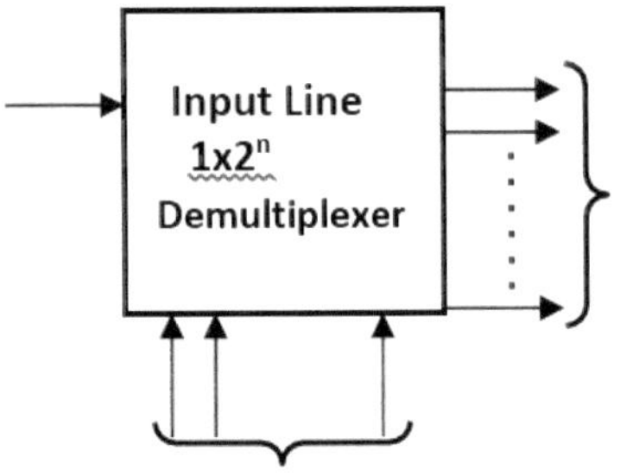

Block Diagram of Demultiplexer

1 x 4 Demultiplexer:

"n" Selection Lines

A 1 x 4 Demultiplexer has 1-input line, 4-output lines and 2-selection lines.

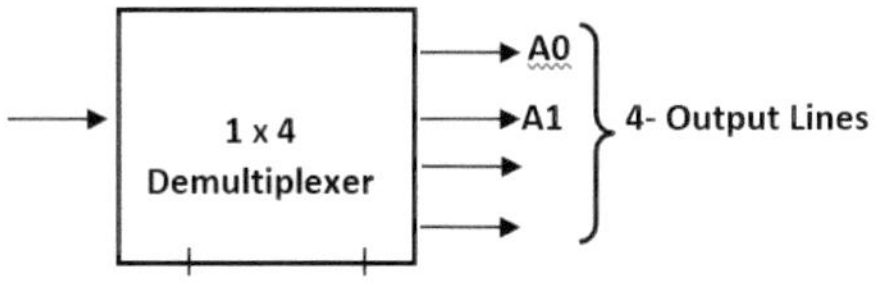

From the block diagram of 1 x 4 Demultiplexer, there is 1- input line (E), 2-selection lines (S_0 and S_1) and 4-output lines (A_0, A_1, A_2, A_3).

Truth Table:

Input	Input Selection Lines		Output Line
	S_1	S_0	
E	0	0	$A_0 = E$
E	0	1	$A_1 = E$
E	1	0	$A_2 = E$
E	1	1	$A_3 = E$

According to the truth table:

1. When the selection lines $S_0 = S_1 = 0$, the input line E is connected to output A_0.
2. When the selection line $S_0 = 1$ and $S_1 = 0$, the input line E is connected to output A_1.
3. When the selection line $S_0 = 0$ and $S_1 = 1$, the input line E is connected to output A_2.
4. When the selection lines $S_0 = S_1 = 1$, the input line E is connected to output A_3.

Output Expression: $A_0 = E.S_0'.S_1'$; $A_1 = E.S_0.S_1'$; $A_2 = E.S_0'.S_1$; $A_3 = E.S_0.S_1$

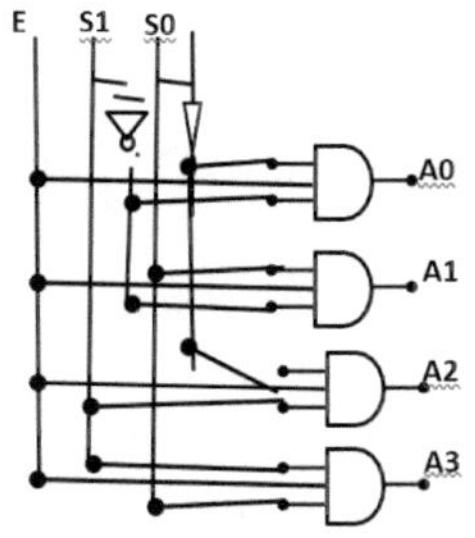

Logic Diagram of 1 x 4 DEMUX

3.10.10. Sequential Circuits

Circuits whose output depends not only on the present input value but also the past input value are known as sequential logic circuits.

Classification of sequential circuits: Sequential circuits may be classified as two types.

- Synchronous sequential circuits; and
- Asynchronous sequential circuits.

Combinational logic refers to circuits whose output is strictly depended on the present value of the inputs. As soon as inputs are changed, the information about the previous inputs is lost, that is, combinational logics circuits have no memory. Although every digital system is likely to have combinational circuits, most systems encountered in practice also include memory elements, which require that the system be described in terms of sequential logic. The mathematical model of a sequential circuit is usually referred to as a sequential machine.

Comparison between combinational and sequential circuits:

SL. No.	Combinational Circuit	Sequential Circuit
1.	It does not contain memory element	It contains memory element.
2.	The output is discovered by the present state of the inputs.	Both the present state input and past state output are used to identify the output.
3.	Combination of operands not necessary in same sequence.	Sequence of operands is necessary in sequential circuit.
4.	Combinational circuits are faster because the delay between the input and output due to propagation delay of gates only.	sequential circuits are comparatively slower than combinational circuits.
5.	Easy to design	Comparatively hard to design
6.	*Example:* Half adder, full adder, encoder, decoder, multiplexer, demultiplexer etc.	Example: Flip-flops, registers, counters, etc.

3.10.11. Flip-Flops

A flip flop is a basic data storage element. A NAND or NOR gate individually acts as a storage element when they are cross coupled with feedback. Such cross coupled NAND or NOR gates with feedback are known as flip flops, as shown in Figures 3.1 and 3.2. A flip flop is a bistable (output will remain permanently either 0 or 1 until it is forced to change the state by an external trigger) circuit. A flip flop has two outputs Q and Q,' and are complement to each other.

3.10.11.1. R-S (Reset-Set)Flip Flop Using NOR Gates

Truth Table:

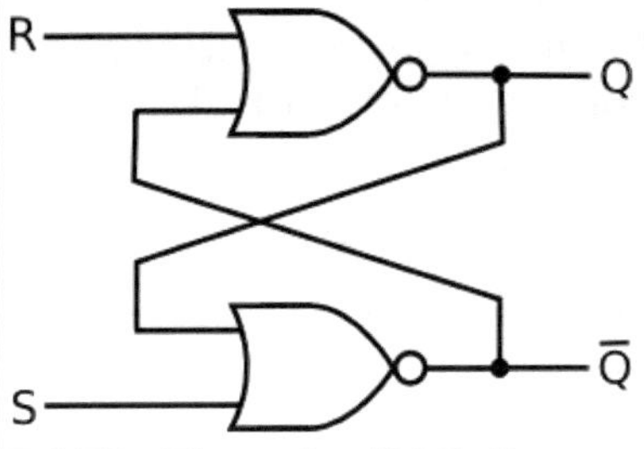

RS Flip-Flop using NOR Gates

S	R	Q (Output)
0	0	No change
1	0	1 (SET)
0	1	0 (Reset)
1	1	Invalid

The truth table shown for NOR gate flip flop is similar to that of transistor flip flop.

3.10.11.2. R-S (Reset-Set) Flip Flop Using NAND Gates

Truth Table:

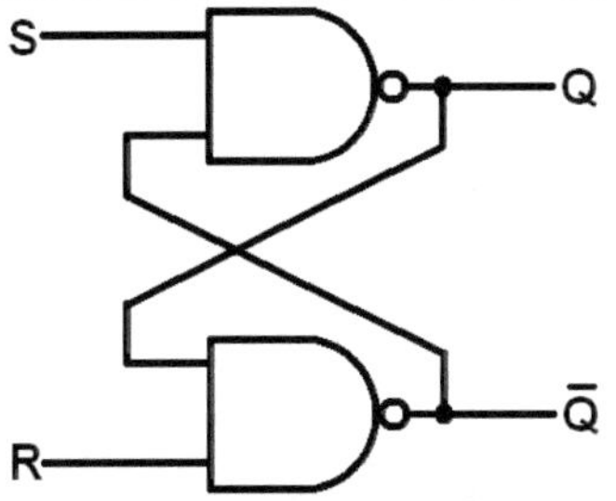

RS Flip Flop using NAND Gates

S	R	Q (Output)
0	0	Invalid
1	0	0 (Reset)
0	1	1 (Set)
1	1	No change

The truth table shown for NAND gate flip flop is inverted to that of NOR gate flip flop, hence inverters gates are used to drive the inputs to the gates as shown in Figure 3.3:

Truth Table:

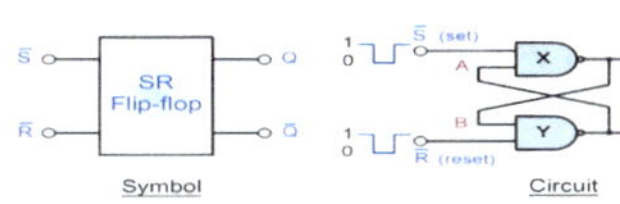

RS Flip Flop using Inverter Gates

S	R	Q (Output)
0	0	No change
1	0	1 (Set)
0	1	0 (Reset)
1	1	Invalid

The truth table for NAND gate flip flop with inverters is similar to that of transistor flip flop, hence this flip flop is used to realize the desired flip flop.

JK-FF (Named for inventor Jack Kilby)

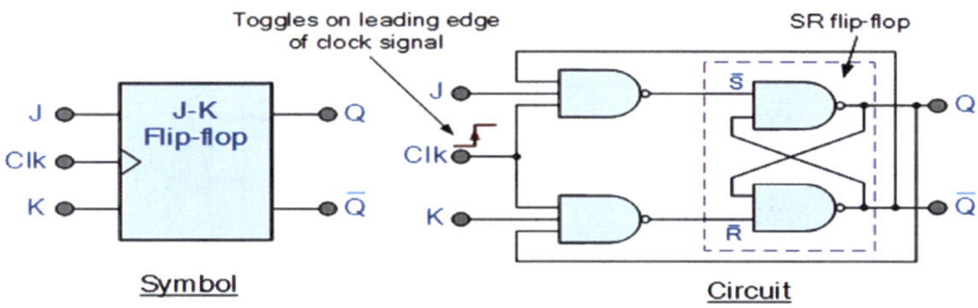

The basic S-R NAND flip-flop circuit has many advantages and uses in sequential logic circuits but it suffers from two basic switching problems.

- The Set = 0 and Reset = 0 condition (S = R = 0) must always be avoided; and
- If Set or Reset change state while the enable (EN) input is high the correct latching action may not occur.

Then to overcome these two fundamental design problems with the SR flip-flop design, the JK flip Flop was developed.

Both the S and the R inputs of the previous SR now been replaced by 2-inputs J and K inputs. The two 2-input AND gates of the gated SR bistable have now been replaced by two 3-input NAND gates with the third input of each gate connected to the outputs at Q and Q. This cross coupling of the SR flip-flop allows the previously invalid condition of S = "1" and R = "1" state to be used to produce a "toggle action" as the two inputs are now interlocked.

3.10.12. Registers

The register capable of shifting its binary information either to the right or to the left is called shift register. Shift register consists of an array of flip flops connected in a cascade. All flip flops receive a common clock pulse which causes the shift from one stage to the next stage. Shift registers are classified depending upon the way data are loaded and retrieved.

Classified as:

1. Serial input serial output shift register;
2. Serial input parallel output shift register;
3. Parallel input serial output shift register;
4. Parallel input parallel output shift register.

3.10.12.1. Serial Input Serial Output Shift Register (SISO)

Figure 3.4 shows the SISO shift register; output of each flip flop is connected to the input of the next flip flop at its right. Each clock pulse shifts the contents of the register one bit to the right.

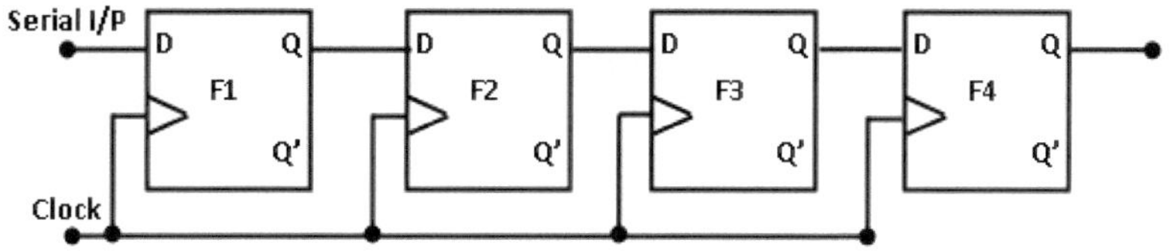

Figure 3.4. *Serial input serial output shift register.*

- **Operation:**

  Serial Loading of Information or Data:

Input Sequence	**F1**	**F2**	**F3**	**F4**	**Clock Pulse**
1 1 0 1	0	0	0	0	Initialstate
	1	0	0	0	After 1CP
	0	1	0	0	After 2CP
	1	0	1	0	After 3CP
	1	1	0	1	After 4CP
Serial loading of data					

- **Serial Retrieving of Information or Data:**

Clock Pulse	**F1**	**F2**	**F3**	**F4**	**Output Sequence**
After 4CP	1	1	0	1	–
After 5CP	X	1	1	0	1

After 6CP	X	X	1	1	01
After 7CP	X	X	X	1	101
After 8CP	X	X	X	X	1101
Serial retrieving of data					

3.10.12.2. Serial Input Parallel Output Shift Register (SIPO)

- **Parallel Output:** In SIPO as shown in Figure 3.5, data is loaded serially, one bit at a time but data can be read simultaneously. Clock pulse stops at the movement the binary information is stored. Each output is available on a separate line, and they may be read simultaneously.

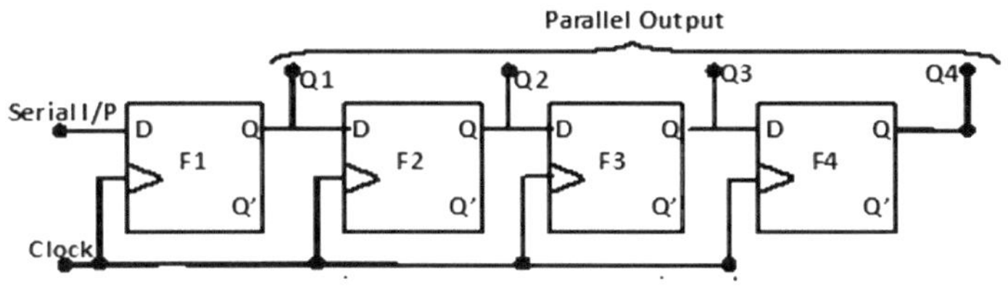

Figure 3.5. *Serial input parallel output shift register.*

3.10.12.3. Parallel Input Parallel Output Shift Register (PIPO)

In PIPO shift register as shown in Figure 3.6, input data D1, D2, D3, and D4 can be loaded into the flip flop simultaneously through the enable pulse and can be retrieved simultaneously also from outputs Q1, Q2, Q3, and Q4.

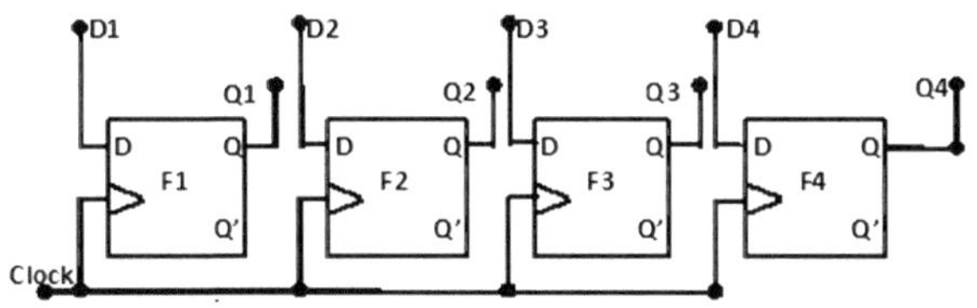

Figure 3.6. *Parallel input parallel output shift register.*

3.10.12.4. Parallel Input Serial Output Shift Register (PISO)

In the PISO shift register as shown in Figure 3.7, all flip flops are preset and the input binary information is written into the register, all bits in parallel, by the preset enable pulse. The stored information may be read serially by applying clock pulses. Since the data can be loaded into the flip flop simultaneously and can be read from the register one bit at a time by clock pulse, this shift register is a parallel to serial converter.

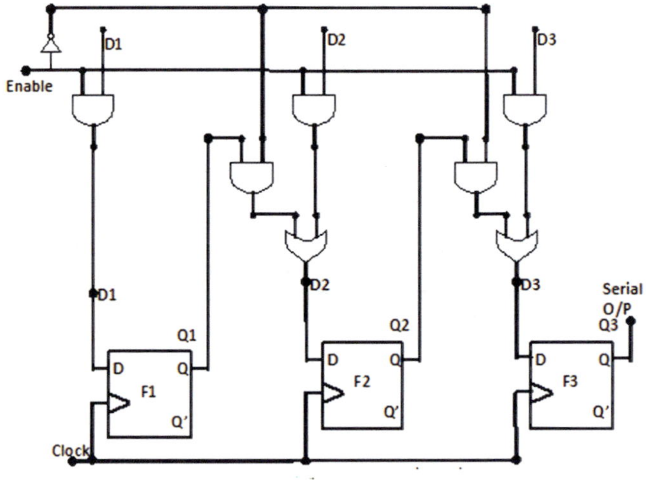

Figure 3.7. Parallel input serial output shift register.

From Figure 3.7 of PISO shift register, data input D1, D2, and D3 are loaded simultaneously, when Enable = 1. When Enable = 0, loaded data is taken out serially from Q3 output of F3 flip flop. On application of clock pulse.

3.10.13. Counters

Counters are digital circuits which are used to count the clock pulses or to generate the sequence of states. Since clock pulses occur at known intervals, the counter can be used for measuring time and therefore period or frequency.

- Asynchronous Counter or Serial Counter:
- Each flip flop is triggered by the previous flip flop. Except the first flip flop.
- Counter is simple and straightforward in operation
- Construction usually requires a minimum amount of hardware.
- Counters have a cumulative settling time.
- **Synchronous Counter or Parallel Counter:**

- Every flip flop is triggered by the clock (in synchronism).
- Increase in speed of operation.
- Construction- Increased in hardware.
- Settling time is equal to the delay time of a single flip flop.

- **Modulus of Counter(MOD):** Modulus of counter is the number of different states before the sequence repeats. Example-3-bit binary counter has 8 different states, so MOD-8 Counter.

Asynchronous Up Counter (Binary Ripple Counter):

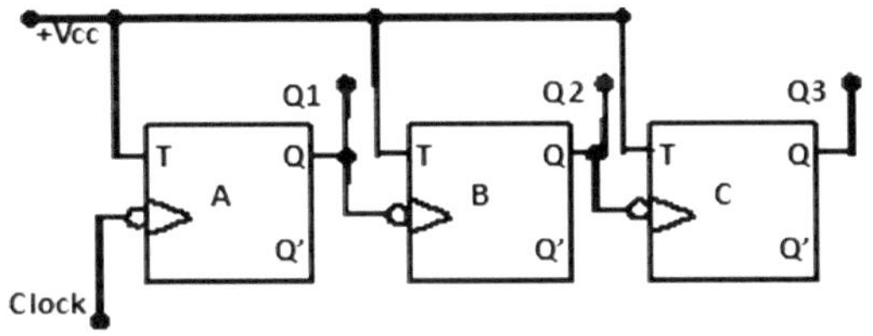

Figure 3.8. *Binary Ripple Counter*

A 3-bit binary ripple counter using T-Flip flop is shown in Figure 3.8 From the figure, the negative edge triggered clock drives the flip flop "A." Output of flip flop "A" drives the flip flop "B" and output of flip flop "B" drives flip flop "C." Flip flop "A" changes state before it can trigger the flip flop "B" and flip flop "B" has to change state before it can trigger the flip flop "C". The trigger moves through the flip flop like a ripple in water, hence the name Ripple Counter.

- **Operation:** Let assume all flip flops are reset to produce "0". Consider flip flop "A" as least significant bit (LSB) and flip flop "C" as most significant bit (MSB), so the content of counter is CBA = 0 0 0.

From the waveform as shown in Figure 3.9, every time there is a negative clock transition, flip flop A will change the state. Since flip flop A output acts as a clock for flip flop B, each time the waveform at A goes low flip flop B will toggle (change the state). Each time the waveform at B goes low flip flop C will toggle (change the state).

Truth Table:

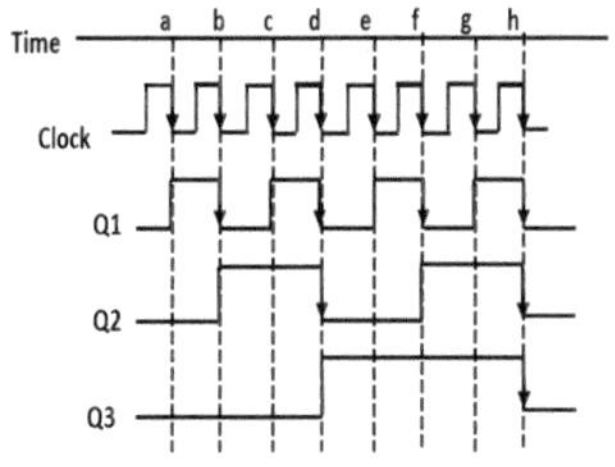

Figure 3.9. *Waveforms.*

Clock	**C**	**B**	**A**	**Count**	
	0	0	0	0	
a	0	0	1	1	
b	0	1	0	2	
c	0	1	1	3	
d	1	0	0	4	
e 1 0 1 5					
f	1	1	0	6	
g	1	1	1	7	
h	0	0	0	0	

3.10.13.1. Synchronous Counter or Parallel Counter

In a ripple counter (asynchronous counter) flip flop delay times are additive and the total settling time for the counter is approximately the delay times the total number of flip flops. This problem is overcome by the use of a synchronous counter or parallel counter. Here every flip flop is triggered in synchronism with the clock.

CHAPTER 4

BASIC COMPUTER ORGANIZATION

Contents

4.1. BASIC ORGANIZATION OF COMPUTER

The organization of the computer is an arrangement of its internal registers, the timing and control units and the set of instructions (program) that it uses to perform certain task. In other words, the organization of a digital computer defined by:

- The set of registers it contains and their function;
- The set of instructions used;
- The timing and control structure.

Basic units for processing of any tasks are as follows:

1. **Program:** A set of instructions that specify the operations, operands, and the sequence by which processing has to occur. The user of a computer can control the process by means of a program. A Program can be defined as a set of instructions that specify the operations, operands, and the sequence by which processing has to occur.
2. **Instruction:** It is the sequence of bits (binary code) that performs an operation. It specifies a sequence of micro-operations (for accomplishment of operation).A Computer Instruction is a binary code that specifies a sequence of micro-operations for the computer.
3. **Instruction Code:** A group of bits that instruct the computer to perform specific operations are known as instructions. An Instruction Code is a group of bits that leads the computer to perform a specific operation. The instruction code is usually divided into many parts, each having its own particular interpretation. The most basic part of an instruction code is its operation part.

Opcode Part (to specify type of operation)	**Operand Part (to specify operand's address, on which operation is to be done)**
The Operation Code is groups of bits that specifies nature of operations such as add, subtract, multiply, shift, and complement.	The operand part specifies the location or address of operation. For example, operation may be performed on some data stored in the processor register or in memory. Therefore, this part of instruction shows the registers or the memory words where the operands are to be found, as well as the register or memory word where the result is to be stored, in addition to the type of operation to be executed.

4.2. COMPUTER REGISTERS

Register are used to quickly accept, store, and transfer data and instructions that are being used immediately by the CPU, there are various types of Registers those are used for various purpose.

4.2.1. General Purpose Registers

These are numbered as R_0, R_1, R_2, …, R_{n-1}, and used to store temporary data during any ongoing operation. Its content can be accessed by assembly programming. Modern CPU architectures tends to use more GPR so that register-to-register addressing can be used more, which is comparatively faster than other addressing modes.

4.2.2. Memory Address Register

This register holds the memory addresses of data and instructions. This register is used to access data and instructions from memory during the execution phase of an instruction. Suppose the CPU wants to store some data in the memory or to read the data from the memory. It places the address of the-required memory location in the MAR.

4.2.3. Program Counter (PC)

The program counter (PC) commonly called the instruction pointer (IP) in Intel x86 microprocessors, and sometimes called the instruction address register, or just part of the instruction sequencer in some computers, is a processor register It is a 16 bit special function register in the 8085 microprocessor. It keeps track of the next memory address of the instruction that is to be executed once the execution of the current instruction is completed. In other words, it holds the address of the memory location of the next instruction when the current instruction is executed by the microprocessor.

4.2.4. Accumulator Register

This Register is used for storing the Results that are produced by the System. When the CPU will generate Some Results after the Processing then all the Results will be Stored into the AC Register.

4.2.5. Memory Data Register (MDR)

MDR is the register of a computer's control unit that contains the data to be stored in the computer storage (RAM), or the data after a fetch from the computer storage. It acts like a buffer and holds anything that is copied from the memory ready for the processor to use it. MDR hold the information before it goes to the decoder. The Memory Data Register is half of a minimal interface between a micro program and computer storage; the other half is a memory address register.

4.2.6. Index-Register

A hardware element which holds a number that can be added to (or, in some cases, subtracted from) the address portion of a computer instruction to form an effective address. Also known as **base register**.

4.2.7. Memory Buffer Register (MBR)

MBR stand for memory buffer register. This register holds the contents of data or instruction read from, or written in memory. It means that this register is used to store data/instructions coming from the memory or going to the memory.

4.2.8. Data Register

A register used in microcomputers to temporarily store data being transmitted to or from a peripheral device.

4.2.9. Condition Code Registers (CCR)

Condition code registers contain different flags that indicate the status of any operation, for instance let us suppose an operation caused creation of a negative result or zero.

4.2.10. Instruction Register (IR)

The IR holds the instruction which is just about to be executed. The instruction from the PC is fetched and stored in IR. As soon as the instruction is placed in IR, the CPU starts executing the instruction and the PC points to the next instruction to be executed.

4.3. COMPUTER INSTRUCTIONS

Computer instructions are a set of machine language instructions that a particular processor understands and executes. A computer performs tasks according to instructions provided.

4.3.1. Fields of Computer Instructions

There are three basic fields of each instruction in a computer. Let us look at the following diagram of 16-bit instruction.

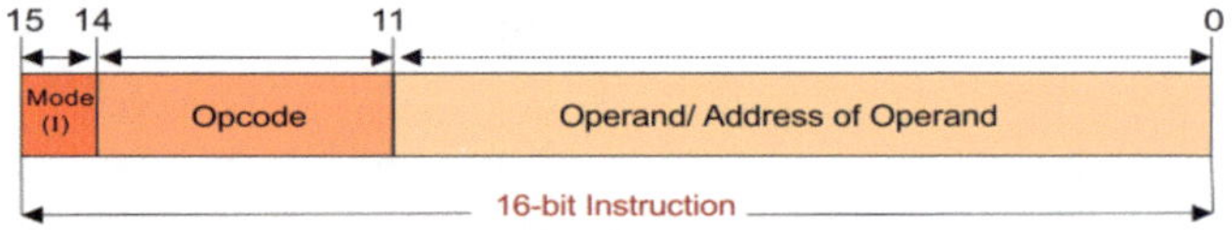

- The Operand is a data. But the operand field may contain actual data or address of that data. Address of data means the location of a register or memory where actual data is present.
- The Opcode field tells the operation which will be performed on data, i.e., +, -, x, <, etc.
- The Mode field tells about the addressing modes. It is a source to find the operand. It tells whether the operand field contains the actual data or address of memory, address of the register, or address of address, etc. i.e., if Mode bit = 0 then it is direct addressing and if Mode bit =1 then it is an indirect addressing mode. We will cover all of this in detail in addressing modes.

4.4. INSTRUCTIONS FORMATS

A basic computer has three instruction code formats.

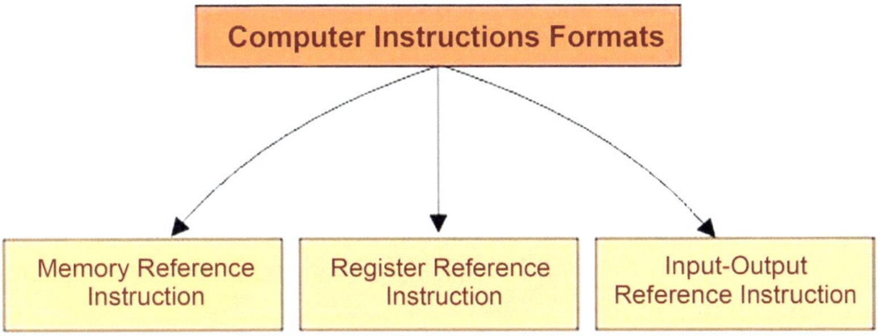

4.4.1. Memory Reference Instruction

The instruction format of memory reference instructions is:

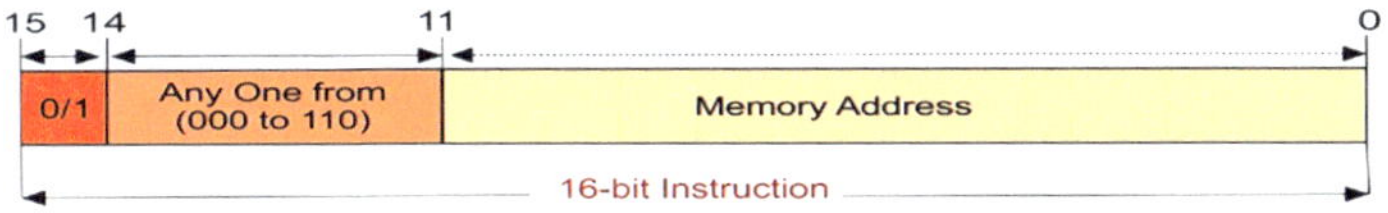

- Where the 15th bit is I. This value of I will be 0, to represent direct addressing mode, or 1 to represent indirect addressing mode.
- 12 to 14 bits represent the Op-code value. Op-code value will be in between 000 to 110. These 7 values (000 to 110) represent the 7 decode operations. Decode operations represented by D0 to D6 as shown in the following diagram.

Symbol	Operational Decoder	Symbolic Description
AND	000 (D0)	AC ← AC ∧ M[AR]
ADD	001 (D1)	AC ← AC + M[AR], E ← Cout
LDA	010 (D2)	AC ← M[AR]
STA	011 (D3)	M[AR] ← AC
BUN	100 (D4)	AR ← PC
BSA	101 (D5)	M[AR] ← PC, PC← AR+1
ISZ	110 (D6)	M[AR] ← M[AR]+1, if M[AR]+1 = 0

- When the value of Opcode = 001 (D1) then ADD operation will perform on the operand.
- 0 to 11 bits represent the address of memory location or operand itself.

4.4.2. Register–Reference Instruction

The instruction format of memory reference instructions is:

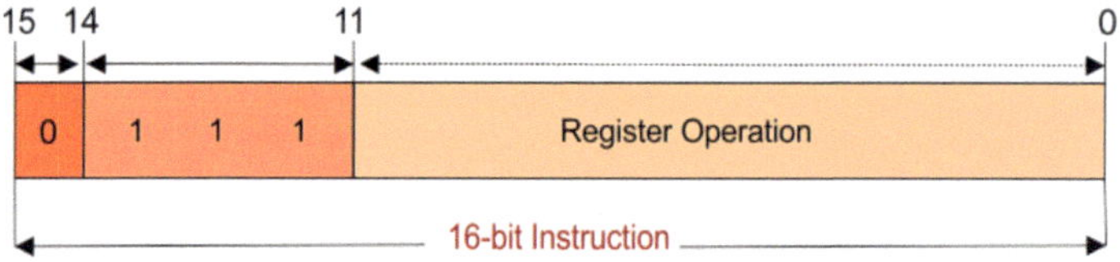

- Where the 15th bit which is I will always equal 0 to represent register addressing mode.
- 12 to 14 bits represent the Opcode value. Opcode value will always equal 111.
- 0 to 11 bits of operand represents the register operation. Different operations can be performed on the register by setting the value 1 of any location from 0 to 11 bits. So, 12 operations can be performed on registers by setting 1 to different locations (B0 to B11).

Symbol	Operational Decoder	Symbolic Description
HLT	000000000001 (IR0)	S ← 0 (S is start-stop flip-flop)
SZE	000000000010 (IR1)	if (E=0) then PC ← PC+1
SZA	000000000100 (IR2)	if (AC=0) then PC ← PC+1
SNA	000000001000 (IR3)	if (AC(15)=1) then PC ← PC+1
SPA	000000010000 (IR4)	if (AC(15)=0) then PC ← PC+1
INC	000000100000 (IR5)	AC ← AC+1
CIL	000001000000 (IR6)	AC ← shl AC, AC(0) ← E, E ← AC(15)
CIR	000010000000 (IR7)	AC ← shr AC, AC(15) ← E, E ← AC(0)
CME	000100000000 (IR8)	E ← E'
CMA	001000000000 (IR9)	AC ← AC'
CLA	010000000111 (IR10)	E ← 0
CLE	100000000111 (IR11)	AC ← 0

4.4.3. Input-Output Instruction

The instruction format of memory reference instructions is:

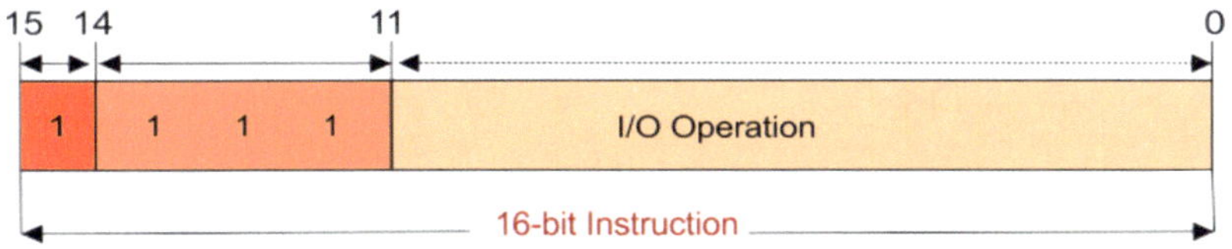

- Where the 15th bit which is I will always equal to 1 to represent I/O addressing mode.
- 12 to 14 bits represent the Op-code value. Op-code value will always equal 111.
- 0 to 5 bits of operand will always be zero and 6–11 bits represents the I/O operation. Different operations can be performed on I/O by setting the value 1 of any location from 6 to 11 bits. So, 6 operations can be performed on I/O by setting 1 to different locations (B6 to B11).

Symbol	Operational Decoder	Symbolic Description
IOF	000001000000 (IR6)	IEN ← 0 // interrupt enable off
ION	000010000000 (IR7)	IEN ← 1 // interrupt enable ON
SKO	000100000000 (IR8)	if (FGO=1) then PC ← PC+1 // skip on output flag
SKI	001000000000 (IR9)	if (FGI=1) then PC ← PC+1 // skip on input flag
OUT	010000000111 (IR10)	OUTR ← AC(0-7), FGO ← 0 // Output character from AC
INP	100000000111 (IR11)	AC(0-7)← INPR, FGI← 0 // Input character to AC

4.5. TIMING AND CONTROL

4.5.1. Control Unit

The block diagram of the control unit is shown · Components of Control unit are:

- Two decoders;
- A sequence counter;
- Control logic gates an instruction read from memory is placed in the instruction register (IR).

The IR is divided into three parts: I bit, the operation code (bits 12–14), and bits 0 through 11. The operation code in bits 12 through 14 is decoded with a 3 x 8 decoder. Bit 15 of the instruction is transferred to a flip-flop designated by the symbol I (Figure 4.1).

- The eight outputs of the decoder are designated by the symbols D0 through D7. Bits 0 through 11 are applied to the control logic gates. The 4-bit sequence counter can count in binary from 0 through 15. The outputs of the counter are decoded into 16 timing signals T0 through T15.
- The sequence counter SC can be incremented or cleared synchronously. Most of the time, the counter is incremented to provide the sequence of timing signals out of 4 x 16 decoders. Occasionally, the counter is cleared to 0, causing the next timing signal to be T0.
- Consider the case where SC is incremented to provide timing signals T0, T1, T2, T3, and T4 in sequence. At time T4, SC is cleared to 0 if the decoder output D3 is active. This is expressed symbolically by the statement D3T4: SC ← 0.

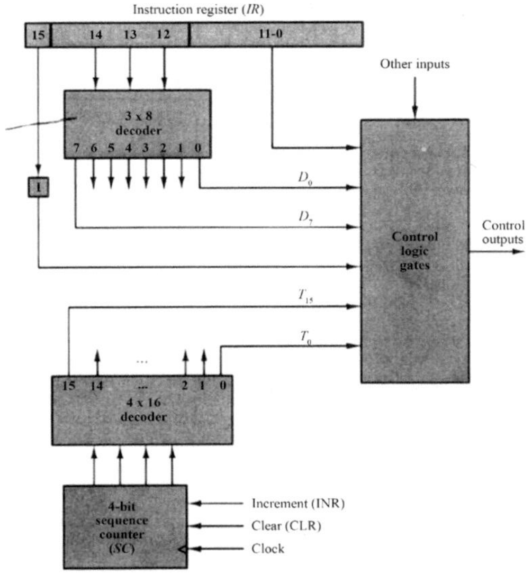

Figure 4.1. *Control unit with timing diagram.*

4.5.2. Timing Diagram

The timing diagram (Figure 4.1) shows the time relationship of the control signals.

- The sequence counter SC responds to the positive transition of the clock.

- Initially, the CLR input of SC is active.
- The first positive transition of the clock clears SC to 0, which in turn activates the timing.
- T0 out of the decoder. T0 is active during one clock cycle. The positive clock transition labeled T0 in the diagram will trigger only those registers whose control inputs are connected to timing signal T0.
- SC is incremented with every positive clock transition unless its CLR input is active.
- This produces the sequence of timing signals T0, T1, T2, T3, and T4, and so on. If SC is not cleared, the timing signals will continue with T5, T6, up to T15 and back to T0.

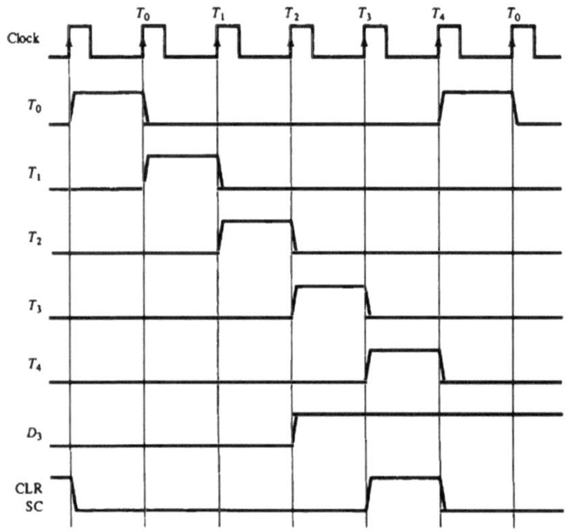

- The last three waveforms show how SC is cleared when D3T4 = 1. Output D3 from the operation decoder becomes active at the end of timing signal T2. When timing signal T4 becomes active, the output of the AND gate that implements the control function D3T4 becomes active.
- This signal is applied to the CLR input of SC. On the next positive clock transition the counter is cleared to 0. This causes the timing signal T0 to become active instead of T5 that would have been active if SC were incremented instead of cleared.

4.6. INSTRUCTION CYCLES

A program that exists inside a computer's memory unit consists of a series of instructions. The processor executes these instructions through a cycle for each instruction (Figure 4.2).

In the basic computer, each instruction cycle includes the following procedures:

- It can fetch instruction from memory;
- It is used to decode the instruction;
- It can read the effective address from memory if the instruction has an indirect address;
- It can execute the instruction.

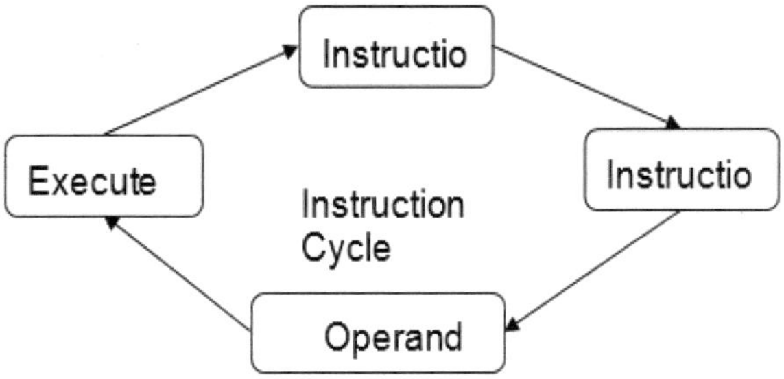

Figure 4.2. *Instruction cycle.*

4.6.1. Registers Involved in Each Instruction Cycle

1. **Memory Address Registers (MAR):** It is connected to System Bus address lines. It specifies the address of a read or write operation in memory.
2. **Memory Buffer Register (MBR)**: It is connected to the data lines of the system bus.: It is connected to the system bus Data Lines. It holds the memory value to be stored, or the last value read from the memory.
3. **Program Counter (PC):** Holds the address of the next instruction to be fetched. Instruction
4. **Register (IR)**: Holds the last instruction fetched.

4.6.2. Fetch Cycle

The address of the next instruction to execute is in the Program Counter (PC) at the beginning of the fetch cycle.

- **Step 1:** The address in the program counter is transferred to the Memory Address Register (MAR), as this is the only register that is connected to the system bus address lines.
- **Step 2:** The address in MAR is put on the address bus, now a Read order is provided by the control unit on the control bus, and the result appears on the data bus and is then copied into the memory buffer register. Program counter is incremented by one, to get ready for the next instruction. These two acts can be carried out concurrently to save time.
- **Step 3:** The content of the MBR is moved to the instruction register (IR).

  T1: MAR ← PC

  T2: MBR ← Memory

  PC ←PC + step size or length of instruction

  T3: IR ←MB R

4.6.3. Decode Instruction Cycle

The next move is to fetch source operands once an instruction is fetched. Indirect addressing (it can be obtained by any addressing mode, here it is done by indirect addressing) is obtained by Source Operand. You do not need to fetch register-based operands. If the opcode is executed, it will require a similar process to store the result in main memory. Micro-operations take place:

T1: MARIR (address) T2: MBR Memory

T3: IR (address) (MBR(Address))

- **Step 1:** The instruction address field is passed to the MAR. This is used to fetch the operand's address.
- **Step 2**: The address field of the IR is updated from the MBR.
- **Step 3:** The IR is now in the state. Now IT is ready for the execution cycle.

4.6.4. Execute Instruction Cycle

The initial three cycles (Fetch, Indirect, and Interrupt) are predictable and quick. Each requires simple, small, and fixed micro-operation sequences. The same micro-operation is repeated every time around in each event. The Execution instruction cycle is different from them. Like, there is NO different series of micro-operations that can occur for a computer with different N opcodes.

Example:

ADD R, X

T1: MAR (IR(address)) T2: MBR Memory

T3: R (R) + (MBR)

- **Step 1:** The address portion of IR is loaded into the MAR.
- **Step 2:** The address field of the IR is updated from the MBR, so the reference memory location is read.
- **Step 3:** Now, the contents of R and MBR are added by the ALU.

4.7. MEMORY REFERENCE INSTRUCTION

There can be a far better acknowledgment that a computer dwells of both software and hardware. All that need is to bring in them synchronize with each other and expending computer programs, constructing the hardware to do the task and that is an authentic dispute. At the instant, let us converse about some chores that are executed by machines while taught by software programs. A stepper motor spreads out at exacting time intervals.

So, why are we discoursing all these examples and how are these concerned with the memory reference instruction? All right, by means of applying assembly language, we can carry out the above-mentioned tasks.

As per an assembly language, memory reference instructions are known to be one among the most vital and extensively used instructions in approximately every assembly program. Consequently, let us talk concerning the memory reference instructions in computer architecture and that too in a thorough manner.

Memory reference instructions are those commands or instructions which are in the habit to construct a reference to the memory and consent to a program to have access to the commanded data and that states as to from where the data is stashed away. It becomes very much necessary to make out that an instruction comprises of an operand and operand code is that which delimitates the data that is to be functioned or misrepresented.

An address is too an instruction part if it is very well expended in direct addressing mode and this address very well exemplifies the position of the value in the memory. There are 7 memory reference instructions as mentioned below (Figure 4.3):

- LDA
- STA
- AND
- ADD

- BUN
- BSA
- ISZ

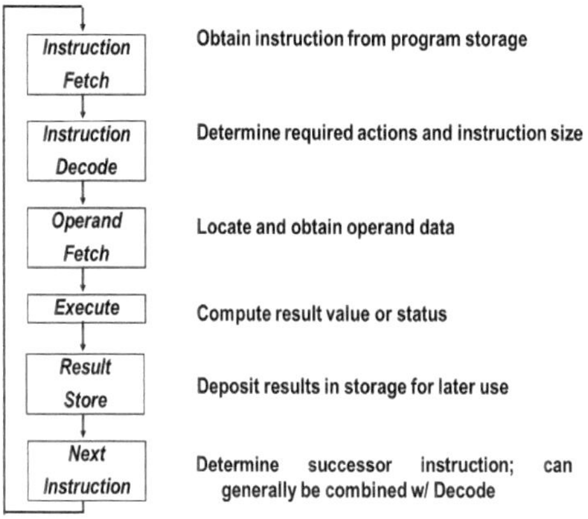

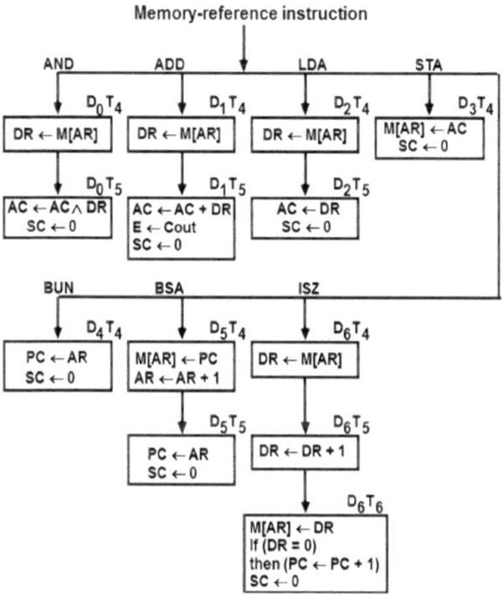

Figure 4.3. *Flow chart of memory reference instruction.*

4.7.1. LDA

LDA // this instruction gets utilized so as to stack the Accumulator with a worth that gets turned up at an explicit memory location. In addition to this, the approved practice of this command is when we write in an assembly language and is as follows:

Example of LDA 2500 H

This command articulates that load the value that is put in at the memory location 2500 into the accumulator. H constitutes that an enrolled address is a hexadecimal memory address. So, when a value gets salted away in the accumulator, further operations are executed as needed by the user on that particular value. Moreover, the changes ready to the value stored in the accumulator are modified in regular time intervals. In surplus, this instruction comes under direct addressing mode that is the address or memory location of the operand and is written in the instruction itself.

Opcode	**Operand**	**Description**
LDA	16-bit address	Load the accumulator

4.7.2. STA

This instruction is accurately opposite to the exceeding one as this memory reference instruction stores the value that is at hand in the accumulator into a precise memory address that chipped into the instruction.

Example of STA 2600 H

This respective command pronounces that store the value that is put in the accumulator to the memory location 2600. When the accumulator is to be attributed with a new-fangled value and the present value is to be remitted to some memory location, this instruction is utilized. In excess, this instruction also comes under direct addressing mode.

Opcode	Operand	Description
STA	16-bit address	Store accumulator direct AND

4.7.3. AND (Logical AND Operation)

The AND instruction implements the AND logic operation on the bit collection from the register and the memory word that is determined by the effective address. The result of this operation is moved back to the register.

Example of ANA M //do not confuse, AND is written as ANA but not AND.

This command enunciates that to perform logical AND operation on the value stored in an accumulator and at the memory location defined by M as an operand. At this point, in the above example, the rightmost A in ANA represents the accumulator and M stands for memory location exemplified with the H-L pair. Examine the below table.

Opcode	Operand	Description
ANA	R M	Logical AND with register or memory with accumulator.

4.7.4. ADD (Add to Accumulator)

ADD //this instruction executes an arithmetic operation on the values stored in the accumulator and memory location. The follow-on after the addition is put in the accumulator by substituting the older value. Not only this, but the instruction is also written as below in order to carry out addition on two values.

Example of ADD B

This respective command contributes the value stored in the accumulator with value at memory location defined by B as an operand. The operand can be a letter that makes up the memory location of the value. At this point, it is taken as B. There is a range of types of additions which are hashed out below:

Opcode	Operand	Description
ADD	B	Put in register or memory to accumulator

ADC M //this instruction executes addition with carrying by adding up the values in accumulator and memory location defined by M as an operand.

ADI 45 H // this instruction utter to add instant the value stored in the accumulator with the 8-bit data.

ACI 45 H //this instruction says that add immediate the length of with carrying.

DAD B // If we want to make a hexadecimal addition, we use this instruction. This instruction performs addition of the 16-bit value in the register pair with the value in the H-L pair.

Example of D4T4: PC <-AR, SC <-0 //Observe the below table to comprehend the functionality of BUN instruction.

Opcode	Operand	Description
BUN	16-bit address	Branch unconditionally

4.7.5. BSA

BSA // BSA instruction in computer architecture holds still for branch and save return address which has in mind that it executes two functions. Branching intends the instruction is currently being carried out and may have subroutines or procedures inside it and giving back the address in the sense that it entrepots the address of the instruction which should be performed right away after it and is stashed away as the program counter.

Example of D5T4: M[AR] <- PC, AR <- AR + 1 // increases the value of address register (AR) and returns the value of the program counter.

D5T5: PC <- AR, SC <-0

Opcode	Operand	Description
BSA	16-bit address	Branch and save the return address

4.7.6. ISZ

The Increment if Zero (ISZ) instruction increments the word determined by effective address. If the incremental cost is zero, this PC is incremented by 1. A negative value is saved in the memory word through the programmer. It can influence the zero value after getting incremented repeatedly. Thus, the PC is incremented and the next instruction is skipped.

Example of D6T4: DR <- M[AR] // by attributing the memory location applied by address register to data register.

D6T5: DR <- DR + 1 //increments the value of data register.

D6T4: M[AR] <- DR (if DR = 0, then PC = PC+1 and SC=0) //incremented address in data register is now attributed back to address register

Opcode	Operand	Description
ISZ	16-bit address	Increment and skip if zero

The following table to be acquainted with the instructions and their symbolic explanation.

Symbol	**Operation Decoder**	**Symbolic Description**
AND	D0	AC ← AC ∧ M[AR]
ADD	D1	AC ← AC + M[AR] →, E ← Cout
LDA	D2	AC ← M[AR]
STA	D3	M[AR] ← AC
BUN	D4	PC ← AR
BSA	D5	M[AR] ← PC, PC ← AR + 1
ISZ	D6	M[AR] ← M[AR] + 1,

if M[AR] + 1 = 0 then PC ← PC + 1

4.8. INPUT–OUTPUT AND INTERRUPTS

In computer architecture, an interrupt is a signal to the processor emitted by hardware or software indicating an event that needs immediate attention.

Our processor repeatedly keeps on checking for the SIN and SOUR bits for the synchronization in the program. Hence, the processor does not do any useful things other than running the infinite loop. To avoid this situation, input/output devices can have the concept of interrupts. When the input/output device is ready it could signal the processor on a separate line called interrupt request line. On receiving the interrupt, the processor reads the input output device and hence removes the infinite loop waiting mechanism.

4.8.1. Type of Interrupts

1. **Hardware Interrupts:** If the signal for the processor is from an external device or hardware is called hardware interrupts. Example: from the keyboard we will press the key to do some action. This pressing of the keyboard will generate a signal which is given to the processor to do action, such interrupts are called hardware interrupts.

 a. **Maskable Interrupt:** The hardware interrupts which can be delayed or disabled when a much highest priority interrupt has occurred to the processor.

 b. **Non-Maskable Interrupt:** The hardware which cannot be delayed or disabled and should be processed by the processor immediately.

2. **Software Interrupts:** Software interrupt can also divide into two types they are

 a. **Normal Interrupts:** the interrupts which are caused by the software instructions are called software instructions.

 b. **Exception:** unplanned interrupts while executing a program is called Exception. For example: while executing a program if we got a value which should be divided by zero is called an exception.

4.8.2. Interrupt Service Routine and Its Working

The routine that gets executed when an interrupt request is made is called an interrupt service routine.

- **Step 1:** When the interrupt occurs, the processor is currently executing i^{th} instruction and the program counter will be currently pointing to $(i + 1)^{th}$ instruction.
- **Step 2:** When the interrupt occurs the program counter value is stored on the processes stack.

- **Step 3:** The program counter is now loaded with the address of interrupt service routine.
- **Step 4:** Once the interrupt service routine is completed the address on the processes stack is popped and placed back in the program counter.
- **Step 5:** Execution resumes from $(i + 1)^{th}$ line of COMPUTE routine.

4.8.3. I/O Interface and Mode of Data Transfer

1. **I/O Interface:** The method that is used to transfer information between internal storage and external I/O devices is known as I/O interface. The CPU is interfaced using special communication links by the peripherals connected to any computer system. These communication links are used to resolve the differences between CPU and peripheral. Type of I/O interface:

i. **Non-Programmed I/O Interface:** In Non-programmed I/O interface, configuration is pre-defined during the design time.

ii. **Programmed I/O Interface:** In programmed I/O interface, configuration is defined in the command word register.

There exists special hardware components between CPU and peripherals to supervise and synchronize all the input and output transfers that are called interface units.

2. **Mode of Data Transfer:** The binary information that is received from an external device is usually stored in the memory unit. The information that is transferred from the CPU to the external device originates from the memory unit. The CPU merely processes the information but the source and target is always the memory unit. Data transfer between CPU and the I/O devices may be done in different modes.

The binary information that is received from an external device is usually stored in the memory unit. The information that is transferred from the CPU to the external device originates from the memory unit. The CPU merely processes the information but the source and target is always the memory unit. Data transfer between CPU and the I/O devices may be done in different modes. Data transfer to and from the peripherals may be done in any of the three possible ways:

i. **Programmed I/O:** It is due to the result of the I/O instructions that are written in the computer program. Each data item transfer is initiated by an instruction in the program. Usually, the transfer is from a CPU register and memory. In this case it requires constant monitoring by the CPU of the peripheral devices.

ii. **Interrupt–Initiated I/O:** Since in the above case we saw the CPU is kept busy unnecessarily. This situation can very well be avoided by using an interrupt driven method for data transfer. By using interrupt facility and special commands to inform the interface to issue an interrupt request signal whenever data is available from any device. In the meantime, the CPU can proceed for any other program execution. The interface meanwhile keeps monitoring the device. Whenever it is determined that the device is ready for data transfer it initiates an interrupt request signal to the computer. Upon detection of an external interrupt signal the CPU stops momentarily the task that it was already performing, branches to the service program to process the I/O transfer, and then returns to the task it was originally performing.

iii. **Direct Memory Access:** The data transfer between a fast storage media such as magnetic disk and memory unit is limited by the speed of the CPU. Thus, we can allow the peripherals to directly communicate with each other using the memory buses, removing the intervention of the CPU. This type of data transfer technique is known as DMA or direct memory access. During DMA, the CPU is idle and it has no control over the memory buses. The DMA controller takes over the buses to manage the transfer directly between the I/O devices and the memory unit.

iv. **I/O Channels and Processors:** The evolution of the I/O function

- Processor directly controls peripheral device
- Addition of a controller or I/O module – programmed I/O
- Same as 2 – interrupts added
- I/O module direct access to memory using DMA
- I/O module enhanced to become processor like – I/O channel
- I/O module has local memory of its own – computer like – I/O processor
- More and more the I/O function is performed without processor involvement. The processor is increasingly relieved of I/O related tasks – improved performance.

• **Characteristics of I/O Channels Extension of the DMA Concept**

- Ability to execute I/O instructions – special-purpose processor on I/O
- Channel – complete control over I/O operations Processor does not execute I/O instructions itself – processor initiates

I/O

- Transfer by instructing the I/O channel to execute a program in memory
- Error condition actions.

4.9. INSTRUCTION FORMATS

The computer can be used to perform a specific task, only by specifying the necessary steps to complete the task. The collection of such ordered steps forms a 'program' of a computer. These ordered steps are the instructions. Computer instructions are stored in central memory locations and are executed sequentially one at a time. The control reads an instruction from a specific address in memory and executes it. It then continues by reading the next instruction in sequence and executes it until the completion of the program.

A computer usually has a variety of Instruction Code Formats. It is the function of the control unit within the CPU to interpret each instruction code and provide the necessary control functions needed to process the instruction. An n bit instruction that k bits in the address field and m bits in the operation code field come addressed 2k location directly and specify 2m different operations (Figure 4.4).

- The bits of the instruction are divided into groups called fields.
- The most common fields in instruction formats are:
- An operation code field that specifies the operation to be performed.
- An Address field that designates a memory address or a processor register.
- A Mode field that specifies the way the operand or the effective address is determined.

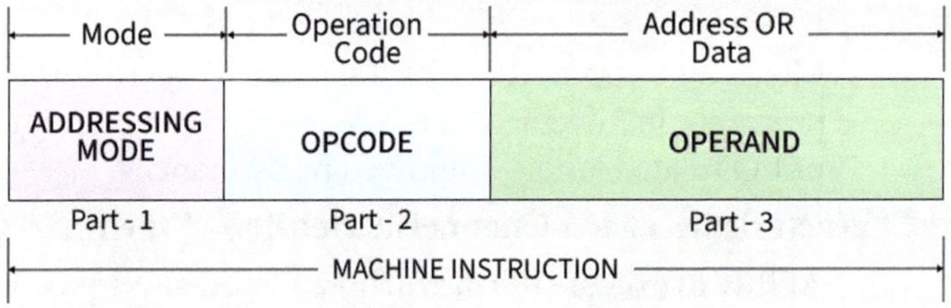

Figure 4.4. *Instruction format.*

The operation code field (Opcode) of an instruction is a group of bits that define various processor operations such as add, subtract, complement, shift etcetera. The bits that define the mode field of an instruction code specify a variety of alternatives for choosing the operands from the given address. Operation specified by an instruction is executed on some data stored in the processor register or in the memory location. Operands residing in memory are specified by their memory address. Operands residing in the processor register are specified with a register address.

4.9.1. Types of Instruction

- Computers may have instructions of several different lengths containing varying numbers of addresses.
- The number of address fields in the instruction format of a computer depends on the internal organization of its registers.
- Most computers fall into one of 3 types of CPU organizations.

An instruction is of various lengths depending upon the number of addresses it contains. Generally,CPU organization is of three types on the basis of number of address fields:

- Single Accumulator organization;
- General register organization;
- Stack organization.

In the first organization operation is done involving a special register called accumulator. Second, multiple registers are used for the computation purpose. In the third organization the work is on stack basis operation due to which it does not contain any address field. It is not necessary that only a single organization is applied; a blend of various organizations is mostly what we see generally. On the basis of number of address instruction are classified as:

$$X = (A + B) \times (C + D)$$

- **Zero Address Instructions:** A stack-based computer does not use address fields in instruction. To evaluate an expression first it is converted to reverse Polish Notation i.e., Post fix Notation.

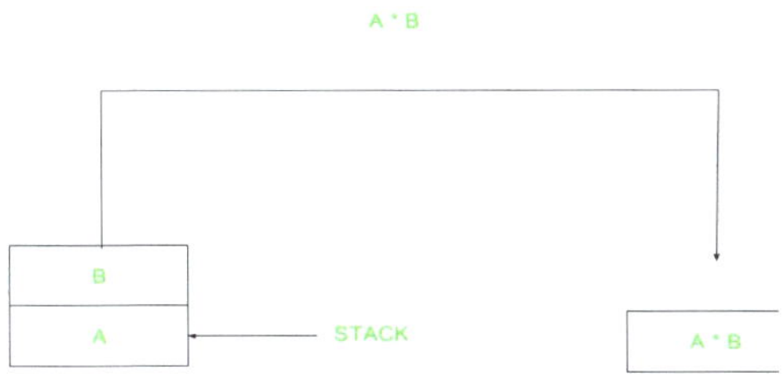

Expression: X = (A + B) × (C + D)

Postfixed: X = AB + CD*

TOP means top of stack

M[X] is any memory location

PUSH	A	TOP = A
PUSH	B	TOP = B
ADD		TOP = A + B
PUSH	C	TOP = C
PUSH	D	TOP = D
ADD		TOP = C + D
MUL		TOP = (C + D) × (A + B)
POP	X	M[X] = TOP

- **One Address Instructions:** This uses an implied ACCUMULATOR register for data manipulation. One operand is in the accumulator and the other is in the register or memory location. Implied means that the CPU already know that one operand is in accumulator so there is no need to specify it:

Expression: X = (A + B) × (C + D)

AC is accumulator.

M[] is any memory location.

M[T] is temporary location.

LOAD	A	AC = M[A]
ADD	B	AC = AC + M[B]
STORE	T	M[T] = AC
LOAD	C	AC = M[C]
ADD	D	AC = AC + M[D]
MUL	T	AC = AC × M[T]
STORE	X	M[X] = AC

Note:

- In this type of instruction, we can use (load) and (store) beside the arithmetic operations.
- This method requires more steps than previous methods to represent the same instruction.

- For temporary storage use a memory location and is not a register.

- **Two Address Instructions:** This is common in commercial computers. Here two addresses can be specified in the instruction. Unlike earlier in one address instruction the result was stored in an accumulator, here the result can be stored at a different location rather than just accumulator, but requires more bits to represent the address.

opcode	Destination address	Source address	mode

Expression: X = (A + B) × (C + D)

R1, R2 are registers.

M[] is any memory location.

MOV	R1, A	R1 = M[A]
ADD	R1, B	R1 = R1 + M[B]
MOV	R2, C	R2 = C
ADD	R2, D	R2 = R2 + D
MUL	R1, R2	R1 = R1 × R2
MOV	X, R1	M[X] = R1

Note:

- In this type of instruction, we can use (mov) beside the arithmetic operations.
- This method requires more steps than the previous method to represent the same Instruction.
- For temporary storage use a register

- **Three Address Instructions:** This has three address fields to specify a register or a memory location. Programs created are much shorter in size but the number of bits per instruction increases. These instructions make creation of program much easier but it does not mean that program will run much faster because now instruction only contain more information but each micro-operation (changing content of register, loading address in address bus etc.) will be performed in one cycle only.

opcode	Destination address	Source address	Source address	mode

Expression: X = (A + B) × (C + D)

R1, R2 are registers.

M[] is any memory location.

ADD	R1, A, B	R1 = M[A] + M[B]
ADD	R2, C, D	R2 = M[C] + M[D]
MUL	X, R1, R2	M[X] = R1 × R2

Homework: Execute the following instruction using all previous instruction format types:

1. X = (A + B) × (C + D)
2. S = F – (C × B) + M
3. N= (A + B × C)/(F × E)

4.10. ADDRESSING MODES

The operation field of an instruction specifies the operation to be performed. And this operation must be performed on some data. So, each instruction needs to specify data on which the operation is to be performed. But the operand (data) may be in the accumulator, general purpose register or at some specified memory location. So, appropriate location (address) of data needs to be specified, and in computers, there are various ways of specifying the address of data. These various ways of specifying the address of data are known as "Addressing Modes."

Why addressing modes are so important are:

1. First, the way the operand data are chosen during program execution is dependent on the addressing mode of the instruction.
2. Second, the address field(or fields) in a typical instruction format are relatively small and sometimes we would like to be able to reference a large range of locations, so here to achieve this objective i.e., to fit this large range of location in address field, a variety of addressing techniques has been employed. As they reduce the number of fields in the addressing field of the instruction

ISA= Addressing Modes are very vital in Instruction Set Architecture A= Contents of an address field in the instruction

R = Contents of an address field in the instruction that refers to a register

EA = Effective Address(Actual address) of location containing the referenced operand. (X)= Contents of memory location x or register X

Or

"The technique for specifying the address of the operands "

And

And in computers the address of operand i.e., the address where operand is actually found is known as "Effective Address."

4.10.1. Types of Addressing Modes

1. **Implied and Immediate Addressing Modes:** Although most Addressing modes need the address field of the instruction, but implied and immediate addressing modes are the only addressing modes that need no address. Now we will discuss each of them in detail one by one.

a. **Implied Addressing Mode:** Implied Addressing Mode also known as "Implicit" or "Inherent" addressing mode is the addressing mode in which no operand (register or memory location or data) is specified in the instruction. As in this mode the operands are specified implicitly in the definition of instruction.

"Complement Accumulator" is an Implied Mode instruction because the operand in the accumulator register is implied in the definition of instruction. In assembly language it is written as:

CMA: Take complement of content of AC Similarly, the instruction,

RLC: Rotate the content of Accumulator is an implied mode instruction.

In addition to this, all Register-Reference instructions that use an accumulator and Zero-Address instruction in a Stack Organized Computer are implied mode instructions, because in Register reference operand implied in accumulator and in Zero-Address instruction, the operand implied on the Top of Stack.

b. **Immediate Addressing Mode:** In this mode, the operand is specified in the instruction itself. In other words, an immediate-mode instruction has an operand field instead of an address field. The operand field includes the actual operand to be used in conjunction with the operation determined in the instruction. Immediate- mode instructions are beneficial for initializing registers to a constant value.

As an example:

MVI 06 Move 06 to the accumulator.

ADD 05 ADD 05 to the content of accumulator.

2. **Stack Addressing Mode:** In this addressing mode, the operand is contained at the top of the stack.

   Operand is contained at the top of the stack.

10
20
30
40
50
60
70
80

EX: ADD

- This instruction simply pops out two symbols contained at the top of the stack.
- The addition of those two operands is performed.
- The result obtained after addition is pushed again at the top of the stack.

4. **Direct and Indirect Addressing Modes:** Direct Addressing Mode is also known as "Absolute Addressing Mode." In this mode the address of data (operand) is specified in the instruction itself. That is, in this type of mode, the operand resides in memory and its address is given directly by the address field of the instruction. Means, in other words, in this mode, the address field contain the Effective Address of operand EA=A

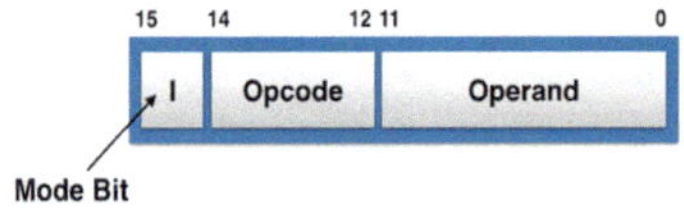

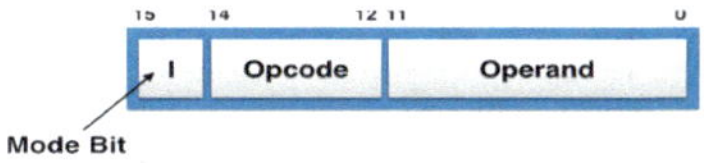

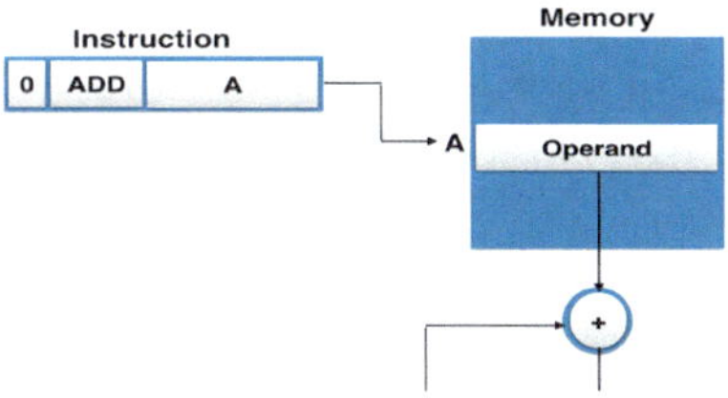

It consists of 3-bit opcode, 12-bit address and a mode bit designated as(I).The mode bit (I) is zero for Direct Address and 1 for Indirect Address. Now we will discuss about each in detail one by one.

As an example:

ADD A Means add contents of cell A to accumulator.

5. **Indirect Addressing Mode:** In this mode, the address field of instruction gives the memory address where on, the operand is stored in memory. That is, in this mode, the address field of the instruction gives the address where the "Effective Address" is stored in memory EA=(A).

   ADD (A) Means adds the content of cell pointed to contents of A to Accumulator

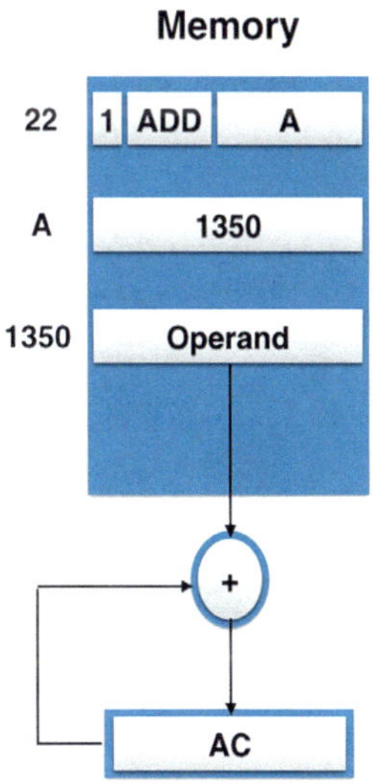

AC <-- M [M [A]]   [M=Memory]

(A)=1350=EA

6. **Register Addressing Mode:** In Register Addressing Mode, the operands are in registers that reside within the CPU. That is, in this mode, instruction specifies a register in CPU, which contains the operand. It is like Direct Addressing Mode; the only difference is that the address field refers to a register instead of memory location, i.e., EA=R

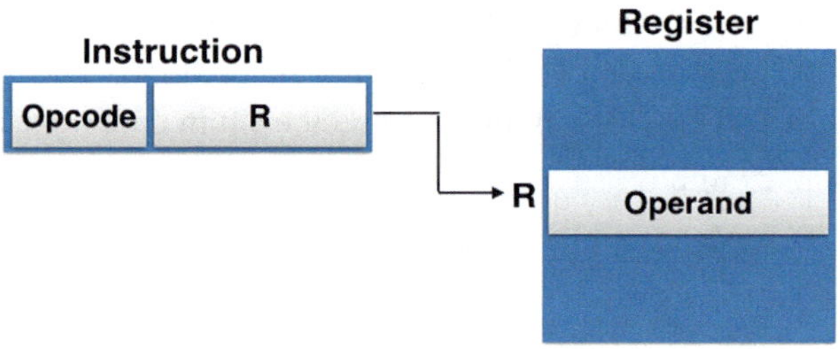

MOV AX, BX   Move contents of Register BX to AX

ADD AX, BX   Add the contents of register BX to AX

Here, AX, BX are used as register names which are 16-bit registers.

7. **Register Indirect Addressing Mode:** In Register Indirect Addressing Mode, the instruction specifies a register in CPU whose contents give the operand in memory. In other words, the selected register contains the address of operand rather than the operand itself. That is, EA=(R) Means, control fetches instruction from memory and then uses its address to access Register and looks in Register(R) for effective address of operand in memory.

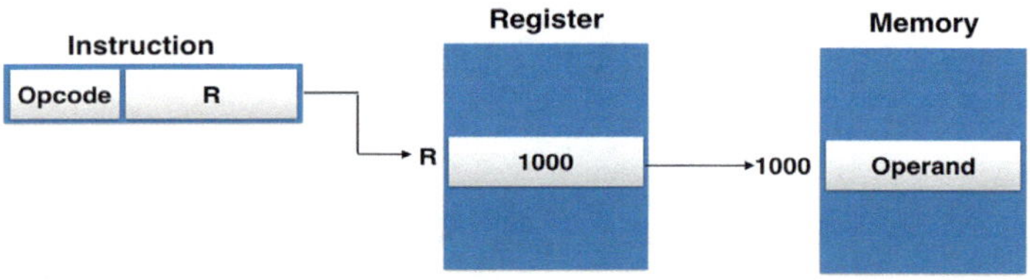

Example:

MOV AL, [BX]

Code example in Register:

MOV BX, 1000H

MOV 1000H, operand

From above example, it is clear that, the instruction(MOV AL, [BX]) specifies a register[BX], and in coding of register, we see that, when we move register [BX], the register contain the address of operand(1000H) rather than address itself.

8. **Auto-Increment and Auto-Decrement Addressing Modes:** These are similar to Register indirect Addressing Mode except that the register is incremented or decremented after (or before) its value is used to access memory. These modes are required because when the address stored in register refers to a table of data in memory, then it is necessary to increment or decrement the register after every access to table so that next value is accessed from memory. Thus, these addressing modes are common requirements in computers.

i. **Auto-Increment Addressing Mode:** Auto-increment Addressing Mode are similar to Register Indirect Addressing Mode except that the register is incremented after its value is loaded (or accessed) at another location like accumulator (AC). That is, in this case also, the Effective Address is equal to EA=(R)

Example:

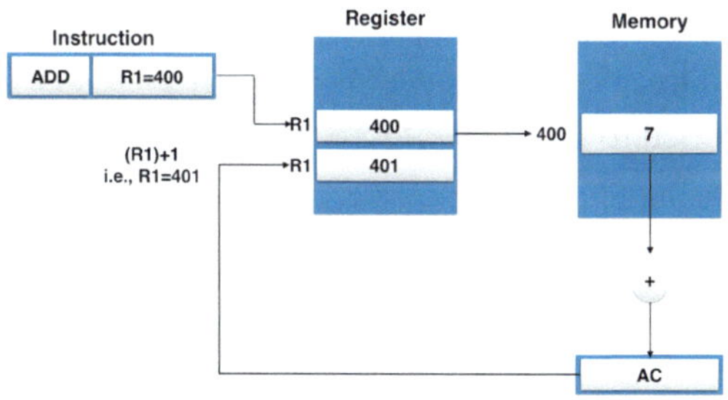

We see that effective address is (R)=400 and operand in AC is 7 And after loading R1 is incremented by 1. It becomes 401 Means, here we see that, in the Auto-increment mode, the R1 register is increment to 401 after execution of instruction.

ii. **Auto-Decrement Addressing Mode:** Auto-decrement Addressing Mode is reverse of auto-increment, as in it the register is decrement before the execution of the instruction. That is, in this case, effective address is equal to EA = (R) – 1

Example:

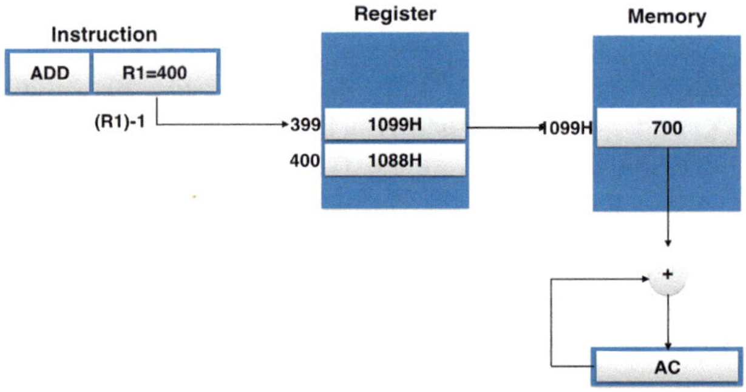

In the Auto-decrement mode, the register R1 is decremented to 399 prior to execution of the instruction, means the operand is loaded to accumulator, is of address 1099H in memory, instead of 1088H. Thus, in this case effective address is 1099H and contents loaded into accumulator is 700.

9. **Displacement-based Addressing Modes:** It is a powerful addressing mode as it is a combination of direct addressing or register indirect addressing mode. EA=A+(R), Means, Displacement Addressing Modes requires that the instruction have two address fields, at least one of which is explicit means, one is address field indicate direct address and other indicate indirect address. That is, value contained in one addressing field is A, which is used directly and the value in other address field is R, which refers to a register whose contents are to be added to produce effective address.

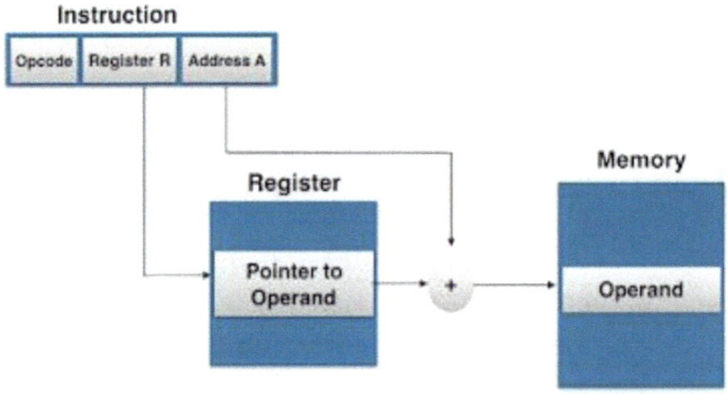

There are three areas where Displacement Addressing modes are used. In other words, Displacement Based Addressing Modes are of three types. These are:

1. **Relative Addressing Mode:** In Relative Addressing Mode, the contents of the program counter are added to the address part of instruction to obtain the Effective Address. That is, in Relative

Addressing Mode, the address field of the instruction is added to implicitly reference register Program Counter to obtain effective address *EA = A + PC.*

Example:

Assume that PC contains the no. – 825 and the address part of instruction contain the no. – 24, then the instruction at location 825 is read from memory during fetch phase and the Program Counter is then incremented by one to 826. The effective address computation for relative address mode is 826 + 24 = 850

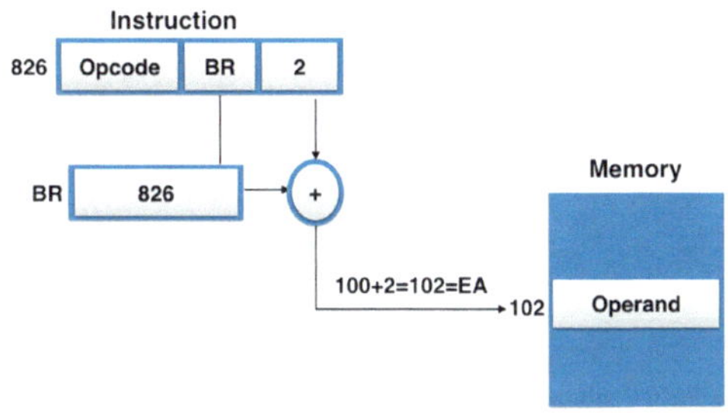

2. **Index Register Addressing Mode:** In indexed addressing mode, the content of Index Register is added to direct address part (or field) of instruction to obtain the effective address. Means, in it, the register indirect addressing field of instruction point to Index Register, which is a special CPU register that contain an Indexed value, and direct addressing field contain base address.

   Indexed type instructions make sense that the data array is in memory and each operand in the array is stored in memory relative to the base address. And the distance between the beginning address and the address of operand is the indexed value stored in the indexed register.

   EA=A+ Index

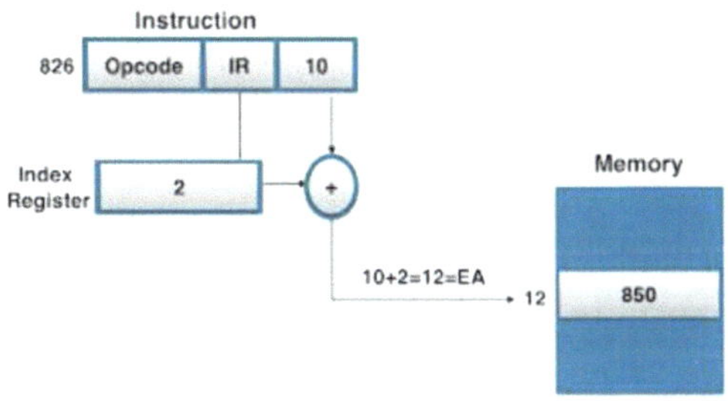

3. **Base Register Addressing Mode:** In this mode, the content of the Base Register is added to the direct address part of the instruction to obtain the effective address. Means, in it the register indirect address field points to the Base Register and to obtain EA, the contents of Instruction Register, is added to the direct address part of the instruction. This is similar to indexed addressing mode except that the register is now called Base Register instead of Index Register. EA=A+ Base.

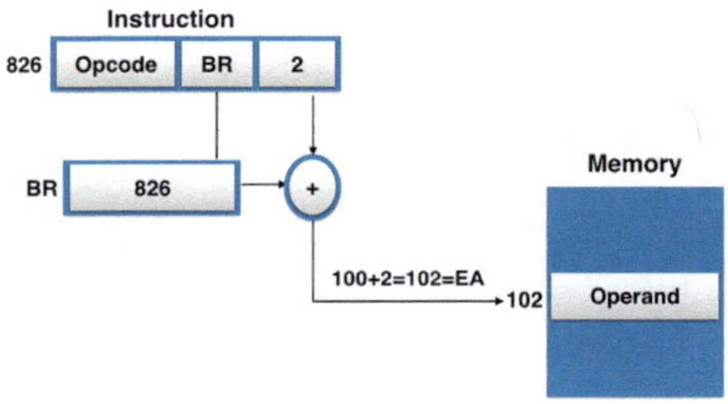

Thus, the difference between Base and Index mode is in the way they are used rather than the way they are computed. An Index Register is assumed to hold an index number that is relative to the address part of the instruction. And a Base Register is assumed to hold a base address and the direct address field of instruction gives a displacement relative to this base address.

4.11. MACHINE LANGUAGE

Humans can understand High-level programming languages. It is not necessary to have a deep understanding of the internal CPU, to program using high-level languages.

They follow syntax similar to the English language. Java, C, C++, and Python are some high-level programming languages. A computer recognizes machine language but does not understand high-level languages. Therefore, those programs should be converted to computer understandable machine language. This translation is done using a compiler or an interpreter. A machine language consists of binary digits which are zeros and once. A computer is a digital electronic device, so it uses binary for operations. One indicates the true state / on state while zero indicates the false state / off state. The way of converting a program from high-level language to machine language depends on the CPU.

4.12. WHAT IS ASSEMBLY LANGUAGE?

Assembly language is the intermediate language between high-level programming languages and machine language. It is one level above machine language. Assembly language is easier to understand than machine language but harder than high-level programming languages. This language is also known as a low-level language because it is close to the hardware level. In order to write effective programs using Assembly, the programmer should have a good understanding of the computer architecture and the register structure. A special compiler known as an assembler is used to convert assembly language instructions to machine code or object code.

Assembly language statements have four sections. They are a label, mnemonic, operand, comment. Labels and comments are optional. Mnemonic is the instruction to execute and operands are parameters for the command. Assembly language also supports macros. A macro can be defined as a set of instructions with a name. It can be used elsewhere in the program.

Some examples of Assembly language statements are as follows:

MOV SUM, 50 – This instruction copies the value 50 to the variable SUM. ADD VALUE1, 20 – This is to add 20 to the VALUE1 variable.

ADD AH, BH – This instruction is to copy the content in AH register to BH register. INC COUNT – This is to increment the variable COUNT by one.

AND VALUE1, 100 – This is to perform AND operation on variable VALUE1 and 100.

MOV AL, 20 – This is to copy value 20 to AL register.

4.12.1. Characteristics of Assembly Language

- Assembly language makes use of symbols, codes and numbers to represent various instructions and make the code human readable.
- In order to code in assembly programming language, the programmer must have knowledge about the hardware of the device like its architecture, registers present etc.
- The execution of assembly language is slow since it needs to be converted to machine language for the device to understand it.
- These codes can be easily memorized by humans since the opcodes need not be memorized.
- Assembly level code is closer to hardware level and thus hardware dependent.

What is the Difference between Machine Language and Assembly language?

Machine Language	Assembly Language
Machine language is only understood by the computers.	Assembly language is only understood by human beings, not by computers.
In machine language data is only represented with the help of binary format (0s and 1s), hexadecimal and octal, decimal.	In assembly language data can be represented with the help of mnemonics such as Mov, Add, Sub, End etc.
Machine language is very difficult to understand by human beings.	Assembly language is easy to understand by human beings as compared to machine language.
Modifications and error fixing cannot be done in machine language.	Modifications and error fixing can be done in assembly language.
Machine language is very difficult to memorize so it is not possible to learn the machine language.	Easy to memorize the assembly language because some alphabets and mnemonics are used.
Execution is fast in machine language because all data is already present in binary format.	Execution is slow as compared to machine language.
There is no need for a translator. The machine understandable form is the machine language.	Assembler is used as a translator to convert mnemonics into machine understandable form.
Machine language is hardware dependent.	Assembly language is machine dependent and it is not portable.

4.13. REGISTER TRANSFER AND MICROOPERATIONS

1. **Register:** It is a Storage device Where the Data is Stored for Time being which will be Process Shortly by the Processor.
2. **Microoperation:** The Operation Executed on Data Stored in a register is called Micro Operation. A Micro Operation is an Elementary Operation Perform on the Information stored in one or more Register.
3. **Register Transfer:** The Register that holds an address for the memory unit is a memory unit called memory address (MAR). The Most Common way to represent a register is by a rectangular box with the name of register inside. it is denoted by capital letters.

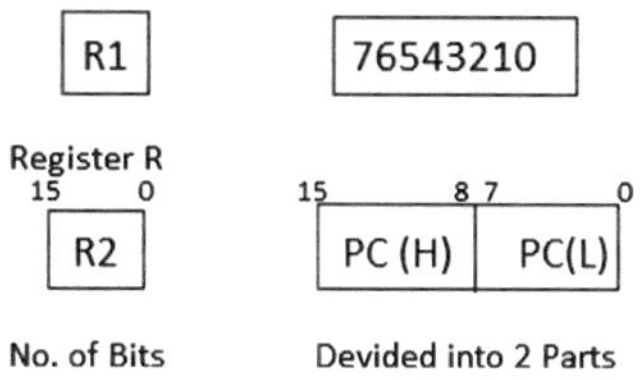

i. The Numbering of bits in 16 bits in Register in Partition into Two parts 0 to 7 are assign the symbol (L) Low and 8 to 15 are assign the Symbol (H) High.

ii. Information Transfer one Register to Another.

iii. Replacement of the Source register R1 does not change after the transfer.

4. Arithmetic Micro Operation: It is an Elementary performance with the Data Stored in the Register. These are of Four Types.

i. Register Transfer Micro Operation: It is Transfer the Binary Information from One Register to Other Register.

R2 ←R1

ii. Arithmetic Transfer Micro Operation: It performs Arithmetic Micro Operation. Where Numeric Data Stored in the Register.

R3 ←R2 + R1 (Here R2 and R1 is Transferring to R3) R3 ← R1 – R2

iii. Logic Micro Operation: It Performs Manipulation Operation on Non- Numeric Data Stored in the Register.

R1 ← R2, if R2 > R3, R2 = 50, R3 = 10

iv. Shift Micro Operation: It Performs Shift Operation of Data Stored in Register. Register Transfer Micro Operation does not change the Information content when the Binary Information moves from to the Source Destination Register.

R2 ← Sh l (Shift Left) R1 R2 ← Sh r (Shift Right) R1

4.13.1. Register Transfer Language

Computers are the electronic devices which have several sets of digital hardware which are interconnected to exchange data. Digital hardware comprises VLSI Chips which are used for both data processing as well as data storage facilities. Each of the Digital hardware is defined as the digital module. Digital modules are considered as the devices which store the data using the registers available in them and process the data based on micro-operational codes. These Micro operational codes will be used to coordinate the data transfer as well as for data processing. Register transfer can be defined as the process of moving the data between the registers which are controlled by the micro-operations.

Therefore, in order to define the micro-operations, we normally use the descriptive language. We explain each micro-operation in detail. This type of writing is better for explanatory purposes, but to write a program this kind of writing is not sufficient.

Therefore, like in other computer programming languages, we use the symbols for denoting an operation. Like to load some data into the registers we use "LOAD 5 → R0" This will be a self-explanatory mnemonic. This type of program writing is called the Register Transfer Language.

As the register transfer language deals with the internals of the hardware we should first know what the internal hardware organization is.

The internal hardware organization of a digital computer is best defined by specifying:

- The set of registers it contains and their function.
- The sequence of micro-operations performed on the binary information stored in the registers.
- The control that initiates the sequence of micro-operations.

4.13.1.1. The Contents of Register Transfer Language

Register Transfer language syntax will contain the micro-operations along with the source and target registers on which the data modification will be performed with a set of control signals.

For Example:

P: LOAD 5 → R0. The command given here is used to load a data 5 to the register R0.

LOAD → Micro Operation 5→ Data (Source Data)

R0 → General Purpose Register (Target Register)

P → Control Signal initiated to run the micro-operation. "→" → Data transfer from source to destination.

4.13.2. Register Transfer

Before we see how the data is transferred from one register to another register, we will see the construction of a register and its various diagrams. Registers are the fast data storage devices which are constructed using VLSI Chips with the technology of FLIPFLOPs. In a simple 8-bit register, there will be 8 flip-flops which will be holding the data, the design of the flip-flops are based on the manufacturer's specification. Several registers are present in the CPU. Such as MAR → used to store the address of the particular data. MDR → which is used to store the data of a particular address stored in MAR. PC → is used to point to the next instruction to be executed.

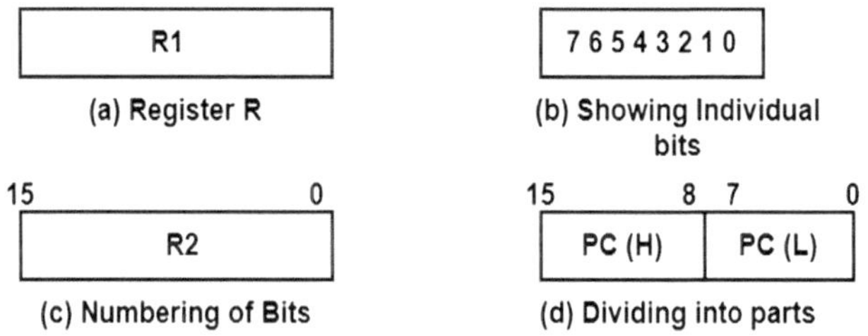

(a) Register R (b) Showing Individual bits (c) Numbering of Bits (d) Dividing into parts

Next, we will see how the Register transfer actually works. We will take the example syntax and then see how the register transfer takes place.

Ex: if (P==1) then (R2 ← R1)

Here "P" is the control signal generated by the control unit which should be true if the data transfer from R1 to R2 should take place.

Steps of execution:

- First n outputs of R1 are connected with n inputs of R2.
- Register R2 has a Load Input which is activated when the control signal P==1;

Basic Symbols for Register Transfers		
Symbol	Description	Examples
Letters & numerals	Denotes a register	MAR, R2
Parenthesis ( )	Denotes a part of a register	R2(0-7), R2(L)
Arrow ←	Denotes transfer of information	R2 ← R1
Comma ,	Separates two microoperations	R2 ← R1, R1 ← R2

4.13.3. Bus and Memory Transfer

In a digital computer all the devices are interconnected using a bus. All the devices will be using these bus paths as the data paths through which the data will be exchanged. So, if we are constructing a system which has several devices(Registers) and each register has to have its own path, there will be a lot of bus(set of wires). This is not a good design, because providing a communication path for each and every device means the time taken to exchange information will be long if the bus path is very long or else the bus management will be very difficult. To avoid this kind of problem we use "Common Bus Structure." In this all the buses available will be shared among all the devices. Therefore, only two devices can communicate at a time using the common bus structure in-order to avoid data inconsistency.

To solve this problem, we have discussed the method of buffers. But this solution also solves the problem only to a certain point. Consider the following problem. You have a system which has 16-bit bus lines, through which you want to send 16 signals of 16-bit data. That is a total of 256 bit of data has to be sent from 16 registers. So, in this type of problem, we use multiplexers.

Multiplexers are the one which convert the no. of input data signals into a small no of output signals. Ex: 16x1 multiplexer can convert 16 signals into one signal based on the selection modes. The diagram below will represent how 4x1 multiplexers are used to transfer 4 signals of 4 bits each using only a 4-bit bus (Figure 4.5).

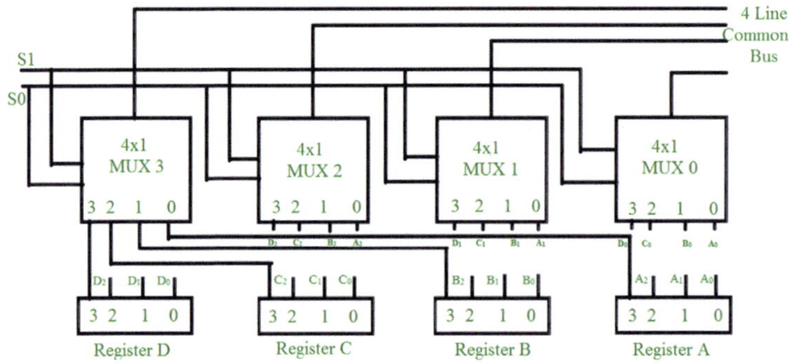

Figure 4.5. *4×1 multiplexer.*

The description below explains how the 4x1 multiplexer is used in the above scenario. The above setup has 2 select signals named "S0" and "S1", along with 4 sets of registers which are 4 bits long (store 4 bits of data). In this diagram we can see that the first multiplexer has inputs from the first bits of all the respective registers. Likewise, the second multiplexer will have all the inputs from the second bit of all the registers. Likewise, third and fourth multiplexers have the third bit and fourth bit input from the respective registers.

4.14. ARITHMETIC MICRO-OPERATIONS

The increment and decrement micro-operations are symbolized by plus-one and minus-one operations, respectively. These micro-operations are implemented with a combinational circuit or with a binary up-down counter.

The arithmetic operations of multiply and divide are not listed in symbolic and its description. These two operations are valid arithmetic operations but are not included in the basic set of micro- operations. The only place where these operations can be considered as micro-operations is in a digital system, where they are implemented by means of a combinational circuit. In such a case, the signals that perform these operations propagate through gates, and the result of the operation can be transferred into a destination register by a clock pulse as soon as the output signal propagates through the combinational circuit. In most computers, the multiplication operation is implemented with a sequence of add and shift micro-operations. Division is implemented with a sequence of subtract and shift micro-operations. To specify the hardware in such a case requires a list of statements that use the basic micro-operations of add, subtract and shift.

1. **Arithmetic Microoperations:** The basic arithmetic micro-operations are addition, subtraction, increment and decrement.
2. Add Microoperation:

   $R3 \leftarrow R1 + R2$

   The above statement states that the contents of register R1 are added to the contents of register R2 and the sum transferred to register R3.
3. Subtract Microoperation:

   $R3 \leftarrow R1 + R2 + 1$

   In the above statement R2 is the symbol for the 1's complement of R2. Adding 1 to the 1's complement produces the 2's complement. Adding the contents of R1 to the 2's complement of R2 is equivalent to R1 – R2.

The increment and decrement micro-operations are symbolized by plus-one and minus- one operations, respectively.

Symbolic Representation	Description
$R3 \leftarrow R1 + R2$	The contents of R1 plus R2 are transferred to R3.
$R3 \leftarrow R1 - R2$	The contents of R1 minus R2 are transferred to R3.

R2 ← R2'	Complement the contents of R2 (1's complement)
R2 ← R2' + 1	2's complement the contents of R2 (negate)
R3 ← R1 + R2' + 1	R1 plus the 2's complement of R2 (subtraction)
R1 ← R1 + 1	Increment the contents of R1 by one
R1 ← R1 – 1	Decrement the contents of R1 by one

4.14.1. Binary Adder

To implement the add micro-operation with hardware, we need the registers that hold the data and the digital component that performs the arithmetic addition.

The binary adder is constructed with full-adder circuits connected in cascade, with the output carry from one full-adder connected to the input carry of the next full-adder (Figure 4.6).

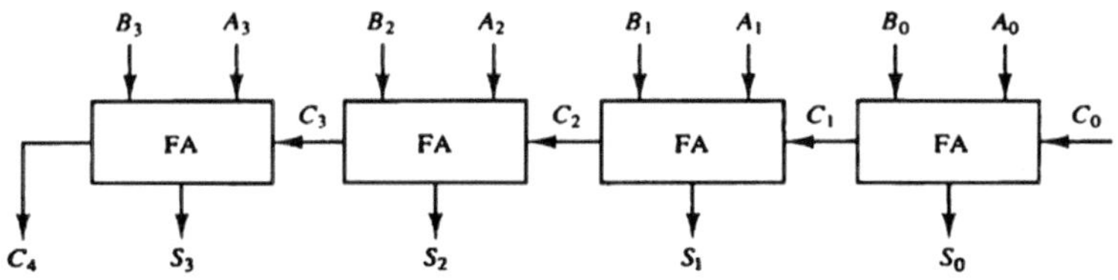

Figure 4.6. *4-bit binary adder.*

The S outputs of the full adders generate the required sum bits.

An n-bit binary adder requires n full-adders. The output carry from each full-adder connected to the input carry of the next-higher-order full-adder.

4.14.1.1. Binary Adder-Subtractor

The addition and subtraction operations can be combined into one common circuit by including an exclusive-OR gate with each full-adder.

A 4-bit adder-subtractor circuit is shown in Figure 4.7.

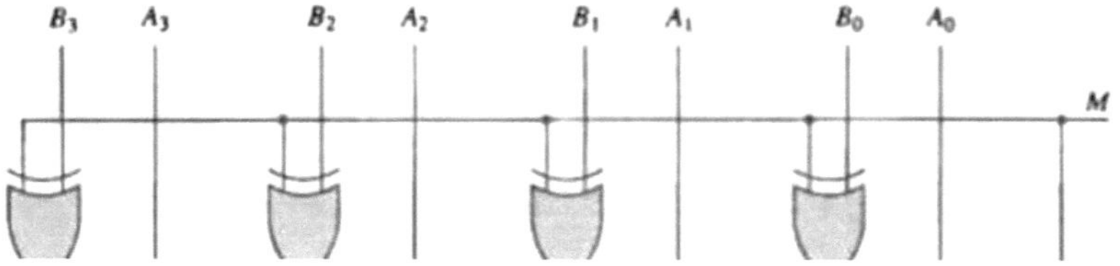

Figure 4.7. *Adder-subtractor.*

- Each exclusive-OR gate receives input M and one of the inputs B. When M = 0, we have B 0 = B. The full adders receive the value of B, the input carry is 0, and the circuit performs A + B.
- When M = 1, we have B 1 = B’ and C0 = 1. The B inputs are all complemented and 1 is added through the input carry. The circuit performs the operation A + 2’s complement of B. In Figure 4.7, mode input M controls the operation.

When M = 0 the circuit is an adder and when M = 1 the circuit becomes a subtractor.

4.14.1.2. Binary Incremented

The increment micro-operation adds one to a number in the register. The diagram of a 4-bit incrementer circuit is shown below. One of the inputs of the least significant half-adder (HA) circuit is connected to logic-1 and the other input is connected to the least significant bit of the number to be incremented (Figure 4.8).

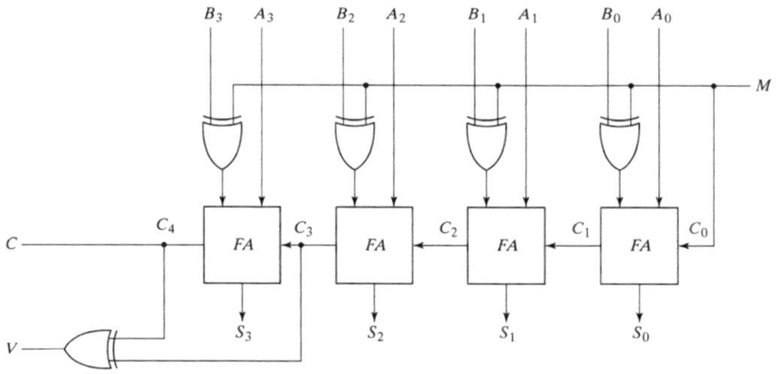

Figure 4.8. *4-bit binary incrementer.*

The output carried from one half-adder is connected to one of the inputs of the next-higher- order half-adder. The circuit receives the four bits from A0 through A3, adds one to it, and generates the incremented output S0 through S3.

4.14.2. Logic Micro-Operations

- Logic micro-operations specify binary operations for strings of bits stored in registers. These operations consider each bit of the register separately and treat them as binary variables.
- For example, the exclusive-OR micro-operation on the contents of two registers R 1 and R2 is symbolized by the statement.

  P: R1 R1 R2
- The above specifies a logic micro-operation to be executed on the individual bits of the registers provided that the control variable P = 1.
- As a numerical example, assume that each register has four bits. Let the content of R1 be 1010 and the content of R2 be 1100. The exclusive-OR micro-operation stated above symbolizes the following logic computation:

1010	Content of R1
1100	Content of R2
0110	Content of R1 if P = 1

- The symbol V will be used to denote an OR micro-operation and the symbol to denote an AND micro-operation. The complement micro-operation is the same as the 1's complement and uses a bar on top of the symbol that denotes the register name.
- **List of Logic Microoperations:** There are 16 different logic operations that can be performed with two binary variables. They can be determined from all possible truth tables obtained with two binary variables (Table 4.1).

Table 4.1. *Sixteen Logic Microoperations*

Boolean function	Microoperation	Name
$F_0 = 0$	$F \leftarrow 0$	Clear
$F_1 = xy$	$F \leftarrow A \wedge B$	AND
$F_2 = xy'$	$F \leftarrow A \wedge \overline{B}$	
$F_3 = x$	$F \leftarrow A$	Transfer A
$F_4 = x'y$	$F \leftarrow \overline{A} \wedge B$	
$F_5 = y$	$F \leftarrow B$	Transfer B
$F_6 = x \oplus y$	$F \leftarrow A \oplus B$	Exclusive-OR
$F_7 = x + y$	$F \leftarrow A \vee B$	OR
$F_8 = (x + y)'$	$F \leftarrow \overline{A \vee B}$	NOR
$F_9 = (x \oplus y)'$	$F \leftarrow \overline{A \oplus B}$	Exclusive-NOR
$F_{10} = y'$	$F \leftarrow \overline{B}$	Complement B
$F_{11} = x + y'$	$F \leftarrow A \vee \overline{B}$	
$F_{12} = x'$	$F \leftarrow \overline{A}$	Complement A
$F_{13} = x' + y$	$F \leftarrow \overline{A} \vee B$	
$F_{14} = (xy)'$	$F \leftarrow \overline{A \wedge B}$	NAND
$F_{15} = 1$	$F \leftarrow$ all 1's	Set to all 1's

- In Table 4.2, each of the 16 columns F0 through F15 represents a truth table of one possible Boolean function for the two variables x and y. Note that the functions are determined from the 16 binary combinations that can be assigned to F.

Table 4.2. *Truth Tables for 16 Functions of Two Variables*

x	y	F_0	F_1	F_2	F_3	F_4	F_5	F_6	F_7	F_8	F_9	F_{10}	F_{11}	F_{12}	F_{13}	F_{14}	F_{15}
0	0	0	0	0	0	0	0	0	0	1	1	1	1	1	1	1	1
0	1	0	0	0	0	1	1	1	1	0	0	0	0	1	1	1	1
1	0	0	0	1	1	0	0	1	1	0	0	1	1	0	0	1	1
1	1	0	1	0	1	0	1	0	1	0	1	0	1	0	1	0	1

- **Hardware Implementation for Logic Microoperations:** The hardware implementation of logic microoperations requires that logic gates be inserted for each bit or pair of bits in the registers to perform the required logic function.

Figure 4.9 shows one stage of a circuit that generates the four basic logic microoperations. It consists of four gates and a multiplexer.

The outputs of the gates are applied to the data inputs of the multiplexer. The two selection inputs S1 and S0 choose one of the data inputs of the multiplexer and direct its value to the output.

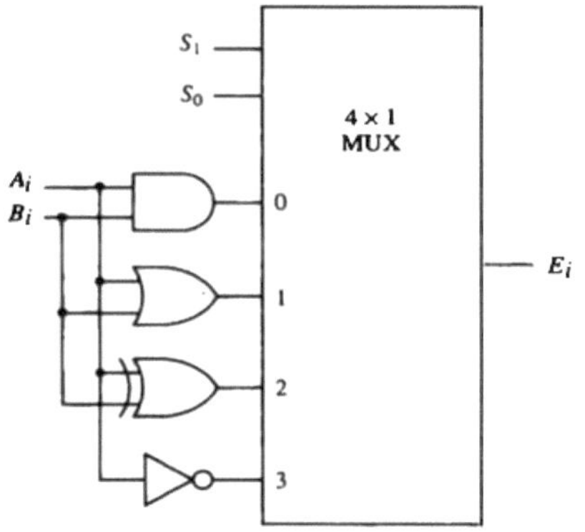

(a) Logic diagram

S_1	S_0	Output	Operation
0	0	$E = A \wedge B$	AND
0	1	$E = A \vee B$	OR
1	0	$E = A \oplus B$	XOR
1	1	$E = \overline{A}$	Complement

(b) Function table

Figure 4.9. *One stage of logic circuit.*

4.14.2.1. Applications of Logic Microoperations

1. **Selective-Set:** The selective-set operation sets to 1 the bits in register A where there are corresponding 1's in register B. It does not affect bit positions that have 0's in B. The following numerical example

clarifies this operation:

1010	A before
1100	B (logic operand)
1110	A after

2. **Selective-Complement:** The selective-complement operation complements bits in A where there are corresponding l's in B. It does not affect bit positions that have 0's in B. For example:

1010	A before
1100	B (logic operand)
0110	A after

3. **Selective-Clear:** The selective-clear operation clears 0 the bits in A only where there are corresponding 1's in B.

For example:

1010	A before
1100	B (logic operand)
0010	A after

4. **Mask:** The mask operation is similar to the selective-clear operation except that the bits of A are cleared only where there are corresponding 0'sin B. The mask operation is an AND micro-operation as seen from the following numerical example:

1010	A before
1100	B (logic operand)
1000	A after masking

5. **Insert:** The insert operation inserts a new value into a group of bits. This is done by first masking the bits and then ORing them with the required value.

For example, an A register contains eight bits, 0110 1010. To replace the four leftmost bits by the value 1001.

First mask the four unwanted bits.

0110 1010	A before masking
0000 1111	B (mask)
0000 1010	A after masking
Now insert the new value	
0000 1010	A before insert
1001 0000	B (insert)
1001 1010	A after insertion

**The mask operation is an AND microoperation and the insert operation is an OR microoperation.

6. **Clear:** The clear operation compares the words in A and B and produces an all 0's result, if the two numbers are equal.

   This operation is achieved by an exclusive-OR microoperation as shown by the following example.

1010	A
1010	B
0000	A

4.14.3. Shift Micro-Operations

1. Shift micro-operations are used for serial transfer of data.
2. They are also used in conjunction with arithmetic, logic, and other data-processing operations.
3. The contents of a register can be shifted to the left or the right.
4. There are three types of shifts:

i. Logical Shift: A logical shift is one that transfers 0 through the serial input to fill the vacancy created by shift operation.

The symbol *shl* is used for logical shift-left micro-operation.

Shr is used for shift-right micro-operation.

shl: Example: R1←shl R1

The above statement shifts the content of register R1 by 1-bit.

Example: R1 = 0110

After performing shift left, R1 has the content 1100

shr: Example: R.←shr R1

The above statement right shifts the content of register R1 by 1-bit.

Example: R1 = 1100

After performing shift left, R1 has the content 0110

ii. **Circular Shift:** The circular shift is also known as a rotate operation.

It circulates the bits of the register around the two ends without loss of information. The symbols *cil* used for logical circular shift-left micro-operation.

cir used for circular shift-right microoperation.

cil: Example: R1←cil R1

The above statement specifies a circular shift left of the content of register R1. Here all the bits are shifted one bit position to LEFT, the Leftmost bit (MSB) was circulated to the Right most bit (LSB).

Example: R1 = 1011

After performing circular shift left, R1 has the content 0111.

cir: Example: R1←cir R1

The above statement specifies circular shift right of the content of register R1. Here all the bits are shifted one bit position to RIGHT, the Rightmost bit (LSB) was circulated to the Left most bit (MSB).

Example: R1 = 1011

After performing circular shift right, R1 has the content 1101.

iii. **Arithmetic Shift:** An arithmetic shift is a microoperation that shifts a signed binary number to the left or right.

After the shift micro-operation, the sign of the number is to be restored.

The symbols ash*l* used for logical arithmetic shift-left micro-operation.

ashr used for arithmetic shift-right microoperation.

ashl:

Example: R1←ashl R1

The above statement specifies arithmetic shift left of the content of register R1 Here all the bits except the MSB, shift one bit position to LEFT. The second Left most bit was discarded and right most bit (LSB) was loaded by 0.

Example: R1 = 1011

After performing arithmetic shift left, R1 has the content 1110.

ashr: Example: R1←ashr R1

The above statement specifies arithmetic shift right of the content of register R1 Here all the bits shifted one bit position to RIGHT. The Leftmost bit (MSB) remains.

Example: R1 = 1011

After performing arithmetic shift right, R1 has the content 110 (Table 4.3).

Table 4.3. *Shift Microoperations*

Symbolic Designation	Description
R ← shl R	Shift-left register R
R ← shr R	Shift-right register R
R ← cil R	Circular shift-left register R
R ← cir R	Circular shift-right register R
R ← ashl R	Arithmetic shift-left R
R ← ashr R	Arithmetic shift-right R

CHAPTER 5

PROCESSOR AND CONTROL UNIT

Contents

A control unit is a combination of circuits in a processor that controls the input as well as output. It receives instructions from a program, and then passes them to the arithmetic logic unit (ALU). The ALU performs the appropriate operation and sends the resulting values back to the control unit.

5.1. HARDWIRED VS. MICROPROGRAMMED CONTROL UNIT

1. **Hardwired:** It is a control mechanism; the control unit generates the control signals needed for the processor using logic circuits; It

is created as a sequential logic circuit. The final circuit is generated by physically linking the components including gates, flip flops, and drums are known as the hardwired controller.

2. **Microprogrammed Control Unit:** A control unit with its binary control values stored as words in memory is called microprogrammed control. Each word in the control memory contains microinstruction that specifies one or more microoperations for the system. A sequence of microinstructions constitutes a micro program.

   What are the advantages and disadvantages of Hardwired control unit:

- Instruction set, the control logic is directly implemented.
- Requires change in wiring if the design has to be controlled.
- An occurrence of an error is more.
- Complex decoding and sequencing logic.
- It requires a more chip area, therefore, it is a costlier control unit.

What are the advantages and disadvantages of Micro programmed?

- **Advantage:** A simpler design means the control unit is cheaper and less error-prone to implement. It is also flexible, as changes can be easily made to the design.
- **Disadvantage:** It is slower than a hardwired unit of comparable technology. A hardwired control unit is used for RISC architecture because it is faster.

Hardwired Control Unit	**Microprogrammed Control Unit**
Speed is fast	Speed is slow
Costlier	Cheaper
Occurrence of error is more	Occurrence of error is less
Control functions implemented in hardware	Control functions implemented in software
Not flexible to accommodate new system specification or new instruction redesign is required.	More flexible to accommodate new system specifications or new instructions.
Difficult to handle complex instruction sets.	Easier to handle complex instruction sets
Complicated design process.	Orderly, systematic and simple design process.
Complex decoding and sequencing logic.	Easier decoding and sequencing logic
Application: Mostly RISC microprocessors.	Application: Mainframes some microprocessors

5.2. GENERAL REGISTER

Generally, CPU has seven general registers. Register organization shows how registers are selected and how data flows between register and ALU. A decoder is used to select a particular register. The output of each register is connected to two multiplexers to form the two buses A and B. The selection lines in each multiplexer select the input data for the particular bus. The A and B buses form the two inputs of an ALU. The operation select lines decide the micro-operation to be performed by ALU. The result of the micro-operation is available at the output bus. The output bus connected to the inputs of all registers, thus by selecting a destination register it is possible to store the result in it (Figure 5.1).

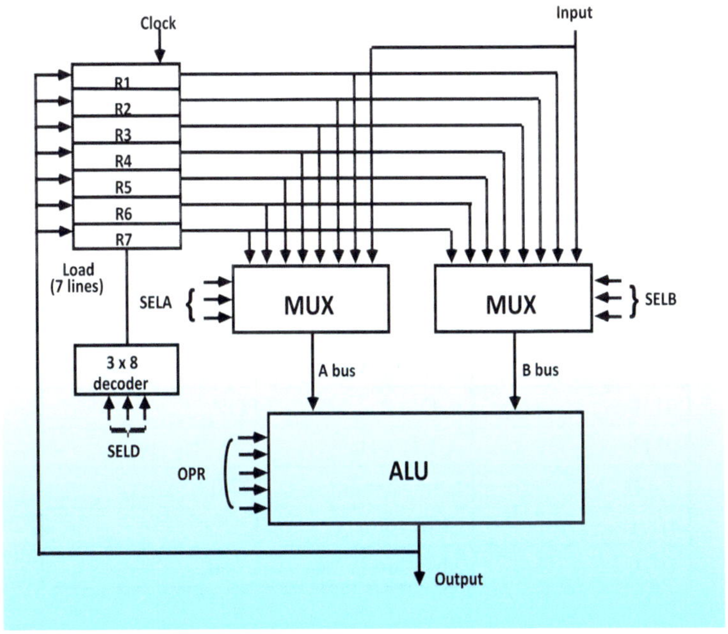

Figure 5.1. *General register.*

Example: To perform the operation R3 = R1 + R2 We have to provide following binary selection variable to the select inputs.

1. SEL A: 001 -To place the contents of R1 into bus A.
2. SEL B: 010 - to place the contents of R2 into bus B
3. SEL OPR: 10010 – to perform the arithmetic addition A + B
4. SEL REG or SEL D: 011 – to place the result available on output bus in R3.

Binary Code	SELA	SELB	SEL-D or SEL-REG
000	Input	Input	–
001	R1	R1	R1
010	R2	R2	R2
011	R3	R3	R3
100	R4	R4	R4
101	R5	R5	R5
110	R6	R6	R6
111	R7	R7	R7

Operation with Symbol:

Operation Selection Code	Operation	Symbol
0000	Transfer A	TSFA
0001	Increment A	INC A
0010	A + B	ADD
0011	A-B	SUB
0100	Decrement A	DEC
0101	A AND B	AND
0110	A OR B	OR
0111	A XOR B	XOR
1000	Complement A	COM A
1001	Shift right A	SHR
1010	Shift left A	SHL

5.3. STACK ORGANIZATION

A stack is an ordered linear list in which all insertions and deletions are made at one end, called top. It uses Last in First out (LIFO) access method which is the most popular access method in most of the CPU. A register is used to store the address of the topmost element of the stack which is known as Stack pointer (SP) because its value always points at the top item in the stack. In this organization, ALU operations are performed on stack data.

The main two operations that are performed on the operands of the stack are Push and Pop. These two operations are performed from one end only (Figure 5.2).

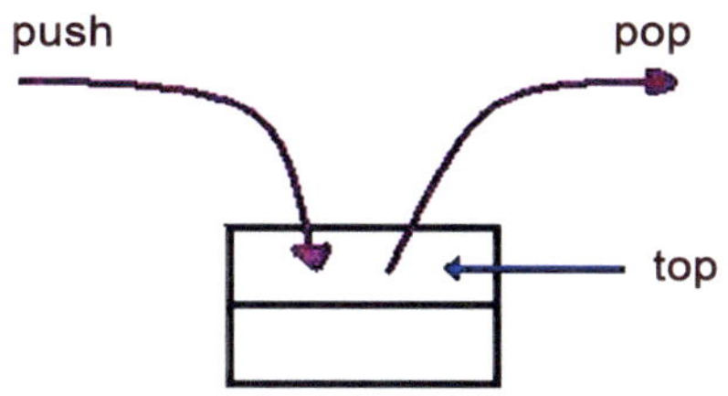

Figure 5.2. *The stack are push and pop.*

- Push operation - The operation of inserting an item onto a stack is called push operation.
- Pop operation- The operation of deleting an item onto a stack is called pop operation

Applications:

- Evaluation of mathematical expressions using Reverse Polish Notation
- To reverse a word. A given word is pushed to stack - letter by letter - and then popped out letters from the stack.
- An "undo" mechanism in text editors; this operation is accomplished by keeping all text changes in a stack
- Backtracking. This is a process when it is required to access the most recent data element in a series of elements.
- space for parameters and local variables is created internally using a stack.
- The compiler's syntax check for matching braces is implemented by using stack.
- **Implementation of Stack:**

1. **Register Stack:** A stack can be organized as a collection of a finite number of registers that are used to store temporary information during the execution of a program. The stack pointer (SP) is a register that holds the address of the top element of the stack.
2. **Memory Stack:** A stack can be implemented in a random-access memory (RAM) attached to a CPU. The implementation of a stack in the CPU is done by assigning a portion of memory to a stack operation and using a processor register as a stack pointer. The starting memory location of the stack is specified by the processor register as stack pointer (Figure 5.3).

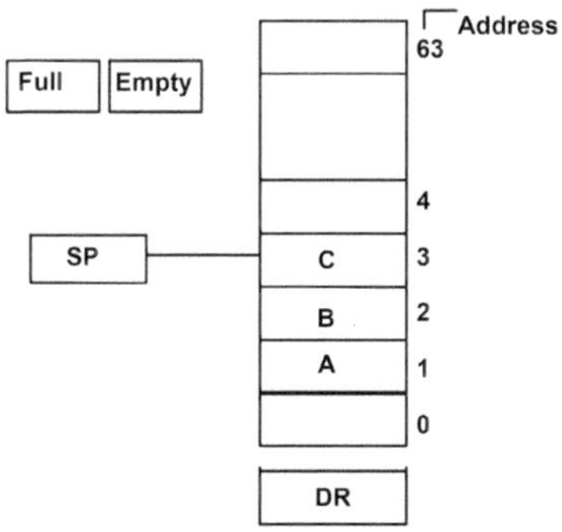

Figure 5.3. *64 word register stack.*

There are 64 registers used to make a register stack. The numbers 0, 1, 2, 3, up to 63 denote the addresses of different registers. SP is a pointer that points to the top of the stack, i.e., it currently points to the item at the top. Two more registers, called FLAG and EMPTY, are used. The FULL and EMPTY registers are made up of flip-flops. They indicate whether the stack is full or not.

If FULlL = 1, then EMPTY = 0 it means that the stack is full.

If FULlL = 0, then EMPTY= 1 it means that stack is empty.

Similarly, the EMPTY flag states whether the stack is empty or not because while retrieving the data from the stack it may happen that the stack is empty.

DR is the data register through which data is transferred to and fro from the stack. Operations

- Push Operation:

  SP ← SP + 1

  //stack pointer is incremented by one

  M[SP] ← DR

  // the content of the data register is stored at the current memory pointed by the stack pointer.

  IF (SP = 0) then (FULL

  ←1) (EMPTY ←0)

  // The values of flag registers are set.

- **Pop operation:**

  DR

  ←M[SP]

// the content of current memory pointed by the stack pointer is stored to data register SP = SP-1

//stack pointer is decremented

by one If (SP = 0) then (EMPTY

←1) FULL ←0

Since the addresses of 64 registers are numbered from 0, 1, 2, 3, …, up to 63. The binary value of 63 is 111111, which is 6 bits. When the stack pointer is incremented after 63, it becomes 64, corresponding to the binary value 1000000, which is 7 bits. But in this case, the address of each register is 6 bits; hence, 1 is discarded from the binary value of 64. The stack pointer points to the 000000-address register. This implies that the stack is full. Zero address instructions are used in register stack organization. The address does not contain the address of the operands.

Example: (a + b) × (c + d)

Following are the instructions to execute it Push a

Push b

Add. // Zero address instruction Push c

Push d

Add. // Zero address instruction Mul. // Zero address instruction

Memory stack – the RAM is divided into three logical parts:

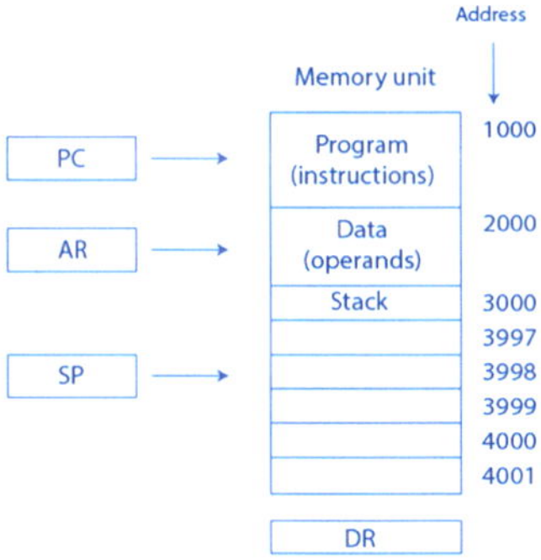

- Program- The logical part of RAM where programs are stored. The program section address starts from 1000.
- Data - It is the logical part of RAM where data (operands) are stored. The data section address starts from 2000.
- Stack - It is the part of RAM used to implement stack. Its address starts from 3000 and continues up to 4001.

It is not necessary that the sequence and address of each part is fixed. It is logically decided by the manufacturer. Program counter (PC) is used to point the program counter. Data register is used to store data. Data is pointed by the address pointer or register. There is also a stack pointer.

- **Push Operation:**

  $SP \leftarrow SP - 1.$

  $M[SP]. \leftarrow DR.$

- **POP Operation:**

  $DR \leftarrow M[SP]$

  $SP \leftarrow SP + 1$

Consider its application - Evaluation of mathematical expressions using Reverse Polish Notation. The common mathematical method of writing arithmetic expressions imposes difficulties when evaluated by a computer. The Polish mathematician Lukasiewicz showed that arithmetic expressions: can be represented in prefix notation as well as postfix notation.

Infix	Prefix or Polish	Postfix or Reverse Polish Notation
A + B	+AB.	AB+

Example: $(3 \times 4) \times (5 \times 6)$.   34*56**

						→	6				
→	4			→	5		5	→	30		
3	3	→	12		12		12		12	→	360

Actually, this is how a computer evaluates mathematical expressions. It is one of the applications of stack.

5.4. INSTRUCTION FORMA

- A 16-bit instruction code format could consist of a 4-bit operation code (opcode) and a 12-bit memory address, where the 4 bits are divided into 2 parts as shown in the figure below.
- The bits 12–14 represent the operation code and the 15th bit which is represented with I states whether the given address is Direct or Indirect.

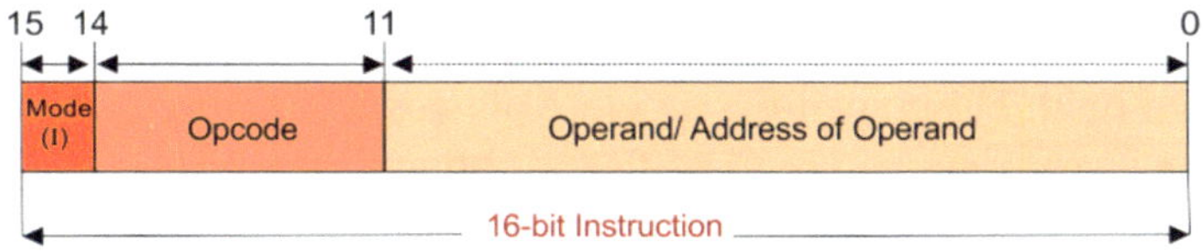

Instruction Format

- If the value of I = 0 then the given address is Direct address and if the value of I = 1 then the given address is Indirect address.
- Direct: Instruction code contains address of operand.
- Immediate: Instruction code contains operand
- Indirect : Instruction code contains address of address of operand.
- Effective address = actual address of the data in memory (Figure 5.4).

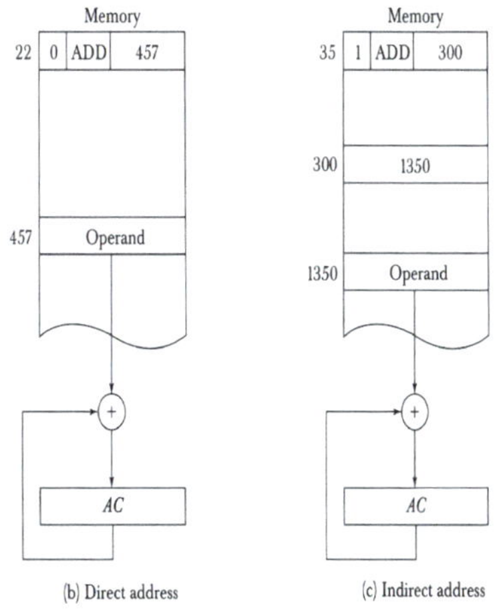

Figure 5.4. *Demonstration of direct and indirect address.*

5.5. DATA TRANSFER AND MANIPULATION

Computer systems consist of a set of instructions that help the users to easily carry out their computational tasks. The instruction set differs from one computer system to another. The operations are represented by binary codes and the binary code assignment in the operation field of the instruction can be different in different computers. However, the actual operations in the instruction set are not very different from one computer system to another. The symbolic names of the instruction (assembly language notation) may also differ from one computer to another. An instruction usually contains op code, addressing field, and operand field. There are different types of opcodes and based on the type of opcode, the instructions can be classified as follows:

1. Data transfer instructions;
2. Data manipulation instructions;
3. Program control instructions.

Data transfer instructions transfer data from one location to another without causing any change in the content present in the binary form. Data manipulation instructions perform arithmetic, logic, and shift operations. Program control instructions provide decision making abilities and are able to change the execution sequence.

5.5.1. Data Transfer Instructions

Data transfer instructions move the data between memory and processor registers, processor registers and I/O devices, and from one processor register to another. There are eight commonly used data transfer instructions. Each instruction is represented by a mnemonic symbol (Table 5.1).

Table 5.1. *Data Transfer Instructions*

Name	Mnemonic Symbols
Load	LD
Store	ST
Move	MOV
Exchange	XCH
Input	In
Output	OUT
Push	PUSH
Pop	POP

The instructions can be described as follows:

- Load – the load instruction is used to transfer data from the memory to a processor register, which is usually an accumulator.
- Store – the store instruction transfers data from processor registers to memory.
- Move – the move instruction transfers data from processor register to memory or memory to processor register or between processor registers itself.

- Exchange – the exchange instruction swaps information either between two registers or between a register and a memory word.
- Input – the input instruction transfers data between the processor register and the input terminal.
- Output – the output instruction transfers data between the processor register and the output terminal.
- Push and Pop – the push and pop instructions transfer data between a processor register and memory stack.

5.5.2. Data Manipulation Instructions

Data manipulation instructions perform operations on data and provide the computational capabilities for the computer. The data manipulation instructions in a typical computer are usually divided into three basic types as follows:

1. **Arithmetic instructions:** The four basic arithmetic operations are addition, subtraction, multiplication, and division. Most computers provide instructions for all four operations.
2. **Logical and Bit Manipulation Instructions:** Logical instructions carry out binary operations on the bits stored in the registers. In logical operations, each bit of the operand is treated as a Boolean variable. Logical instructions can change bit value, clear a group of bits, or can even insert new bit value into operands that are stored in registers or memory words. Each logical instruction is represented by mnemonic symbols.

Name	Mnemonics
Clear	CLR
Complement	COM
AND	AND
OR	OR
Exclusive-OR	XOR
Clear carry	CLRC
Set carry	SETC
Complement carry	COMC
Enable interrupt	EI
Disable interrupt	DI

Clear instruction replaces the specific operand with 0's. The complement instruction inverts all the bits of the operand and produces 1's complement.

The AND, OR, and XOR instructions perform logical operations on each bit or group of bits of the operand. AND instruction can clear a bit or group of bits of an operand. For the Boolean variable, a, the relationship 'ab0 = 0' and 'ab1 = a' indicates that the binary variable when ANDed with 0 changes the value to 0. OR instruction can set a bit or group of bits of an operand. For the Boolean variable, a, the relationship 'a + 1 =1' and 'a + 0 = a' indicates that the binary variable, when ORed with 1, changes the value to 1. XOR instruction can complement bits of an operand. For the Boolean variable, a, the relationship 'a + 1 = a' and 'a + 0 = a' indicates that the binary variable is complemented when XORed with 1. However, the variable does not change the value when XORed with 0. The carry bits can be cleared, set, or complemented with appropriate instructions.

3. **Shift Instructions:** Shifts are operations in which the bits of a word are moved to the left or right. Shift instructions may specify logical shifts, arithmetic shifts, or rotate-type operations.

Typical Shift Instructions:

Name	Mnemonic
Logical shift right	SHR
Logical shift left	SHL
Arithmetic shift right	SHRA
Arithmetic shift left	SHLA
Rotate right	ROR
Rotate left	ROL
Rotate right through carry	RORC
Rotate left through carry	ROLC

5.6. PROGRAM CONTROL

The program control instructions direct the flow of a program and allow the flow of the program to change. It is an important feature of the computers since it provides the control over the flow of the program and provides the capability to branch to different program segments.

call	This instruction calls a subroutine using an immediate value as the subroutine's absolute address, and stores the return address in register ra

callr	This instruction calls a subroutine at the absolute address contained in a register, and stores the return address in register ra. This instruction serves the role of dereferencing a C function pointer.
ret	The ret instruction is used to return from subroutines called by call or call. ret loads and executes the instruction specified by the address in register ra
jmp	The jmp instruction jumps to an absolute address contained in a register. jmp is used to implement switch statements of the C programming language
jmpi	The jmpi instruction jumps to an absolute address using an immediate value to determine the absolute address
br	This instruction branches relative to the current instruction. A signed immediate value gives the offset of the next instruction to execute

The conditional branch instructions compare register values directly, and branch if the expression is true. The conditional branches support the following equality and relational comparisons of the C programming language:

- == and !=
- < and <= (signed and unsigned)
- > and >= (signed and unsigned)

5.7. INTRODUCTORY CONCEPT OF REDUCED INSTRUCTION SET COMPUTER (RISC)

A processor architecture that shifts the analytical process of a computational task from the execution or runtime to the preparation or compile time. By using less hardware or logic, the system can operate at higher speeds. RISC cuts down on the number and complexity of instructions, on the theory that each one can be accessed and executed faster, and that less semiconductor real estate is required to process them. The result is that for any given semiconductor technology, a more powerful microprocessor can be produced with RISC than with complex instruction set computer (CISC) architectures. This simplification of computer instruction sets gains processing efficiencies. That theme works because all computers and programs execute mostly simple instructions. RISC has five design principles:

1. **Single-Cycle Execution:** In most traditional central processing unit (CPU) designs, the peak possible execution rate is one instruction per basic machine cycle, and for a given technology, the cycle time has some fixed lower limit. Even on complex CPUs, most compiler-

generated instructions are simple. RISC designs emphasize single-cycle execution, even at the expense of synthesizing multi-instruction sequences for some less-frequent operations.

2. **Hard-Wired Control, Little or No Microcode:** Microcode adds a layer of interpretive overhead, raising the number of cycles per instruction, so even the simplest instructions can require several cycles.
3. **Simple Instructions, Few Addressing Modes:** Complex instructions and addressing modes, which entail microcode or multi cycle instructions, are avoided.
4. **Load and Store, Register-Register Design:** Only loads and stores access memory; all others perform register-register operations. This tends to follow from the previous three principles.
5. **Efficient, Deep Pipelining:** To make convenient use of hardware parallelism without the complexities of horizontal microcode, fast CPUs use pipelining. An n-stage pipeline keeps up to "n" instructions active at once, ideally finishing one (and starting another) every cycle. The instruction set must be carefully tuned to support pipelining.

A programmer would need to code four lines of assembly:

LOAD	A,	2:3
LOAD	B,	5:2
PROD	A,	B
STORE 2:3, A		

At first, this may seem like a much less efficient way of completing the operation. Because there are more lines of code, more RAM is needed to store the assembly level instructions. The compiler must also perform more work to convert a high-level language statement into code of this form.

5.7.1. Typical Features of RISC Architecture

Pipelining technique of RISC executes multiple parts or stages of instructions simultaneously such that every instruction on the CPU is optimized. Hence, the RISC processors have a Clock per Instruction of one cycle, and this is called One Cycle Execution.

- It optimizes the usage of register with more number of registers in the RISC and more number of interactions within the memory can be prevented.

- Simple addressing modes, even complex addressing can be done by using arithmetic AND/ OR logical operations.
- **Advantages of RISC Processor Architecture:**
- Because of the small set of instructions of RISC, high-level language compilers can produce more efficient code.
- RISC allows freedom of using the space on microprocessors because of its simplicity.
- Instead of using Stack, many RISC processors use the registers for passing arguments and holding the local variables.
- RISC functions uses only a few parameters, and the RISC processors cannot use the call instructions, and therefore, use a fixed length instructions which are easy to pipeline
- **Drawbacks of RISC Processor Architecture:**
- With the increase in length of the instructions, the complexity increases for the RISC processors to execute due to its character cycle per instruction.
- The performance of the RISC processors depends mostly on the compiler or programmer as the knowledge of the compiler plays a major role while converting the CISC code to a RISC code; hence, the quality of the generated code depends on the compiler.
- The first level cache of the RISC processors is also a disadvantage of the RISC, in which these processors have large memory caches on the chip itself. For feeding the instructions, they require very.

5.7.2. CISC (Complex Instruction Set Computer) Architecture

The main intent of the CISC processor architecture is to complete tasks by using a smaller number of assembly lines. For this purpose, the processor is built to execute a series of operations. Complex instruction is also termed as MULT, which operates memory banks of a computer directly without making the compiler to perform storing and loading functions

- **Features of CISC Architecture:**
  - To simplify the computer architecture, CISC supports microprogramming.
  - CISC has a greater number of predefined instructions which makes high level languages easy to design and implement.
  - CISC consists of a smaller number of registers and a greater number of addressing modes, generally 5 to 20.

- CISC processor takes varying cycle time for execution of instructions – multi-clock cycles.
- CISC consists of a greater number of instructions, generally from 100 to 250.
- Operands in memory are manipulated by instructions.

- Advantages of CISC Architecture:
  - Each machine language instruction is grouped into a micro-code instruction and executed accordingly, and then are stored inbuilt in the memory of the main processor, termed as micro-code implementation.
  - As the microcode memory is faster than the main memory, the microcode instruction set can be implemented without considerable speed reduction over hard wired implementation.
  - Entire new instruction set can be handled by modifying the micro program design.
- **Drawbacks of CISC Architecture:**
  - The amount of clock time taken by different instructions will be different – due to this – the performance of the machine slows down.
  - The instruction set complexity and the chip hardware increases as every new version of the processor consists of a subset of earlier generations.
  - Only 20% of the existing instructions are used in a typical programming event, even though there are many specialized instructions in existence which are not even used frequently.

RISC	**CISC**
· RISC stands for Reduced Instruction Set Computer.	· CISC stands for Complex Instruction Set Computer.
· RISC processors have simple instructions taking about one clock cycle. The average clock cycle per instruction (CPI) is 1.5	· CSIC processor has complex instructions that take up multiple clocks for execution. The average clock cycle per instruction (CPI) is in the range of 2 and 15.
· Performance is optimized with more focus on software	· Performance is optimized with more focus on hardware.
· It has no memory unit and uses separate hardware to implement instructions.	· It has a memory unit to implement complex instructions.

· It has a hard-wired unit of programming.	· It has a microprogramming unit.
· The instruction set is reduced i.e.; it has only a few instructions in the instruction set. Many of these instructions are very primitive.	· The instruction set has a variety of different instructions that can be used for complex operations.
· The instruction set has a variety of different instructions that can be used for complex operations.	· CISC has many different addressing modes and can thus be used to represent higher-level programming language statements more efficiently.
· Complex addressing modes are synthesized using the software.	· CISC already supports complex addressing modes
· Multiple register sets are present	· Only has a single register set
· RISC processors are highly pipelined	· They are normally not pipelined or less pipelined
· The complexity of RISC lies with the compiler that executes the program	· The complexity lies in the microprogram
· Execution time is very less	· Execution time is very high
· Code expansion can be a problem	· Code expansion is not a problem
· The decoding of instructions is simple.	· Decoding of instructions is complex
· It does not require external memory for calculations	· It requires external memory for calculations
· The most common RISC microprocessors are Alpha, ARC, ARM, AVR, MIPS, PA-RISC, PIC, Power Architecture, and SPARC.	· Examples of CISC processors are the System/360, VAX, PDP-11, Motorola 68000 family, AMD, and Intel x86 CPUs.
· RISC architecture is used in high-end applications such as video processing, telecommunications, and image processing.	· CISC architecture is used in low-end applications such as security systems, home automation, etc.

5.7.3. Difference Between RISC Instruction Execution vs. and CISC Instruction Execution

A comparison of instruction execution in RISC and CISC architectures is given in Figure 5.5.

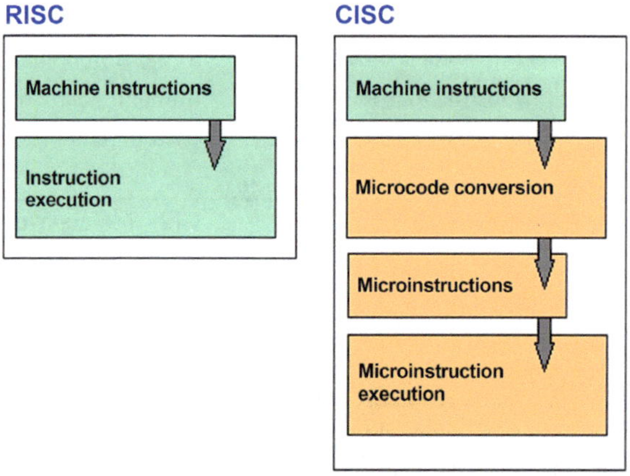

Figure 5.5. *RISC and CISC.*

5.8. PIPELINING

A technique used in advanced microprocessors where the microprocessor begins executing a second instruction before the first has been completed.

Or

Pipelining is a technique of decomposing a sequential process into sub operations with each sub process being executed in a special dedicated segment that operates concurrently with all other segments.

- **Pipelining Works?** The pipeline is divided into segments and each segment can execute its operation concurrently with the other segments. Once a segment completes an operation, it passes the result to the next segment in the pipeline and fetches the next operations from the preceding segment.
- **Characteristics of Pipelines:**
  - **Hardware or Software Implementation** – pipelining can be implemented in either software or hardware.
  - **Large or Small Scale** – Stations in a pipeline can range from simplistic to powerful, and a pipeline can range in length from short to long.
  - **Synchronous or Asynchronous Flow** – a synchronous pipeline operates like an assembly line: at a given time, each station is processing some amount of information. An

asynchronous pipeline, allow a station to forward information at any time.

– **Buffered or Un-Buffered Flow** – One stage of pipeline sends data directly to another one or a buffer is placed between each pair of stage.

– **Finite Chunks or Continuous Bit Streams** – the digital information that passes through a pipeline can consist of a sequence or small data items or an arbitrarily long bit stream. Automatic Data Feed or Manual Data Feed – Some implementations of pipelines use a separate mechanism to move information, and other implementations require each stage to participate in moving information.

IF: Fetches the instruction into the instruction register.

ID: Instruction Decode, decodes the instruction for the opcode. AG: Address Generator generates the address.

DF: Data Fetch fetches the operands into the data register. EX: Execution executes the specified operation.

WB: Write back, writes back the result to the register.

Advantages of Pipelining:

- More efficient use of processor
- Quicker time of execution of large number of instructions.
- Increase in the number of pipeline stages increases the number of instructions executed simultaneously.
- Faster ALU can be designed when pipelining is used.
- Pipelined CPU's works at higher clock frequencies than the RAM.

Disadvantages:

- Pipelining involves adding hardware to the chip
- Inability to continuously run the pipeline at full speed because of pipeline hazards which disrupt the smooth execution of the pipeline.
- Designing of the pipelined processor is complex.
- Instruction latency increases in pipelined processors.
- The throughput of a pipelined processor is difficult to predict.

5.9. PIPELINED DATA PATH AND CONTROL

1. **Pipeline Data Paths:** The goal of pipelining is to allow multiple instructions to be executed at the same time. We may need to perform several operations in a cycle. Increment the PC and add registers at the same time. Fetch one instruction while another one reads or writes data.

   Like the single-cycle Datapath, a pipeline processor needs to duplicate hardware elements that are needed in the same clock cycle.

2. **Pipeline Control Issues and Hardware Control:** Observe that there is nothing to control during instruction fetch and decode (IF and ID). Thus, we can begin our control activities (initialization of control signals) during ID, since control will only be exerted during EX, MEM, and WB stages of the pipeline.

3. **Handling Data Hazards and Control Hazards:**

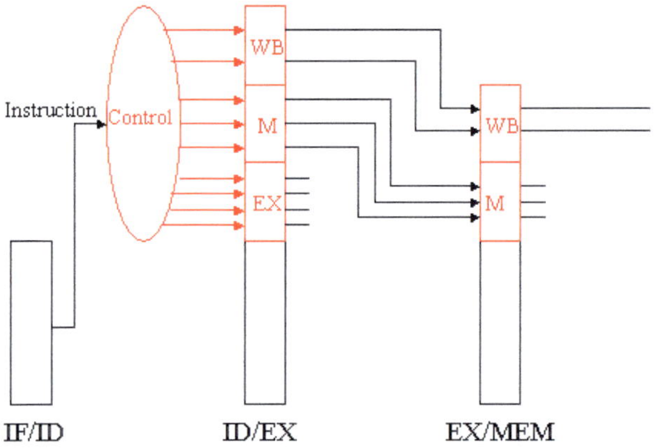

   - IF/ID: Initializes control by passing the rs, rd, and rt fields of the instruction, together with the opcode and funct fields, to the control circuitry.
   - ID/EX: Buffers control for the EX, MEM, and WB stages, while executing control for the EX stage. Control decides what operands will be input to the ALU, what ALU operation will be performed, and whether or not a branch is to be taken based on the ALU Zero output.
   - EX/MEM: Buffers control for the MEM and WB stages, while executing control for the MEM stage. The control lines are set for memory read or write, as well as for data selection for memory write. This stage of control also contains the branch control logic.

- MEM/WB: Buffers and executes control for the WB stage, and selects the value to be written into the register file

5. **Overview of Hazards:**

- Structural hazards occur when different instructions collide while trying to access the same piece of hardware in the same segment of a pipeline. This type of hazard can be alleviated by having redundant hardware for the segments wherein the collision occurs. Occasionally, it is possible to insert stalls or reorder instructions to omit this type of hazard.
- Data hazards occur when an instruction depends on the result of a previous instruction still in the pipeline, which result has not yet been computed. The simplest remedy inserts stalls in the execution sequence, which reduces the pipeline's efficiency. The solution to data dependencies is twofold. First, one can forward the ALU result to the write-back or data fetch stages. Second, in selected instances, it is possible to restructure the code to eliminate some data dependencies.
- Control hazards can result from branch instructions. Here, the branch target address might not be ready in time for the branch to be taken, which results in stalls (dead segments) in the pipeline that have to be inserted as local wait events, until processing can resume after the branch target is executed. Control hazards can be mitigated through accurate branch prediction (which is difficult), and by delayed branch strategies.

6. **Data Hazards:** This occurs when the current instruction requires the result of a preceding instruction, but there are insufficient segments in the pipeline to compute the result and write it back to the register file in time for the current instruction to read that result from the register file.
   - **Forwarding:** In order to resolve a dependency, one adds special circuitry to the pipeline that is comprised of wires and switches with which one forwards or transmits the desired value to the pipeline segment that needs that value for computation. Although this adds hardware and control circuitry, the method works because it takes far less time for the required value(s) to travel through a wire than it does for a pipeline segment to compute its result.
   - **Code Re-Ordering:** Here, the compiler reorders statements in the source code, or the assembler reorders object code, to place one or more statements between the current instruction and

the instruction in which the required operand was computed as a result. This requires an "intelligent" compiler or assembler, which must have detailed information about the structure and timing of the pipeline on which the data hazard would occur. We call this type of software a hardware-dependent compiler.

– **Stall Insertion:** It is possible to insert one or more stalls (no-op instructions) into the pipeline, which delays the execution of the current instruction until the required operand is written to the register file. This decreases pipeline efficiency and throughput, which is contrary to the goals of pipeline processor design. Stalls are an expedient method of last resort that can be used when compiler action or forwarding fails or might not be supported in hardware or software design.

Suppose we have the following sequence of instructions:

sub $2, $1, $3 # Register 2 is the output of sub

and $8, $2, $5 # Operand #1 depends on Register 2 data

or $9, $6, $2 # Operand #2 depends on Register 2 data

add $7, $2, $2 # Add result depends on Register 2 data

sw $6,20($2) # Store (memory write) depends on Register 2

Ans:

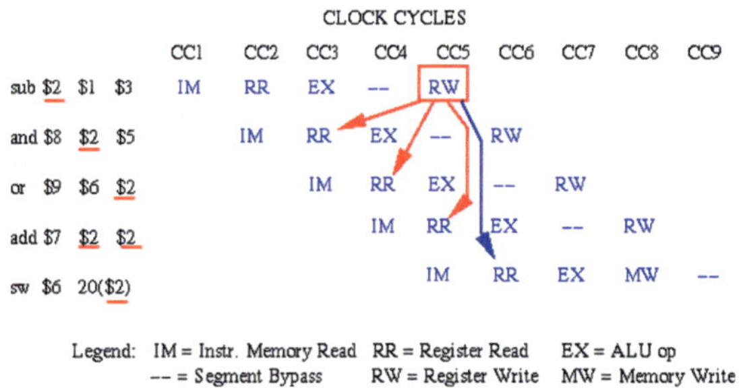

2. **Structural Hazards:** This occurs when there is insufficient hardware to support a computation in a given pipeline segment.

Clock cycle number								
Instr	1	2	3	4	5	6	7	8
Load	IF	ID	EX	MEM	WB			
Instr 1		IF	ID	EX	MEM	WB		
Instr 2			IF	ID	EX	MEM	WB	
Instr 3				IF	ID	EX	MEM	WB

To overcome this problem, we stall the pipeline for 1 clock cycle when a data-memory access takes place. The effect of the stall is in fact to occupy the resources for that instruction slot. The following table denoted how the stalls are in fact implemented.

	Clock cycle number								
Instr	1	2	3	4	5	6	7	8	9
Load	IF	ID	EX	MEM	WB				
Instr 1		IF	ID	EX	MEM	WB			
Instr 2			IF	ID	EX	MEM	WB		
Stall				bubble	bubble	bubble	bubble	bubble	
Instr 3					IF	ID	EX	MEM	WB

Instr 1 suppose not to be data-memory reference (load or store), or else Instr 3 cannot begin execution for the similar reason as shown above.

	Clock cycle number								
Instr	1	2	3	4	5	6	7	8	9
Load	IF	ID	EX	MEM	WB				
Instr 1		IF	ID	EX	MEM	WB			
Instr 2			IF	ID	EX	MEM	WB		
Instr 3				stall	IF	ID	EX	MEM	WB

Introducing stalls reduced performance as we discussed before. Why, then, would the designer permit structural hazards? There are 2 reasons:

- To reduce the latency of the unit. The smaller latency comes from the lack of pipeline registers that introduce overhead.
- To reduce cost. For instance, machines that support an instruction and a cache both access every cycle (to stop the structural hazard of the above instance) need at least twice of the total memory.

3. **Control (Branch) Hazards:** These are the most difficult types of hazards arising from normal operation of a program. In the next section, we will see that exceptions (e.g., overflow) can play particularly interesting types of havoc with smooth pipeline execution.

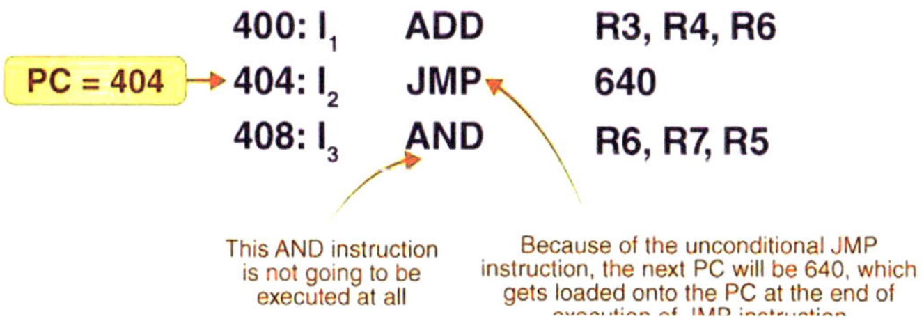

In this scenario, fetching the I3 is pointless. What is the status of the pipeline? The I3 fetch must be terminated while in I2. This can only be determined once I2 has been decoded as JMP. As a result, the pipeline cannot continue at its current rate, resulting in a Control Dependency (hazard). If I3 is fetched in the meantime, it is not just unnecessary work, but it is also possible that some data in registers has been changed and needs to be reversed.

4. **Exceptions as Hazards:** Hardware and software must work together in any architecture, especially in a pipeline processor. Here, the ISA and processor control must be designed so that the following steps occur when an exception is detected:

- Hardware detects an exception (e.g., overflow in the ALU) and stops the offending instruction at the EX-stage.
- Pipeline loader and scheduler allow all prior instructions (e.g., those already in the pipeline in MEM and WB) to complete.
- All instructions that are present in the pipeline after the exception is detected are flushed from the pipeline.
- The address of the offending instruction (usually the address in main memory) is saved in the EPC register, and a code describing the exception is saved in the Cause register.
- Hardware control branches to the exception handling routine (part of the operating system).

CHAPTER 6

SYSTEM-LEVEL ARCHITECTURE: I/O, MEMORY, AND MICROPROCESSOR OPERATIONS

Contents

From the CPU's perspective, an I/O device appears as a set of special-purpose registers, of three general types:

- Status registers provide status information to the CPU about the I/O device. These registers are often read-only, i.e., the CPU can only read their bits, and cannot change them.
- Configuration/control registers are used by the CPU to configure and control the device. Bits in these configuration registers may be write-only, so the CPU can alter them, but not read them back. Most bits in control registers can be both read and written.

- Data registers are used to read data from or send data to the I/O device.

6.1. PERIPHERAL DEVICES

A peripheral device, also sometimes called an auxiliary device, is any connected device (internal or external) that provides a computer with additional functionality. Peripheral devices fall into three main categories.

- Input devices, which send data to the computer.
- Output devices, which receive data from the computer.
- Input/output devices, such as storage devices.

1. **Mouse:** It is an input device that allows you to use point-and-click technology to interact with a computer. Modern mice usually have two buttons with a scroll wheel between them. This device was named a "mouse" because the inventors thought that the wire that connects the device to the computer resembled a mouse tail. Nowadays, mice often connect to the computer using wireless technology.
2. **Keyboard:** These are the most common input device. The user enters letters, numbers, and other symbols to give the computer information and instruction. Using a keyboard to enter a lot of information is called typing.
3. **Webcam:** These input devices are video cameras that connect to a computer. They can be external or built in. Webcams are most often used to enable people to see each other when communicating over the internet, or for recording video blogs, or making other videos.
4. **Microphone:** These are audio input devices. The microphone feeds a sound signal to the computer, where it can be recorded, or streamed across the internet. Microphones are often built into laptops, webcams and mobile phones nowadays.
5. **Monitor:** The most common output device, monitors enable users to interact with a computer more easily. The monitor essentially displays a signal sent by the computer in a visual format.
6. **Speakers:** A computer speaker is another common type of output device. They typically come in pairs to provide stereo sound and sometimes with a subwoofer unit too in order to enhance bass frequency. Computer speakers usually have built-in amplifiers and therefore require a power supply, either from the mains, batteries, or via a USB port.

7. **Projector:** These are optical output devices that enable a roomful of people to see visuals generated by a single computer. As their name suggests, projectors "project" still or moving images onto a screen, blank wall, or other surface.
8. **Printer:** These are another common form of output device. They are used to generate hard copies of electronic data stored on a computer, most often text or images onto paper.

6.2. I/O INTERFACE

The I/O bus is the route used for peripheral devices to interact with the computer processor. A typical connection of the I/O bus to I/O devices is shown in the figure below:

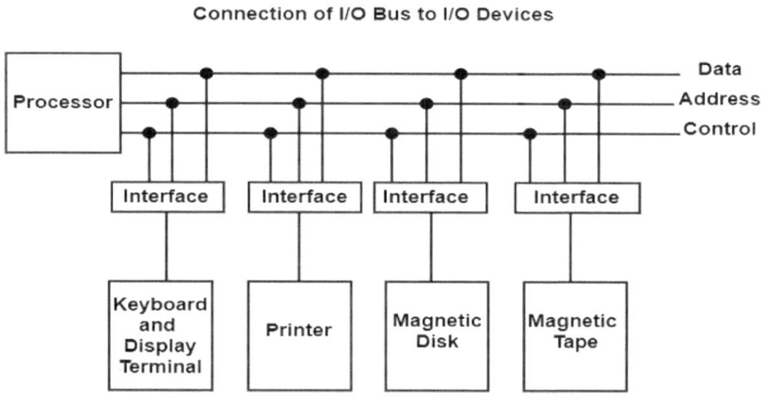

Figure 6.1. *Connection of I/O bus to I/O devices*

The I/O bus includes data lines, address lines, and control lines. In any general-purpose computer, the magnetic disk, printer, and keyboard, and display terminal are commonly employed. Each peripheral unit has an interface unit associated with it. Each interface decodes the control and address received from the I/O bus. When the address is recognized by the interface, it activates the direction between the bus lines and the device that it controls. The interface disables the peripherals whose address does not equivalent to the address in the bus.

1. **Control:** A command control is given to activate the peripheral and to inform its next task. This control command depends on the peripheral, and each peripheral receives its sequence of control commands, depending on its mode of operation.
2. **Status:** A status command can test multiple test conditions in the interface and the peripheral.

3. **Data Output:** A data output command creates the interface counter to the command by sending data from the bus to one of its registers.
4. **Data Input:** The data input command is opposite to the data output command. In data input, the interface gets an element of data from the peripheral and places it in its buffer register.

6.3. DATA TRANSFER SCHEMES

We can connect several I/O devices and memory peripherals to a microprocessor. However, since different technologies are involved, there will be differences in the speed of operation and of data transfer.

Usually, when memory is connected with the microprocessor, there is not a stark difference in the processing speed since semiconductor memories are generally easily compatible with microprocessors. However, this might not always be the case. But the problem often arises when external peripherals are connected as I/O devices. A slow I/O device will not be able to transfer data at a satisfactory rate whenever the microprocessor requests for data transfer. And usually, the peripheral devices do have slower transfer rates than the processor. Maybe the processor might send two units of information per second, but the external device might only accept 1 unit of information per second. Or conversely, perhaps the external device expects quicker transfers, but our microprocessor might be sending information a bit slower.

This might lead to severe data losses, or the devices might get damaged, or there might even be chances for the system to slow down all over, thus affecting the overall efficiency of the system.

To avoid this problem, a number of data transfer techniques have been devised. Since constant communication is required between the external device and the processor, these data transfer techniques play a crucial role in the efficient functioning of the system with the externally connected devices.

- **Data Transfer Schemes:** The data in the serial communication may be sent in two formats:
  - **Asynchronous:** This type of programmed data transfer scheme is used when the speeds of I/O devices and the microprocessor do not match and also when the timing characteristics of the I/O devices are not predictable.
  - **Synchronous:** This type of programmed data transfer scheme is used when the processor and the I/O devices match in speed. Some suitable instructions such as IN and OUT are used for 'to and from' data transfer of I/O devices.

6.3.1. Asynchronous Data Transfer Methods

The asynchronous data transfer between two independent units requires that control signals be transmitted between the communicating units to indicate when they send the data. Thus, the two methods can achieve the asynchronous way of data transfer.

1. **Strobe Control Method:** The Strobe Control method of asynchronous data transfer employs a single control line to time each transfer. This control line is also known as a strobe, and it may be achieved either by source or destination, depending on which initiate the transfer.

i. **Source Initiated Strobe:** In the below block diagram, you can see that strobe is initiated by source, and as shown in the timing diagram, the source unit first places the data on the data bus.

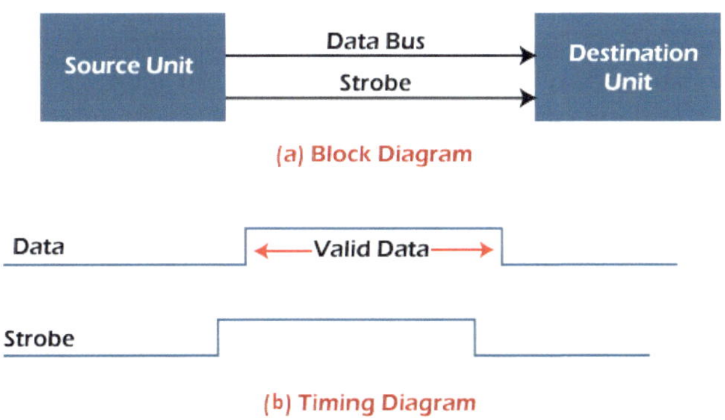

Figure 6.2. Source Initiated Strobe

After a brief delay to ensure that the data resolves to a stable value, the source activates a strobe pulse. The information on the data bus and strobe control signal remains in the active state for a sufficient time to allow the destination unit to receive the data. The destination unit uses a falling edge of strobe control to transfer the contents of a data bus to one of its internal registers. The source removes the data from the data bus after it disables its strobe pulse. Thus, new valid data will be available only after the strobe is enabled again.

In this case, the strobe may be a memory-write control signal from the CPU to a memory unit. The CPU places the word on the data bus and informs the memory unit, which is the destination.

ii. **Destination Initiated Strobe:** In the below block diagram, you see that the strobe initiated by destination, and in the timing diagram, the destination unit first activates the strobe pulse, informing the source to provide the data.

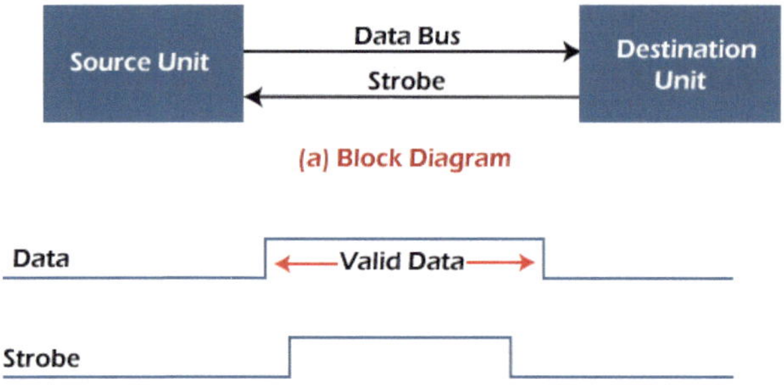

(a) Block Diagram

(b) Timing Diagram

Figure 6.3. *Destination Initiated Strobe*

The source unit responds by placing the requested binary information on the data bus. The data must be valid and remain on the bus long enough for the destination unit to accept it. The falling edge of the strobe pulse can use again to trigger a destination register. The destination unit then disables the strobe. Finally, and source removes the data from the data bus after a determined time interval.

In this case, the strobe may be a memory read control from the CPU to a memory unit. The CPU initiates the read operation to inform the memory, which is a source unit, to place the selected word into the data bus.

2. **Handshaking Method:** The strobe method has the disadvantage that the source unit that initiates the transfer has no way of knowing whether the destination has received the data that was placed in the bus. Similarly, a destination unit that initiates the transfer has no way of knowing whether the source unit has placed data on the bus.

So, this problem is solved by the handshaking method. The handshaking method introduces a second control signal line that replays the unit that initiates the transfer. In this method, one control line is in the same direction as the data flow in the bus from the source to the destination. The source unit uses it to inform the destination unit whether there are valid data in the bus. The other control line is in the other direction from the destination to the source. This is because the destination unit uses it to inform the source whether it can accept data. And in it also, the sequence of control depends on the unit that initiates the transfer. So, it means the sequence of control depends on whether the transfer is initiated by source and destination.

i. **Source Initiated Handshaking:** In the below block diagram, you can see that two handshaking lines are "data valid", which is generated by the source unit, and "data accepted", generated by the destination unit

The timing diagram shows the timing relationship of the exchange of signals between the two units. The source initiates a transfer by placing data on the bus and enabling its data valid signal. The destination unit then activates the data accepted signal after it accepts the data from the bus.

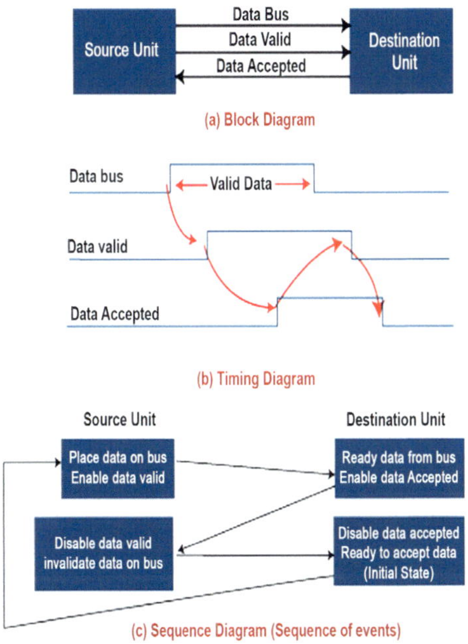

Figure 6.4. *Source Initiated Handshaking*

The source unit then disables its valid data signal, which invalidates the data on the bus. After this, the destination unit disables its data accepted signal, and the system goes into its initial state. The source unit does not send the next data item until after the destination unit shows readiness to accept new data by disabling the data accepted signal. This sequence of events described in its sequence diagram, which shows the above sequence in which the system is present at any given time.

ii. **Destination Initiated Handshaking:** In the below block diagram, you see that the two handshaking lines are "data valid", generated by the source unit, and "ready for data" generated by the destination unit.

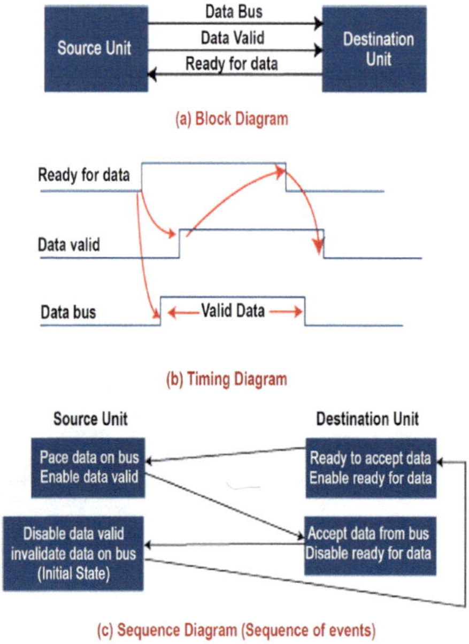

Figure 6.5. *Destination Initiated Handshaking*

The destination transfer is initiated, so the source unit does not place data on the data bus until it receives a ready data signal from the destination unit. After that, the handshaking process is the same as that of the source initiated.

6.3.2. Advantages of Asynchronous Data Transfer

It does not require complex processes by the receiving device. Furthermore, it means that inconsistency in data transfer does not result in a big crisis since the device can keep up with the data stream. It also makes asynchronous transfers suitable for applications where character data is generated irregularly.

6.3.3. Disadvantages of Asynchronous Data Transfer

A large portion of the transmitted data is used to control and identify header bits and thus carries no helpful information related to the transmitted data. This invariably means that more data packets need to be sent.

6.4. INTERRUPT

6.4.1. Interrupt Structures

Data transfer between the CPU and the peripherals is initiated by the CPU. But the CPU cannot start the transfer unless the peripheral is ready to communicate with the CPU. When a device is ready to communicate with the CPU, it generates an interrupt signal. A number of input-output devices are attached to the computer and each device is able to generate an interrupt request. The main job of the interrupt system is to identify the source of the interrupt. There is also a possibility that several devices will request simultaneously for CPU communication. Then, the interrupt system has to decide which device is to be serviced first.

- **Priority Interrupt:** A priority interrupt is a system which decides the priority at which various devices, which generate the interrupt signal at the same time, will be serviced by the CPU. The system has authority to decide which conditions are allowed to interrupt the CPU, while some other interrupt is being serviced. Generally, devices with high-speed transfer such as magnetic disks are given high priority and slow devices such as keyboards are given low priority. When two or more devices interrupt the computer simultaneously, the computer services the device with the higher priority first.
- **Types of Interrupts:**

1. **Hardware Interrupts:** When the signal for the processor is from an external device or hardware then this interrupt is known as hardware interrupt. Let us consider an example: when we press any key on our keyboard to do some action, then this pressing of the key will generate an interrupt signal for the processor to perform certain action. Such an interrupt can be of two types:

i. **Maskable Interrupt:** The hardware interrupts which can be delayed when a much high priority interrupt has occurred at the same time.

ii. **Non-Maskable Interrupt:** The hardware interrupts which cannot be delayed and should be processed by the processor immediately.

2. **Software Interrupts:** The interrupt that is caused by any internal system of the computer system is known as a software interrupt. It can also be of two types:

- **Normal Interrupt:** The interrupts that are caused by software instructions are called normal software interrupts.
- **Exception:** Unplanned interrupts which are produced during the execution of some program are called exceptions, such as division by zero.

6.5. I/O INTERFACE

I/O devices can be interfaced to a computer system I/O in two ways, which are interfacing techniques: (i) memory-mapped I/O; and (ii) I/O-mapped I/O.

Memory mapped I/O – In this technique, the total memory address space is partitioned and part of this space is devoted to I/O addressing as shown in Figure 6.6 When this technique is used, a memory reference instruction that causes data to be fetched from or stored at address specified, automatically becomes an I/O instruction if that address is made the address of an I/O port.

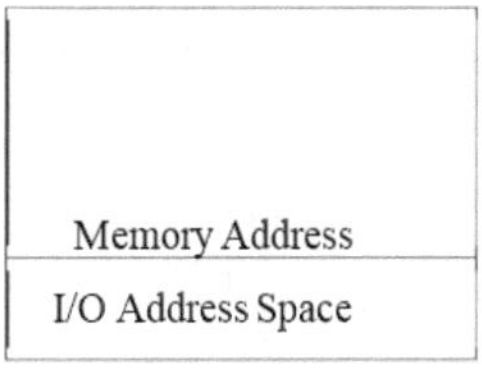

Figure 6.6. *I/O addressing*

- **Advantage:** The usual memory related instructions are used for I/O related operations. The special I/O instructions are not required.
- **Disadvantage:** The memory address space is reduced.

6.5.1. I/O Mapped I/O

If we do not want to reduce the memory address space, we allot a different I/O address space; apart from total memory space which is called I/O mapped I/O technique as shown in Figure 3.6

- **Advantage:** The advantage is that the full memory address space is available.
- **Disadvantage:** The memory related instructions do not work; Therefore, the processor can only use this mode if it has special instructions for No related operations such as I/O read, I/O write (Table 6.1).

Table 6.1. *Memory-Mapped I/O and I/O-Mapped I/O Comparison*

SL. No.	Memory Mapped I/O	I/O Mapped I/O
1.	Memory and I/O share the entire address range of processor.	Processor provides a separate address range for memory and I/O devices.

2.	Usually, the processor provides more address lines for accessing memory. Therefore, more decoding is required for control signals.	Usually, the processor provides less address I/O. Therefore, less decoding is required.
3.	Memory controls signals are used to control read and write I/O operations.	I/O controls signals are used to control read and write I/O operations.

6.6. DMA TRANSFER

The term DMA stands for direct memory access. The hardware device used for direct memory access is called the DMA controller. DMA controller is a control unit, part of I/O device's interface circuit, which can transfer blocks of data between I/O devices and main memory with minimal intervention from the processor.

The DMA transfers the data in three modes which include the following. a) Burst Mode: In this mode DMA handover the buses to CPU only after completion of whole data transfer. Meanwhile, if the CPU requires the bus it has to stay ideal and wait for data transfer.

1. **Burst Mode:** In this mode DMA handover the buses to CPU only after completion of whole data transfer. Meanwhile, if the CPU requires the bus it has to stay ideal and wait for data transfer.
2. **Cycle Stealing Mode:** In this mode, DMA gives control of the buses to the CPU after the transfer of every byte. It continuously issues a request for bus control, makes the transfer of one byte, and returns the bus. This way, the CPU does not have to wait for a long time if it needs the bus for a higher priority task.
3. **Transparent Mode:** Here, DMA transfers data only when the CPU is executing the instruction which does not require the use of buses.

6.6.1. How Are DMA Operations Performed?

Following is the sequence of operations performed by a DMA –

- Primarily, when any device requires to send data between the device and the memory, the device need to send DMA request (DRQ) to DMA controller.
- The DMA controller sends Hold request (HRQ) to the CPU and waits for the CPU to assert the HLDA signal.

- Then the microprocessor tri-states all the data bus, address bus, and control bus. The CPU leaves the control over bus and acknowledges the HOLD request through HLDA signal.

The DMA controller has three registers as follows:

- **Address Register:** It contains the address to specify the desired location in memory.
- **Word Count Register:** It contains the number of words to be transferred.
- **Control Register:** It specifies the transfer mode.

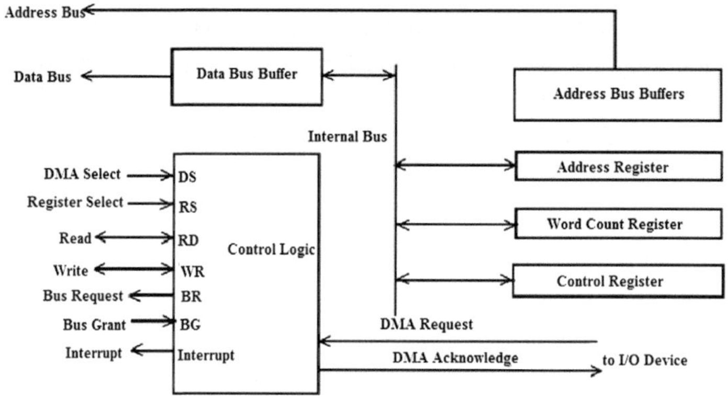

Figure 6.7. *DMA controller*

The CPU initializes the DMA by sending the given information through the data bus:

- The starting address of the memory blocks where the data is available (to read) or where data are to be stored (to write).
- It also sends word count which is the number of words in the memory block to be read or write.
- Control to define the mode of transfer such as read or write.
- A control to begin the DMA transfer.

6.7. I/O PROCESSOR

The DMA mode of data transfer reduces CPU's overhead in handling I/O operations. It also allows parallelism in CPU and I/O operations. Such parallelism is necessary to avoid wastage of valuable CPU time while handling I/O devices whose speeds are much slower as compared to CPU. The concept of DMA operation can be extended to relieve the CPU further from getting involved with the execution of I/O operations. This gives rises to the development of special purpose processor called Input-Output Processor (IOP) or IO channel. The Input Output Processor (IOP) is just like a CPU that handles the details of I/O operations. It is more equipped with facilities than those are available in typical DMA controller. The IOP can fetch and execute its own instructions that are specifically designed to characterize I/O transfers. In addition to the I/O – related tasks, it can perform other processing tasks like arithmetic, logic, branching and code translation. The main memory unit takes the pivotal role. It communicates with processor by the means of DMA (Figure 6.1).

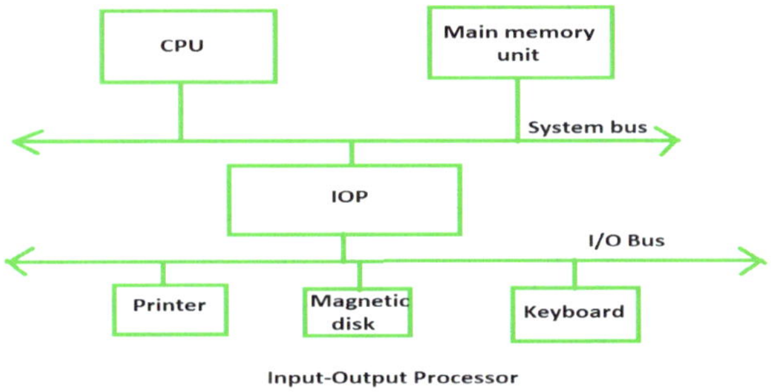

Figure 6.8. *I/O processor.*

The input output processor is a specialized processor which loads and stores data into memory along with the execution of I/O instructions. It acts as an interface between system and devices. It involves a sequence of events to executing I/O operations and then stores the results into the memory.

Advantages:

- The I/O devices can directly access the main memory without the intervention by the processor in I/O processor-based systems.
- It is used to address the problems that arise in Direct memory access method.

6.8. MEMORY HIERARCHY

Memory Hierarchy is a feature in computer system design that helps to organize memory such that access time is reduced. A processor, as well as a huge number of memory devices, was used in the computer systems architecture. However, the fundamental issue is that these components are costly. As a result, memory hierarchy can be used to organize the system's memory. It has many memory levels with varying performance rates. However, any of these can provide a precise objective, reducing the access time. The memory hierarchy was created in response to the program's activity. The memory hierarchy in computer architecture is discussed in this article.

- The memory unit is used for storing programs and data. It fulfils the need for storage of information.
- The additional storage with main memory capacity enhances the performance of the general-purpose computers and makes them efficient.
- Only those programs and data, which are currently needed by the processor, reside in the main memory. Information can be transferred from auxiliary memory to main memory when needed.

6.8.1. Memory Hierarchy Levels

In a computer system, the memory hierarchy design primarily consists of several storage devices. The majority of computers came with extra storage to allow them to run faster than the main memory. Primary (internal) memory and secondary (external) memory are the two forms of the memory hierarchy that are designed. A hierarchical pyramid for computer memory is shown in the diagram below.

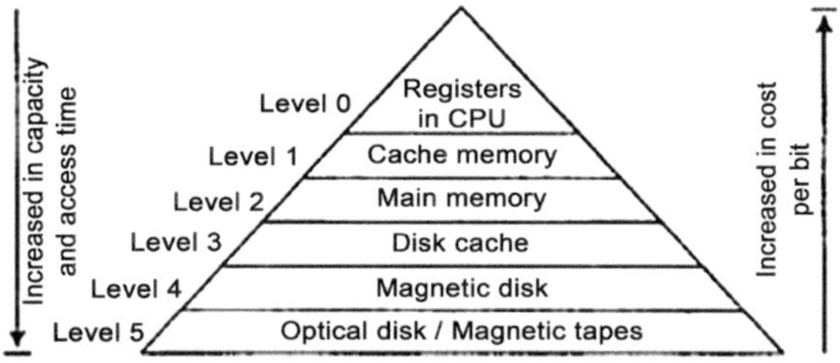

Figure 6.9. *Memory hierarchy levels*

6.8.2. Characteristics of Memory Hierarchy

The following are the main characteristics of memory hierarchy:

1. **Performance:** Initially, computer systems were designed without a memory hierarchy, and the speed gap between main memory and CPU registers grew as a result of the large differential in access time,

resulting in lower system performance. As a result, enhancement was required. Because of the system's increased performance, this was enhanced in the memory hierarchy model.

2. **Ability:** The total quantity of data that the memory hierarchy can store is its capability. Because the memory hierarchy's capacity grows as we move from top to bottom.
3. **Cost Per Bit:** When we move from the bottom to the top of the memory hierarchy, the cost of each bit increases, implying that internal memory is more expensive than external memory.
4. **Access Time:** In the memory hierarchy, the access time is the time delay between data availability and requests to read or write. Because the access time increases as we move from the top to the bottom of the memory hierarchy.

- **Advantages of Memory Hierarchy:** The following are some of the reasons why a memory hierarchy is necessary:
  - Memory distribution is easy and cost-effective.
  - External destruction is removed.
  - Data can be spread all over
  - Allows for pre-paging and demand paging.
  - Swapping will be a lot easier.

6.8.3. Auxiliary Memory

- The most common auxiliary memory devices used in computer systems are magnetic disks and tapes. Other components used, but not as frequently, are magnetic drums, magnetic bubble memory, and optical disks.
- To understand fully the physical mechanism of auxiliary memory devices one must have a knowledge of magnetics, electronics, and electromechanical systems.
- Although the physical properties of these storage devices can be quite complex, their logical properties can be characterized and compared by a few parameters. The important characteristics of any device are its access mode, access time, transfer rate, capacity, and cost.
- The average time required to reach a storage location in memory and obtain its contents is called the access time.
- In electromechanical devices with moving parts such as disks and tapes, the access time consists of a seek time required to position

the read-write head to a location and a transfer time required to transfer data to or from the device. Because the seek time is usually much longer than the transfer time, auxiliary storage is organized in records or blocks.

- A record is a specified number of characters or words. Reading or writing is always done on entire records. The transfer rate is the number of characters or words that the device can transfer per second, after it has been positioned at the beginning of the record.
- Magnetic drums and disks are quite similar in operation. Both consist of high-speed rotating surfaces coated with a magnetic recording medium. The rotating surface of the drum is a cylinder and that of the disk, a round flat plate.
- The recording surface rotates at uniform speed and is not started or stopped during access operations. Bits are recorded as magnetic spots on the surface as it passes a stationary mechanism called a write head.
- Stored bits are detected by a change in magnetic field produced by a recorded spot on the surface as it passes through a read head. The amount of surface available for recording in a disk is greater than in a drum of equal physical size.
- Therefore, more information can be stored on a disk than on a drum of comparable size. For this reason, disks have replaced drums in more recent computers.

6.8.4. Magnetic Disks

- A magnetic disk is a circular plate constructed of metal or plastic coated with magnetized material. Often both sides of the disk are used and several disks may be stacked on one spindle with read/write heads available on each surface.
- All disks rotate together at high speed and are not stopped or started for access purposes. Bits are stored in the magnetized surface in spots along concentric circles called tracks.
- The tracks are commonly divided into sections called sectors. In most systems, the minimum quantity of information which can be transferred is a sector. The subdivision of one disk surface into tracks and sectors is shown in Figure 6.10.

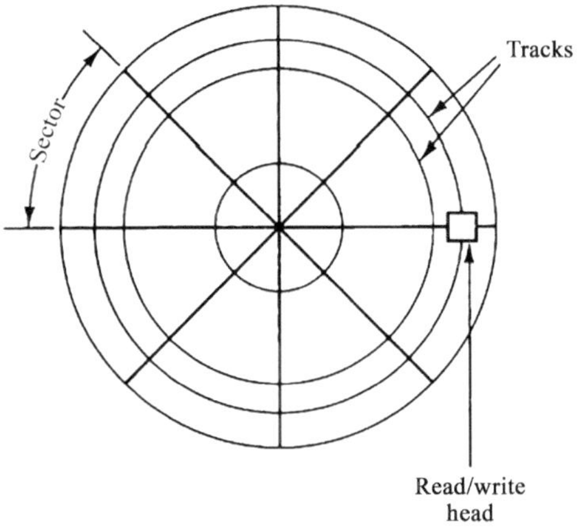

Figure 6.10. *Magnetic Disks*

- Some units use a single read/write head for each disk surface. In this type of unit, the track address bits are used by a mechanical assembly to move the head into the specified track position before reading or writing.
- In other disk systems, separate read/write heads are provided for each track in each surface. The address bits can then select a particular track electronically through a decoder circuit.
- This type of unit is more expensive and is found only in very large computer systems. Permanent timing tracks are used in disks to synchronize the bits and recognize the sectors.
- A disk system is addressed by address bits that specify the disk number, the disk surface, the sector number and the track within the sector. After the read/write heads are positioned in the specified track, the system has to wait until the rotating disk reaches the specified sector under the read/write head.
- Information transfer is very fast once the beginning of a sector has been reached. Disks may have multiple heads and simultaneous transfer of bits from several tracks at the same time.
- A track in a given sector near the circumference is longer than a track near the center of the disk If bits are recorded with equal density, some tracks will contain more recorded bits than others.
- To make all the records in a sector of equal length, some disks use a variable recording density with higher density on tracks near the

center than on tracks near the circumference. This equalizes the number of bits on all tracks of a given sector.

- Disks that are permanently attached to the unit assembly and cannot be removed by the occasional user are called hard disks. A disk drive with removable disks is called a floppy disk. The disks used with a floppy disk drive are small removable disks made of plastic coated with magnetic recording material.
- There are two sizes commonly used, with diameters of 5.25 and 3. 5 inches. The 3.5- inch disks are smaller and can store more data than can the 5.25-inch disks.
- Floppy disks are extensively used in personal computers as a medium for distributing software to computer users.

6.8.5. Magnetic Tape

- A magnetic tape transport consists of the electrical, mechanical, and electronic components to provide the parts and control mechanism for a magnetic-tape unit.
- The tape itself is a strip of plastic coated with a magnetic recording medium. Bits are recorded as magnetic spots on the tape along several tracks.
- Usually, seven or nine bits are recorded simultaneously to form a character together with a parity bit. Read/write heads are mounted one in each track so that data can be recorded and read as a sequence of characters.
- Magnetic tape units can be stopped, started to move forward or in reverse, or can be rewound.
- However, they cannot be started or stopped fast enough between individual characters.
- For this reason, information is recorded in blocks referred to as records. Gaps of unrecorded tape are inserted between records where the tape can be stopped.
- The tape starts moving while in a gap and attains its constant speed by the time it reaches the next record. Each record on tape has an identification bit pattern at the beginning and end.
- By reading the bit pattern at the beginning, the tape control identifies the record number.
- By reading the bit pattern at the end of the record, the control recognizes the beginning of a gap.

- A tape unit is addressed by specifying the record number and the number of characters in the record. Records may be of fixed or variable length.

6.8.6. Associative Memory

- Many data-processing applications require the search of items in a table stored in memory.
- An assembler program searches the symbol address table in order to extract the symbol's binary equivalent.
- An account number may be searched in a file to determine the holder's name and account status.
- The established way to search a table is to store all items where they can be addressed in sequence.
- The search procedure is a strategy for choosing a sequence of addresses, reading the content of memory at each address, and comparing the information read with the item being searched until a match occurs.
- The number of accesses to memory depends on the location of the item and the efficiency of the search algorithm.
- Many search algorithms have been developed to minimize the number of accesses while searching for an item in a random or sequential access memory.
- The time required to find an item stored in memory can be reduced considerably if stored data can be identified for access by the content of the data itself rather than by an address.
- A memory unit accessed by content is called an associative memory or content addressable memory (CAM).
- This type of memory is accessed simultaneously and in parallel on the basis of data content rather than by specific address or location. When a word is written in an associative memory, no address is given.
- The memory is capable of finding an empty unused location to store the word.
- When a word is to be read from an associative memory, the content of the word, or part of the word, is specified.
- The memory locates all words which match the specified content and marks them for reading.

- Because of its organization, the associative memory is uniquely suited to do parallel searches by data association. Moreover, searches can be done on an entire word or on a specific field within a word.
- An associative memory is more expensive than a random-access memory because each cell must have storage capability as well as logic circuits for matching its content with an external argument.
- For this reason, associative memories are used in applications where the search time is very critical and must be very short.
- The block diagram of an associative memory is shown in Figure 6.11. It consists of a memory array and logic for *m* words with n bits per word. The argument register A and key register K each have n bits, one for each bit of a word.
- The match register M has m bits, one for each memory word. Each word in memory is compared in parallel with the content of the argument register. The words that match the bits of the argument register set a corresponding bit in the match register.
- After the matching process, those bits in the match register that have been set indicate the fact that their corresponding words have been matched.
- Reading is accomplished by a sequential access to memory for those words whose corresponding bits in the match register have been set.
- The key register provides a mask for choosing a particular field or key in the argument word.
- The entire argument is compared with each memory word if the key register contains all 1's.
- Otherwise, only those bits in the argument that have 1's in their corresponding position of the key register are compared.

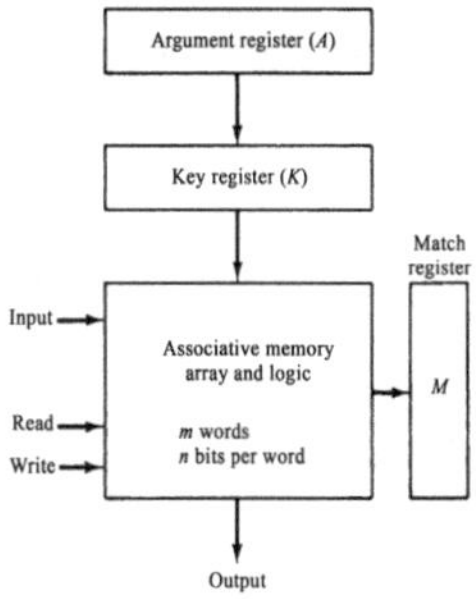

Figure 6.11. *Associative Memory*

6.8.7. Cache Memory

- Analysis of a large number of typical programs has shown that the references to memory at any given interval of time tend to be confined within a few localized areas in memory.
- This phenomenon is known as the property of locality of reference locality of reference.
- The reason for this property may be understood considering that a typical computer program flows in a straight-line fashion with program loops and subroutine calls encountered frequently.
- When a program loop is executed, the CPU repeatedly refers to the set of instructions in memory that constitute the loop. Every time a given subroutine is called, its set of instructions is fetched from memory.
- Thus, loops and subroutines tend to localize the references to memory for fetching instructions. To a lesser degree, memory references to data also tend to be localized.
- Table-lookup procedures repeatedly refer to that portion in memory where the table is stored. Iterative procedures refer to common memory locations and array of numbers are confined within a local portion of memory.
- The result of all these observations is the locality of reference property, which states that over a short interval of time, the addresses generated by a typical program refer to a few localized areas of memory repeatedly, while the remainder of memory is accessed relatively infrequently.
- If the active portions of the program and data are placed in a fast small memory, the average memory access time can be reduced, thus reducing the total execution time of the program.
- Such a fast small memory is referred to as a cache memory. It is placed between the CPU and main memory as illustrated in Figure 6.12.
- The cache memory access time is less than the access time of main memory by a factor of 5 to 10. The cache is the fastest component in the memory hierarchy and approaches the speed of CPU components.
- The fundamental idea of cache organization is that by keeping the most frequently accessed instructions and data in the fast cache memory, the aver-age memory access time will approach the access time of the cache.

- Although the cache is only a small fraction of the size of main memory, a large fraction of memory requests will be found in the fast cache memory because of the locality of reference property of programs.
- The basic operation of the cache is as follows. When the CPU needs to access memory, the cache is examined. If the word is found in the cache, it is read from the fast memory.
- If the word addressed by the CPU is not found in the cache, the main memory is accessed to read the word. A block of words containing the one just accessed is then transferred from main memory to cache memory. The block size may vary from one word (the one just accessed) to about 16 words adjacent to the one just accessed. In this manner, some data are transferred to cache so that future references to memory find the required words in the fast cache memory.
- The performance of cache memory is frequently measured in terms of a quantity called hit ratio. When the CPU refers to memory and finds the word in cache, it is said to produce a hit. If the word is not found in cache, it is in main memory and it counts as a miss.
- The ratio of the number of hits divided by the total CPU references to memory (hits plus misses) is the hit ratio.
- The hit ratio is best measured experimentally by running representative programs in the computer and measuring the number of hits and misses during a given interval of time.
- Hit ratios of 0.9 and higher have been reported. This high ratio verifies the validity of the locality of reference property.
- The average memory access time of a computer system can be improved considerably by use of a cache. If the hit ratio is high enough so that most of the time the CPU accesses the cache instead of main memory, the average access time is closer to the access time of the fast cache memory.
- For example, a computer with cache access time of 100 ns, a main memory access time of 1000 ns, and a hit ratio of 0.9 produces an average access time of 200 ns. This is a considerable improvement over a similar computer without a cache memory, whose access time is 1000 ns.
- The basic characteristic of cache memory is its fast access time. Therefore, very little or no time must be wasted when searching for words in the cache. The transformation of data from main memory to cache memory is referred to as a mapping process.

- The cache is capable of storing 512 of these words at any given time. For every word stored in cache, there is a duplicate copy in main memory.

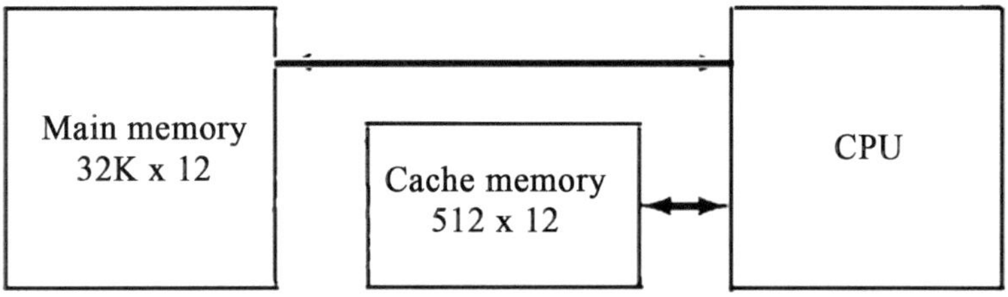

Figure 6.12. *Cache memory*

- The CPU communicates with both memories. It first sends a 15-bit address to cache. If there is a hit, the CPU accepts the 12-bit data from cache. If there is a miss, the CPU reads the word from main memory and the word is then transferred to cache.

6.8.8. Virtual Memory

- In a memory hierarchy system, programs and data are first stored in auxiliary memory. Portions of a program or data are brought into main memory as they are needed by the CPU.
- Virtual memory is a concept used in some large computer systems that permit the user to construct programs as though a large memory space were available, equal to the totality of auxiliary memory.
- Each address that is referenced by the CPU goes through an address mapping from the so-called virtual address to a physical address in main memory.
- Virtual memory is used to give programmers the illusion that they have a very large memory at their disposal, even though the computer actually has a relatively small main memory.
- A virtual memory system provides a mechanism for translating program-generated addresses into correct main memory locations. This is done dynamically, while programs are being executed in the CPU.
- The translation or mapping is handled automatically by the hardware by means of a mapping table.

6.9. PRACTICAL/EXPERIMENTS

6.9.1. Introduction to Microprocessor 8086

- **Microprocessor 8086:** 8086 Microprocessor is an enhanced version of 8085Microprocessor that was designed by Intel in 1976. It is a 16-bit Microprocessor having 20 address lines and 16 data lines that provides up to 1 MB storage. It consists of powerful instruction set, which provides operations like multiplication and division easily.

  It supports two modes of operation, i.e., Maximum mode and Minimum mode. Maximum mode is suitable for system that has multiple processors and Minimum mode is suitable for system having a single processor.

- Features of 8086: The most prominent features of 8086 microprocessor are as follows –
  - It has an instruction queue, which is capable of storing six instruction bytes from the memory resulting in faster processing.
  - It was the first 16-bit processor having 16-bit ALU, 16-bit s, internal data bus, and 16-bit external data bus resulting in faster processing.
  - It is available in 3 versions based on the frequency of operation –

    8086 → 5 MHz

    8086–2 → 8 MHz

    (c)8086–1 → 10 MHz

- It uses two stages of pipelining, i.e., Fetch Stage and Execute Stage, which improves performance.
  - Fetch stage can prefetch up to 6 bytes of instructions and stores them in the queue.
  - Execute stage executes these instructions.
  - It has 256 vectored interrupts.
  - It consists of 29,000 transistors.

- **Comparison between 8085 and 8086 Microprocessor:**
  - **Size** – 8085 is 8-bit microprocessor, whereas 8086 is 16-bit microprocessor.
  - **Address Bus** – 8085 has 16-bit address bus while 8086 has 20-bit address bus.

 - **Memory** – 8085 can access up to 64 Kb, whereas 8086 can access up to 1 Mb of memory.

- **Instruction** – 8085 does not have an instruction queue, whereas 8086 has an instruction queue.
- **Pipelining** – 8085 does not support a pipelined architecture while 8086 supports a pipelined architecture.
- **I/O** – 8085 can address $2^8 = 256$ I/O's, whereas 8086 can access $2^{16} = 65{,}536$ I/O's.
- **Cost** – the cost of 8085 is low whereas that of 8086 is high.

6.9.2. Experiment 1

- **Aim:** WAP to store the result in memory location 2000 after adding two 8-bit numbers.
- **Software required: Emu8086**
  - **Step 1**: This step algorithm is to load the byte from memory location 2000 into AL.
  - **Step 2:** Insert the byte from memory location 2001 into BL.
  - **Step 3:** Add the contents of AL and BL; AL stores the outcome.
  - **Step 4:** Save the outcome at memory locations 2000.
  - **Step 5:** Put an end to
- **Output:**

DATA:	RESULT:
2000: 2001:	2000:

6.9.3. Experiment 2

- **Aim:** WAP to store the result at memory locations 2000 and 2001 after multiplying two 8-bit numbers placed there.
- **Software Required:** Emu8086
- Algorithm:
  - **Step 1:** Load the byte from memory location 2000 into AL.
  - **Step 2:** Insert the byte from memory location 2001 into BL. Multiply AL by BL in Step 3
  - **Step 4:** Save the outcome at memory addresses 2000
  - **Step 5:** Come to an end.

- **Output:**

DATA:	RESULT:
2000: 2001:	2000:

6.9.4. Experiment 3

- **Aim:** To add two 16-bit values, use WAP. Beginning in the year 2000, store the outcome at the memory address.
- **Software Required:** Emu8086.
- **Algorithm:**
  - **Step 1:** Use the first binary number's starting address to load the source index.
  - **Step 2:** Fill AXE with the data bytes that are located in locations 2000 and 2001.
  - **Step 3:** To access the second 16-Bit no existing in 2002, increment the SI value twice.
  - **Step 4:** Load data bytes into BX from locations 2002 and 2003 by SI.
  - **Step 5:** Add the contents of Axe and Bx; Axe stores the result.
  - **Step 6:** Save the outcome in memory locations in 2000.
  - **Step 7:** Come to a halt
- **Output:**

DATA:		RESULT:
2000: 2001:	2002: 2003:	2000:

6.9.5. Experiment 4

- **Aim:** Write an assembly language program to perform subtraction of two 8-bit binary numbers using 2's complement method.
- **Software Required:** Emu8086
- **Algorithm:**
  - **Step 1:** Load the byte (no.) from memory location 0300 into AL.
  - **Step 2:** Transfer data to BL from [0301].

- **Step 3:** To indicate the result's sign, load CL with 00 H. The first complement of BL is step four.
- **Step 5:** To obtain the complement of 2, increase BL by 1.
- **Step 6:** Include the information from AL and BL.
- **Step 7:** Leap to the label: If a carry is generated, skip.
- **Step 8:** Take the 2's complement of the information that is already in AL (if carry is not generated) since the result is negative.
- **Step 9:** Set CL=1; to show that the outcome is negative.
- **Step 10:** Save the final result, or difference, to memory location 0302.
- **Step 11:** To show the sign of the result, store the value of CL in memory position 0303, where 1 = –ve and 0 = +ve.
- **Step 12:** Come to a halt

- **Output:**

DATA:	RESULT:
0300:	0302:
0301:	0303:

6.9.6. Experiment 5

- **Aim:** To translate a given binary number into its grey code, write an assembly language program.
- **Software Required:** Emu8086
- Algorithm:
  - **Step 1:** Enter the quantity of binary numbers that need to be transformed into their grey code into DL.
  - **Step 2:** Load CL with 01 to shift the binary no. to the right once, bit by bit.
  - **Step 3:** Enter the starting address from which the binary numbers are to be retrieved into SI.
  - **Step 4:** Use the beginning address of the result (grey code) places to load DI.
  - **Step 5:** Load the binary number into AL from the location that SI referred to.
  - **Step 6:** Transfer the contents of AL to BL once more.
  - **Step 7:** Move each bit of BL one bit to the right.

- **Step 8:** To obtain grey code in AL, XOR the original binary number (AL) with the shifted one (BL).
- **Step 9:** DI points to the position where grey code is loaded from AL.
- **Step 10:** To indicate the next memory location where binary numbers should be obtained, increment SI by one.
- **Step 11:** To indicate the next memory place where the grey code (result) should be stored, increment DI by one.
- **Step 12:** Reduce by one the count value DL.
- **Step 13:** If the label's DI value is less than zero, jump: Back, that is, to go through the process again of retrieving binary integers and turning them into their grey code.
- **Step 14:** Come to an end.

• **Output:**

DATA:	RESULT:
0300:	0310:
0301:	0311
0302:	0312:
0303:	0313:
0304:	0314:

6.9.7. Experiment 6

• **Aim:** To determine the greatest number in a given string, write an assembly language program.

• **Software Required:** Emu8086

• **Algorithm:**

- **Step 1:** Load SI using the string's starting address.
- **Step 2:** Set up the counter, or CX.
- **Step 3:** The string's first data byte is compared to 00H.
- **Step 5:** Go to location 020E if both bytes are equal or higher.
- **Step 6:** If not, transfer the material to the accumulator.
- **Step 7:** Point to the string's subsequent address.
- **Step 8:** Reduce the counter value (of CX) and verify that CX=0; if not, proceed with the operation.

   - **Step 9:** The memory location 0310 contains the largest number.
   - **Step 10:** Give up.
- **Output:**

DATA:				RESULT:
0300:	0305:	030A:	030F:	0310:
0301:	0306:	030B:		
0302:	0307:	030C:		
0303:	0308:	030D:		
0304:	0309:	030E:		

6.9.8. Experiment 7

- **Aim:** Write an assembly language program to find the smallest number in a given string.
- **Software Required:** Emu8086
- **Algorithm:**
   - **Step 1:** Load SI using the string's starting address.
   - **Step 2:** Set up the counter, or CX.
   - **Step 3:** Set up the eight-bit accumulator.
   - **Step 4:** The string's first data byte is compared to 00H
   - **Step 5:** Go to location 020E if both bytes are equal or less.
   - **Step 6:** If not, transfer the material to the accumulator.
   - **Step 7:** Point to the string's subsequent address.
   - **Step 8:** Reduce the counter value (of CX) and verify that CX=0; if not, proceed with the operation.
   - **Step 9:** The memory location 0310 contains the smallest number.
   - **Step 10:** Come to a halt.
- **Output:**

DATA:				RESULT:
0300:	0305:	030A:	030F:	0310:
0301:	0306:	030B:		
0302:	0307:	030C:		
0303:	0308:	030D:		
0304:	0309:	030E:		

6.9.9. Experiment 8

- **Aim:** Write an assembly language program to sort a string of byte in the descending order.
- **Software Required:** Emu8086
- **Algorithm:**
  - **Step 1:** Set the SI Register's initial value to 0300 in memory.
  - **Step 2:** BX contains the number of bytes from locations 0300 and 0301 that will be used for sorting.
  - **Step 3:** The third step is to reduce the number of bytes by one.
  - **Step 4:** Additionally, CX has the number of bytes from 0300 and 0301 positions.
  - **Step 5:** The fifth step is to reduce the number of bytes by one.
  - **Step 6:** Set the string's starting address (including the first byte) to initialize the SI Register.
  - **Step 7:** Insert the string's initial data byte into AL.
  - **Step 8:** Point to the string's subsequent byte.
  - **Step 9:** Compare the two bytes (one that is pointed by the SI and one that is present in AL).
  - **Step 10:** Jump to label here if two bytes are equivalent or if the first byte is larger than the second:
  - **Step 11:** Else, switch the two bytes in step 11.
  - **Step 12:** To indicate the next lower memory location, decrement SI by one.
  - **Step 13:** Put AL's contents in the next lower memory address that SI points to.
  - **Step 14:** Point to the string's subsequent place.
  - **Step 15:** If the count value of CX is not equal to zero, carry out the previous steps again.
  - **Step 16:** Give up.
- **Output:**

DATA:								**RESULT:**
0300: (LB)						0301: (HB)		
0302:								0302:
0303:								0303:

0304:	0304:							
0305:								0305:
0306:								0306:
0307:								0307:
0308:								0308:
0309:								0309:
030A:								030A:
030B:								030B:

6.9.10. Experiment 9

- **Aim:** To sort a string of bytes in ascending order, write an assembly language program.
- **Software Required:** Emu8086
- **Algorithm:**
  - **Step 1:** Set the SI Register's initial value to memory address 0200.
  - **Step 2:** BX contains the number of bytes from locations 0300 and 0301 that will be used for sorting.
  - **Step 3:** The third step is to reduce the number of bytes by one.
  - **Step 4:** Additionally, CX has the number of bytes from 0300 and 0301 positions.
  - **Step 5:** The fifth step is to reduce the number of bytes by one.
  - **Step 6:** Set the string's starting address (including the first byte) to initialize the SI Register.
  - **Step 7:** Point to the string's subsequent byte.
  - **Step 8:** Compare the two bytes (one that is pointed by the SI and one that is present in AL).
  - **Step 9:** Jump to label here if two bytes are equivalent or if the first byte is less than the second byte:
  - **Step 10:** If not, switch the two bytes in step 10.
  - **Step 11:** To indicate the next lower memory location, decrement SI by one.
  - **Step 12:** Put AL's contents in the next lower memory address that SI points to.
  - **Step 13:** Come to a stop.

- **Output:**

DATA:	RESULT:
0300: (LB)	0302:
0301: (HB)	0303:
0304:	0304:
0302:	0305:
0303:	0306:
0304:	0307:
0305:	0308:
0306:	0309:
0307:	030A:
0308:	030B:
0309:	
030A:	
030B	

6.9.11. Experiment 10

- **Aim:** Program for binary to decimal conversion.

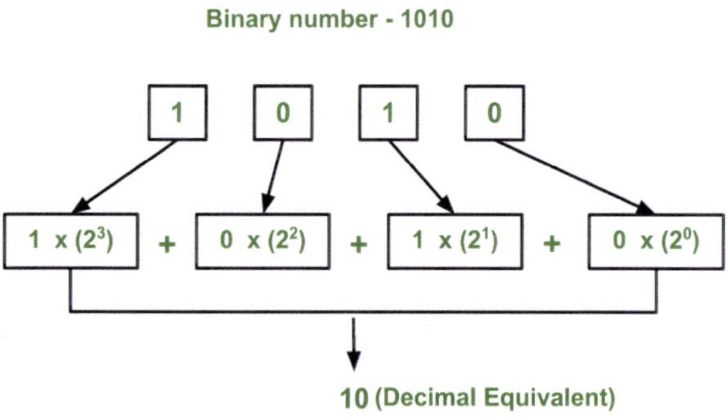


```
// C++ program to convert binary to decimal
#include <iostream>
using namespace std;

        // Function to convert binary to decimal
int binaryToDecimal(int n)
{
        int num = n;
        int dec_value = 0;
```

```
            // Initializing base value to 1, i.e., 2^0
        int base = 1;
        int temp = num;
        while (temp) {
            int last_digit = temp % 10;
            temp = temp / 10;
            dec_value += last_digit * base;
            base = base * 2;
        }
        return dec_value;
    }

// Driver program to test above function
    int main()
    {
        int num = 10101001;
        cout << binaryToDecimal(num) << endl;
    }
```

- Output:

169

6.9.12. Experiment 11

- **Aim:** Program for decimal to binary conversion
- **For Example:**

If the decimal number is 10.

- **Step 1**: Remainder when 10 is divided by 2 is zero. Therefore, arr[0] = 0.
- **Step 2**: Divide 10 by 2. New number is 10/2 = 5.
- **Step 3**: Remainder when 5 is divided by 2 is 1. Therefore, arr[1] = 1.
- **Step 4**: Divide 5 by 2. New number is 5/2 = 2.
- **Step 5**: Remainder when 2 is divided by 2 is zero. Therefore, arr[2] = 0.
- **Step 6**: Divide 2 by 2. New number is 2/2 = 1.
- **Step 7**: Remainder when 1 is divided by 2 is 1. Therefore, arr[3] = 1.
- **Step 8**: Divide 1 by 2. New number is 1/2 = 0.

– **Step 9**: Since number becomes = 0. Print the array in reverse order. Therefore, the equivalent binary number is 1010.

The below diagram shows an example of converting the decimal number 17 to an equivalent binary number.

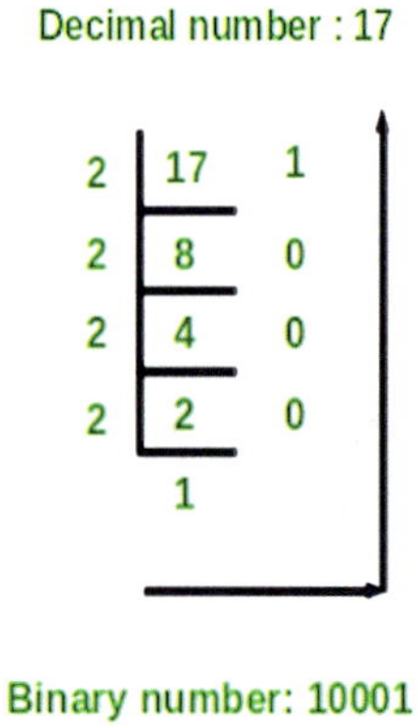


```
// C++ program to convert a decimal
// number to binary number
#include <iostream>
using namespace std;
// function to convert decimal to binary
void decToBinary(int n)
{
        int binaryNum[32];
        // counter for binary array
        int i = 0;
        while (n > 0) {
                binaryNum[i] = n % 2;
                n = n / 2;
                i++;
        }
        // printing binary array in reverse order
        for (int j = i – 1; j >= 0; j--)
        cout << binaryNum[j];
}
// Driver program to test above function
int main()
{
        int n = 17;
```

```
        decToBinary(n);
        return 0;
}
```

- **Output:**

10001

6.9.13. Experiment 12

- **Aim:** Program for decimal to octal conversion

We must create a program that takes a decimal number as input and converts it to an equivalent octal value. For example, change a number with base value 10 to base value 8. The number of digits required to express a numeric value depends on the number system's base value. To represent any numeric value, for instance, the binary number system uses two digits, 0 and 1, the octal number system uses eight digits, 0–7, and the decimal number system uses ten digits, 0–9.

- **Examples:**

Input: 16

Output: 20

Input: 10

Output: 12

- **Algorithm:**
  - Store the remainder when the number is divided by 8 in an array.
  - Divide the number by 8 now
  - Repeat the above two steps until the number is not equal to 0.
  - Print the array in reverse order now.
- **For Example: If the given decimal number is 16.**
  - **Step 1:** When 16 is divided by 8, the remainder equals 0. Consequently, arr[0] = 0.
  - **Step 2:** Divide 16 by 8 in step two. The new figure is 16/8 = 2.
  - **Step 3:** The remainder is 2, which is obtained by dividing 2 by 8. Consequently, arr[1] = 2.
  - **Step 4:** Divide 2 by 8 in step four. The new figure is 2/8 = 0.
  - **Step 5:** Since the number is now equal to 0.

Stop repeating steps and print the array in reverse order. Therefore, the equivalent octal number is 20. The below diagram shows an example of converting the decimal number 33 to an equivalent octal number.

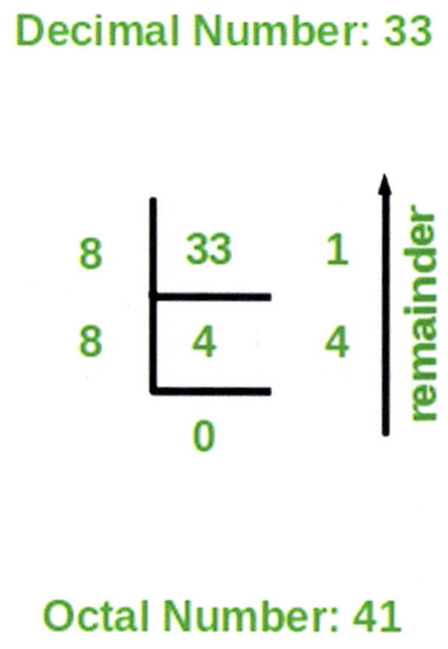


```
// C++ program to convert a decimal
// number to octal number

#include <iostream>
using namespace std;

// function to convert decimal to octal
void decToOctal(int n)
{
        // array to store octal number
        int octalNum[100];
        // counter for octal number array
        int i = 0;
        while (n != 0) {
                // storing remainder in octal array
                octalNum[i] = n % 8;
                n = n / 8;
                i++;
        }
        // printing octal number array in reverse order
```

```
        for (int j = i – 1; j >= 0; j--)
        cout << octalNum[j];
}

// Driver Code
int main()
{
        int n = 33;
        // Function Call
        decToOctal(n);
        return 0;
}
```

6.9.14. Experiment 13

- **Aim:** Program for octal to decimal conversion

```
#include <stdio.h>
#include <math.h>
// Function to convert octal to decimal
int octalToDecimal(int octalNumber) {
        int decimalNumber = 0, i = 0, remainder;
        while (octalNumber != 0) {
                remainder = octalNumber % 10;
                decimalNumber += remainder * pow(8, i);
                ++i;
                octalNumber /= 10;
        }
        return decimalNumber;
}
int main() {
        int octalNumber;
        // Input octal number from user
        printf("Enter an octal number: ");
        scanf("%d", &octalNumber);
        // Convert octal to decimal using function
        int decimalNumber = octalToDecimal(octalNumber);
        // Output the result
        printf("Decimal equivalent: %d\n", decimalNumber);
        return 0;
}
```

6.9.15. Experiment 14

- **Aim: Program for hexadecimal to decimal**

```
#include <stdio.h>
#include <math.h>
#include <string.h>
// Function to convert hexadecimal to decimal
int hexToDecimal(char hex[]) {
        int decimalNumber = 0;
        int length = strlen(hex);
        int base = 1; // Initialize base value to 16^0
        for (int i = length – 1; i >= 0; i--) {
                if (hex[i] >= '0' && hex[i] <= '9') {
                        decimalNumber += (hex[i] - '0') * base;
                }
                else if (hex[i] >= 'A' && hex[i] <= 'F') {
                        decimalNumber += (hex[i] - 'A' + 10) * base;
                }
                else if (hex[i] >= 'a' && hex[i] <= 'f') {
                        decimalNumber += (hex[i] - 'a' + 10) * base;
                }
                // Update base value to 16^1, 16^2, …
                base *= 16;
        }
        return decimalNumber;
}
int main() {
        char hex[20];
        printf("Enter a hexadecimal number: ");
        scanf("%s", hex);
        // Convert hexadecimal to decimal using function
        int decimalNumber = hexToDecimal(hex);

        // Output the result
        printf("Decimal equivalent: %d\n", decimalNumber);
        return 0;
}
```

6.9.16. Experiment 15

- **Aim:** Implement logic gates using NAND and NOR gates.
- **NAND:**

```
#include <stdio.h>
#include <stdlib.h>
int main()
{
        int a[5] = { 1, 0, 1, 0, 1 };
        int b[5] = { 0, 1, 1, 0, 0 };
        int i, ans;
        for (i = 0; i < 5; i++) {
                if (a[i] == 1 && b[i] == 1) ans = 0;
                else
                ans = 1;
                printf("\n %d NAND %d = %d", a[i], b[i], ans);
        }
}
```

- **Output:**

```
1 NAND 0 = 1
0 NAND 1 = 1
1 NAND 1 = 0
0 NAND 0 = 1
1 NAND 0 = 1
```

- **NOR:**

```
#include <stdio.h> #include <stdlib.h>
int main()
{
        int a[5] = { 1, 0, 1, 0, 1 };
        int b[5] = { 0, 1, 1, 0, 0 };
        int i, ans;
        for (i = 0; i < 5; i++) { ans = !(a[i] + b[i]);
                printf("\n %d NOR %d = %d", a[i], b[i], ans);
        }
}
```

- **Output:**

```
1 NOR 0 = 0
0 NOR 1 = 0
1 NOR 1 = 0
0 NOR 0 = 1
1 NOR 0 = 0
```

- **Logic Gate:**

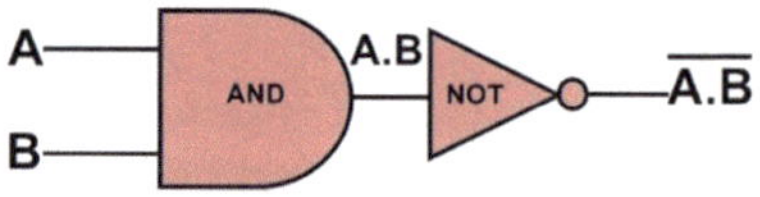

NAND Gate

NOR Gate

6.9.17. Experiment 16

- **Aim: Design a full adder using gates.**

```
#include<stdio.h> #include<conio.h> #include<string.h>
char* addBinary(char* a, char* b)
{
        int la = strlen(a); int lb = strlen(b);
        int lr = la > lb ? la: lb; int carry = 0;
        char *res = (char*)calloc(lr + 2, sizeof(char)); res[lr + 1] =
'\0';
        la--; lb--;
        while (la >= 0 || lb >= 0)
        {
                int ba = la >= 0 ? a[la--] - '0': 0;
                int bb = lb >= 0 ? b[lb--] - '0': 0; int br = ba ^ bb ^
        carry;
                carry = (ba & bb) | (carry & (ba ^ bb)); res[lr--] = br
        + '0';
        }
        if (!carry) return res + 1; res[0] = '1';
        return res;
}
void main()
{
        clrscr(); printf("%s",addBinary("1110","1011")); getch();
}
```

- **Output:**

  11001

- **Logic Gate:**

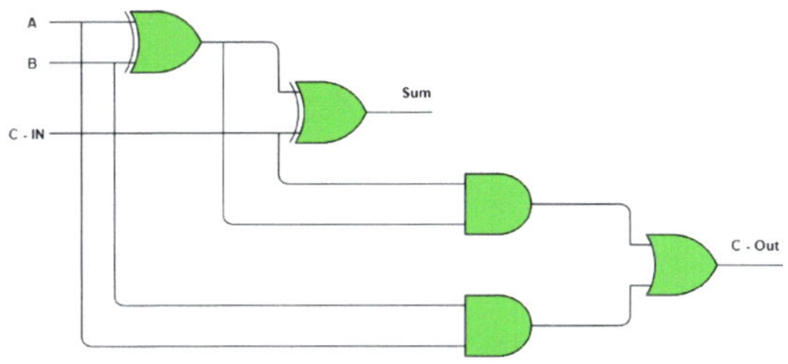

6.9.18. Experiment 17

- **Aim:** To design and implement the 4:1 MUX, 8:1 MUX using gates /ICs.
- Theory: Digital systems greatly benefit from the use of multiplexers. Under the direction of selection signals, they transmit a lot of information units across a limited number of channels, typically just one channel. "Many to one" is what multiplexer means. A circuit that has numerous inputs but just one output is called a multiplexer. Any input to the output can be chosen by employing control signals, often known as select lines. Because the output bit depends on the selected input data bit, multiplexers are also known as data selectors. Two input signals, n control/select signals, and one output signal make up the typical multiplexer circuit.

1. **4:1 Multiplexer**

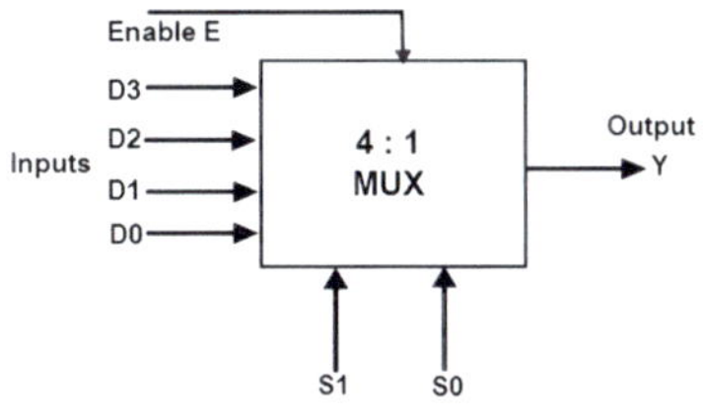

To get the total data output from the multiplexer, all these product terms are to be summed and then the final Boolean expression of this multiplexer is given as:

$$Y = D0\,\overline{S1}\,\overline{S0} + D1\,\overline{S1}\,S0 + D2\,S1\,\overline{S0} + D3\,S1\,S0$$

- **Logic Gate:**

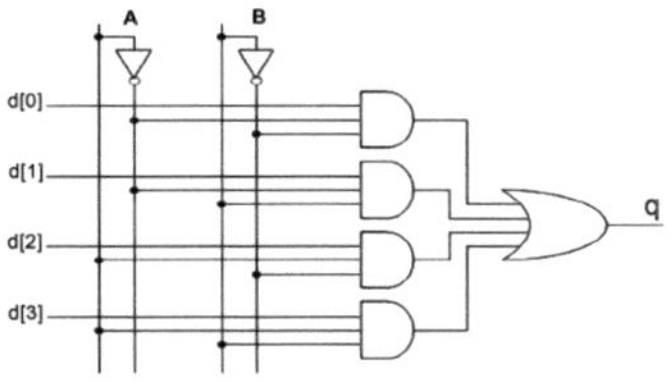

- **Pin Diagram:**

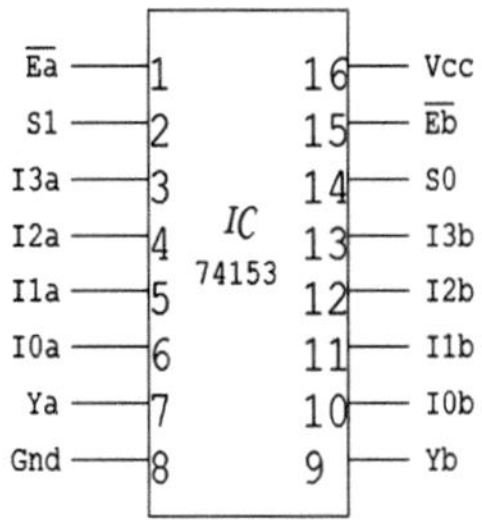

- **Truth Table:**

Select inputs		Enable input	Inputs				Output
S1	S0	E	I0	I1	I2	I3	Y
X	X	1	X	X	X	X	0
0	0	0	0	X	X	X	0
0	0	0	1	X	X	X	1
0	1	0	X	0	X	X	0
0	1	0	X	1	X	X	1
1	0	0	X	X	0	X	0
1	0	0	X	X	1	X	1
1	1	0	X	X	X	0	0
1	1	0	X	X	X	1	1

- **Procedure:**
  - Connect the circuit as shown in figure.
  - Apply Vcc and ground signal to every IC.
  - Observe the input and output according to the truth table.

2. **8:1 Multiplexer Aim:** To verify the truth table of Multiplexer.

- Theory: The TTL/MSI SN54/74LS151 is a fast digital multiplexer with eight inputs. It offers the option to choose one piece of information from up to eight sources in a single bundle. Any logic function involving four variables can be produced using the LS151 as a universal function generator. Outputs for assertion and denial are offered.

- The Schottky Process for rapidity
- The ability to perform multiple tasks
- Select logic decoding on-chip.
- Completely buffered outputs that complement each other
- The consequences of high speed termination are limited by input clam diodes.

- Functional Description: The status of three select inputs, s0, s1, and s2, controls the switch position in the LS151, a logical implementation of a single pole, eight-position switch. Outputs for assertion and denial are offered. Active LOW is the state of the enable input (E). Regardless of all other inputs, the negation output is HIGH and the assertion output is LOW when it is not active.

CONNECTION DIAGRAM DIP (TOP VIEW)

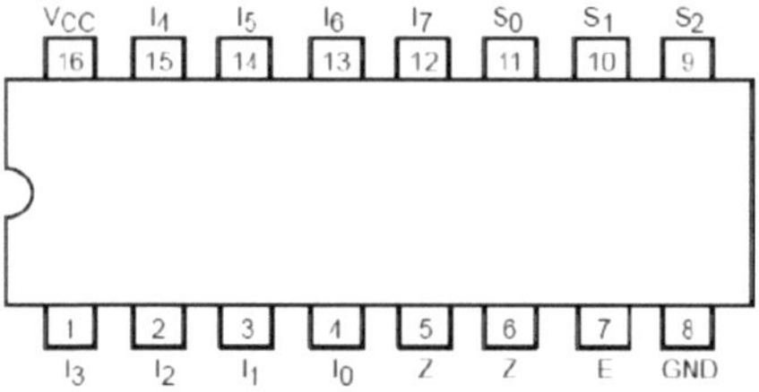

- **Truth Table:**

TRUTH TABLE

$\overline{E}$	S_2	S_1	S_0	I_0	I_1	I_2	I_3	I_4	I_5	I_6	I_7	$\overline{Z}$	Z
H	X	X	X	X	X	X	X	X	X	X	X	H	L
L	L	L	L	L	X	X	X	X	X	X	X	H	L
L	L	L	L	H	X	X	X	X	X	X	X	L	H
L	L	L	H	X	L	X	X	X	X	X	X	H	L
L	L	L	H	X	H	X	X	X	X	X	X	L	H
L	L	H	L	X	X	L	X	X	X	X	X	H	L
L	L	H	L	X	X	H	X	X	X	X	X	L	H
L	L	H	H	X	X	X	L	X	X	X	X	H	L
L	L	H	H	X	X	X	H	X	X	X	X	L	H
L	H	L	L	X	X	X	X	L	X	X	X	H	L
L	H	L	L	X	X	X	X	H	X	X	X	L	H
L	H	L	H	X	X	X	X	X	L	X	X	H	L
L	H	L	H	X	X	X	X	X	H	X	X	L	H
L	H	H	L	X	X	X	X	X	X	L	X	H	L
L	H	H	L	X	X	X	X	X	X	H	X	L	H
L	H	H	H	X	X	X	X	X	X	X	L	H	L
L	H	H	H	X	X	X	X	X	X	X	H	L	H

H = HIGH Voltage Level
L = LOW Voltage Level
X = Don't Care

- **Procedure:**
  - Connect Inputs S2,S1,S0,I0,I1,I2,I,3I4,I5,I6,I7 and Enable(E) to Logic Input Sockets.
  - Connect Output terminal Z & Z to Logic Output Sockets.
  - Verify output with given Truth Table.
- **Conclusion:** Hence verified the truth table of Multiplexer.

6.9.19. Experiment 18

- **Aim:** To design and implement a 3 to 8 decoder using gates.
- Theory: A decoder is a device which does the reverse operation of an encoder, undoing the encoding so that the original information can be retrieved. The same method used to encode is usually just reversed in order to decode. It is a combinational circuit that converts binary information from n input lines to a maximum of 2n unique output lines. In digital electronics, a decoder can take the form of a multiple-input, multiple-output logic circuit that converts coded inputs into coded outputs, where the input and output codes are different. e.g. *n*-to-2*n*, binary-coded decimal decoders. Enable inputs must be on for the decoder to function, otherwise its outputs assume a single "disabled" output code word. In case of decoding all combinations of three bits eight (23=8) decoding gates are required. This type of decoder is called 3–8 decoder because 3 inputs and 8 outputs. For any input combination decoder outputs are 1. This decoder circuit gives 8 logic outputs for 3 inputs and has a enable pin. The circuit is designed with AND and NAND logic gates. It takes 3 binary inputs and activates one of the eight outputs. 3 to 8 line decoder circuit is also called as binary to an octal decoder.

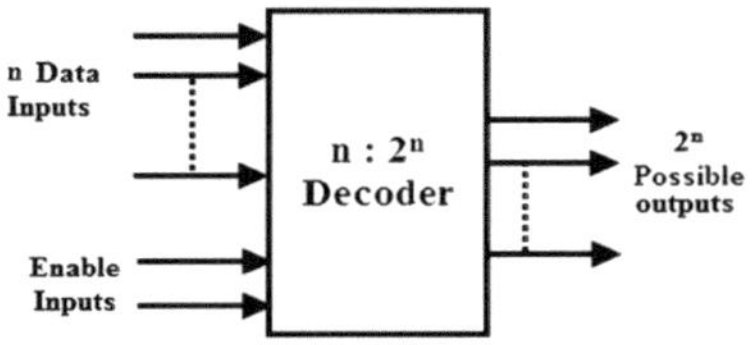

Pin Diagram of 74138 IC

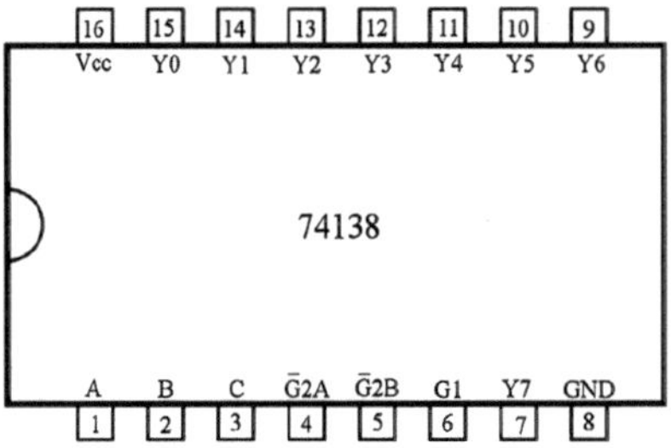

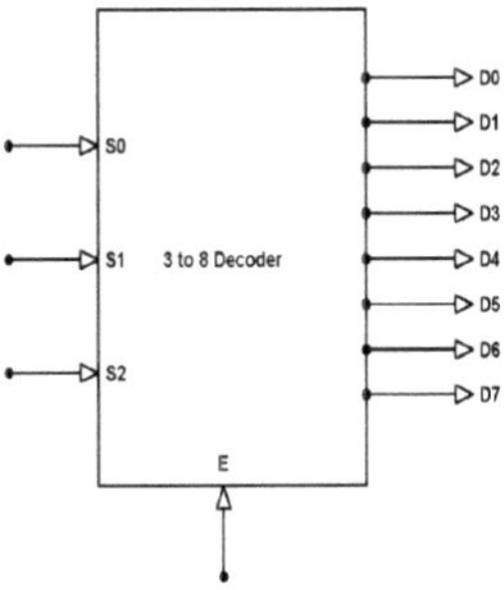

3 Line to 8 Line Decoder

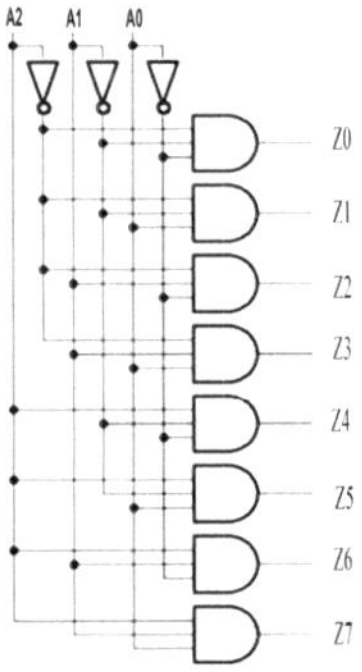

Logic Diagram

- **Truth Table:**

Inputs				Outputs							
EN	A	B	C	Y_7	Y_6	Y_5	Y_4	Y_3	Y_2	Y_1	Y_0
0	×	×	×	0	0	0	0	0	0	0	0
1	0	0	0	0	0	0	0	0	0	0	1
1	0	0	1	0	0	0	0	0	0	1	0
1	0	1	0	0	0	0	0	0	1	0	0
1	0	1	1	0	0	0	0	1	0	0	0
1	1	0	0	0	0	0	1	0	0	0	0
1	1	0	1	0	0	1	0	0	0	0	0
1	1	1	0	0	1	0	0	0	0	0	0
1	1	1	1	1	0	0	0	0	0	0	0

- **Procedure:**
  - Connections are given as per circuit diagram
  - Logical inputs are given as per circuit diagram.
  - The decoder circuit works only when the Enable pin (E) is

high.

- S0, S1 and S2 are three different inputs and D0, D1, D2, D3. D4. D5. D6. D7 are the eight outputs.
- When the Enable pin (E) is low all the output pins are low.
- Observe the output and verify the truth table.

• **Result:** Hence verified the truth table of 3:8 decoders.

6.9.20. Experiment 19

• **Aim:** To verify the truth table of 4-bit Comparator.

- Theory: The SN54/74LS85 is a 4-Bit Magnitude comparator which compares two 4-bit words (A,B), each word having four parallel inputs (A0-A3, B0-B3); A3,B3being the most significant inputs. Operation is not restricted to binary codes; the device will work with any monotonic code. Three outputs are provided: "A greater than B" (OA>B), "A less than B" (OA<B), "A equal to B" (OA=B). Three expander inputs IA>B, IA<B, IA=B, allow cascading without external gates. For proper compare operation, the expander inputs to the least significant position must be connected as follows: IA<B= IA>B=L, IA=B=H. For serial (ripple) expansion, OA>B, OA<B, and OA=B outputs are connected respectively to the IA>B,IA<B, and IA=B inputs of the next most significant comparator. Refer to application section of data sheet for high speed method of comparing large words.

  The truth table on the following page describes the operation of SN54/74LS85 under all possible logic conditions. The upper 11 lines describe the normal operation under all conditions that will occur in a single device or in a series expansion scheme. The lower five lines describe the operation under abnormal conditions on the cascading inputs. These conditions occur when the parallel expansion technique is used.
- Easily expandable.
- Binary or BCD comparison
- OA>B, OA<B, and OA=B outputs available.

• **4-Bit Magnitude Comparator:**

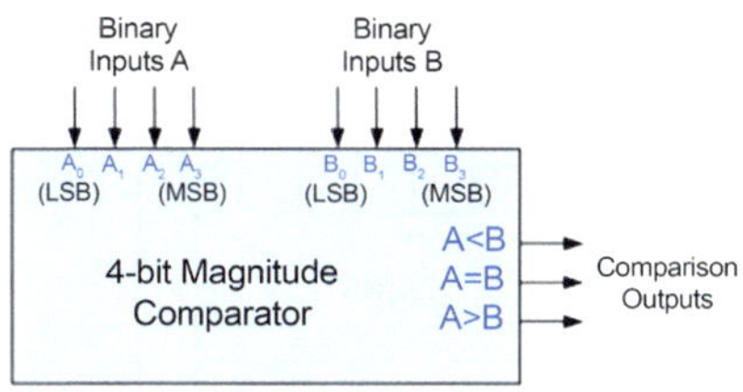

- Some commercially available digital comparators such as the TTL74LS85 or CMOS4063 4-bit magnitude comparator have additional input terminals that allow more individual comparator strobe "cascaded" together to compare words larger than 4-bits with magnitude comparators of "n"-bits being produced. These cascading inputs are connected directly to the corresponding outputs of the previous comparator as shown to compare 8,16 or even 32-bit words.
- When comparing large binary or BCD numbers like the example above, to save time the comparator starts by comparing the highest-order bit(MSB) first. If equality exists, A=B then it compares the next lowest bit and so on until it reaches the lowest-order bit, (LSB). If equality still exists then the two numbers are defined as being equal.
- If in equality is found, either A > B or A < B the relationship between the two numbers is determined and the comparison between any additional lower order bits tops. Digital Comparator is used widely in Analogue-to-Digital converters, (ADC) and Arithmetic Logic Units, (ALU) to perform a variety of arithmetic operations. Magnitude Comparator is a logical circuit, which compares two signals A and B and generates three logical outputs, whether A>B, A=B, or A<B. IC7485 is a high speed 4-bit Magnitude comparator, which compares two 4-bit words. The A=B Input must be held high for proper compare operation.

- **Pin Diagram:**

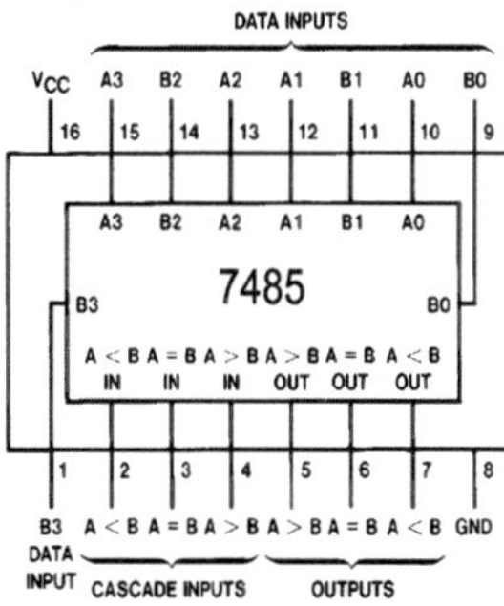

- **Procedure:**
  - Connect Inputs (A0,A1,A2,A3,B0,B1,B2,B3) to Input Switches
  - Connect Cascade Inputs(A<B,A>B,A=B)to Input Switches
  - Connect Outputs (A<B,A>B,A=B)to Output Switches
  - Observe the Truth Table.
- **Truth Table:**

COMPARING INPUTS				CASCADINGINPUTS			OUTPUTS		
A3,B3	A2,B2	A1,B1	A0,B0	A>B	A<B	A=B	A>B	A<B	A=B
A3>B3	X	X	X	X	X	X	H	L	L
A3<B3	X	X	X	X	X	X	L	H	L
A3=B3	A2>B2	X	X	X	X	X	H	L	L
A3=B3	A2<B2	X	X	X	X	X	L	H	L
A3=B3	A2=B2	A1>B1	X	X	X	X	H	L	L
A3=B3	A2=B2	A1<B1	X	X	X	X	L	H	L
A3=B3	A2=B2	A1=B1	A0>B0	X	X	X	H	L	L
A3=B3	A2=B2	A1=B1	A0<B0	X	X	X	L	H	L
A3=B3	A2=B2	A1=B1	A0=B0	H	L	L	H	L	L
A3=B3	A2=B2	A1=B1	A0=B0	L	H	L	L	H	L
A3=B3	A2=B2	A1=B1	A0=B0	L	L	H	L	L	H
A3=B3	A2=B2	A1=B1	A0=B0	X	X	H	L	L	H
A3=B3	A2=B2	A1=B1	A0=B0	H	H	L	L	L	L
A3=B3	A2=B2	A1=B1	A0=B0	L	L	L	H	H	L

- **Conclusion:** Verified the truth table of 4- bit Comparator.

6.9.21. Experiment 19

- **Aim:** To verify the truth table of universal shift register.
- Theory: A register is simply a group of flip flops that can be used to store a binary number. A shift register is a group of flip flops connected such that the binary number can be entered (shifted) into the register and possibly shifted out. There are two ways to shift the data (bits in the binary number) from one place to another. The first method involves shifting the data 1 bit at a time in a serial fashion, beginning with either MSB or LSB. This technique is referred to as serial shifting. These methods involve shifting all the data bits simultaneously and are referring red to as parallel shifting. There are two ways to shift data into a register (serial or parallel) and similarly two ways to shift data out of the register. This leads to the construction off our basic types of registers.
  - Serial in–Serial out shift register.
  - Serial in–Parallel out shift register.
  - Parallel in–Serial out shift register.
  - Parallel in–Parallel out shift register.

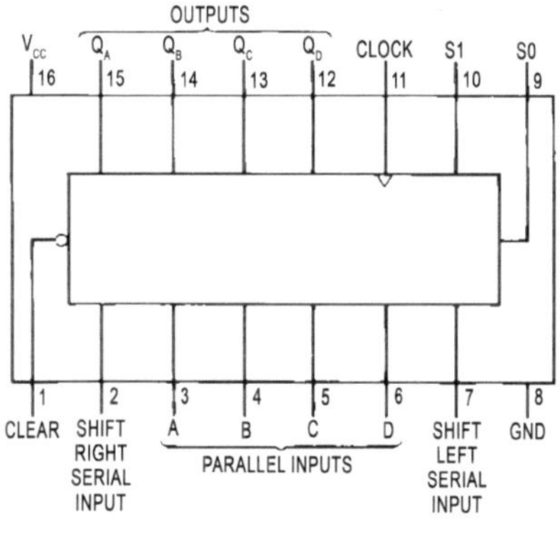

- Modes of Operation:

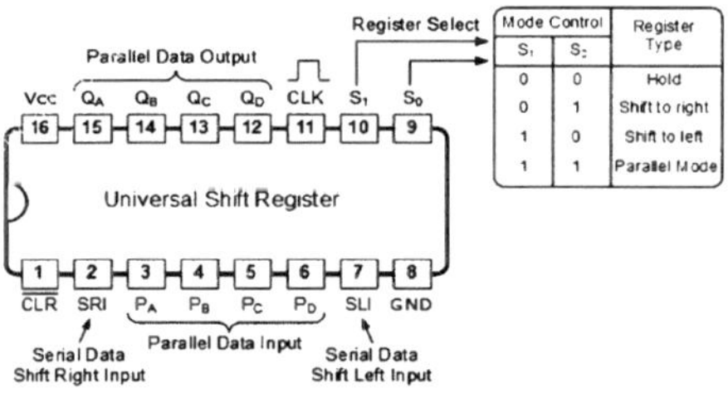

- ## Internal Diagram of 74194:

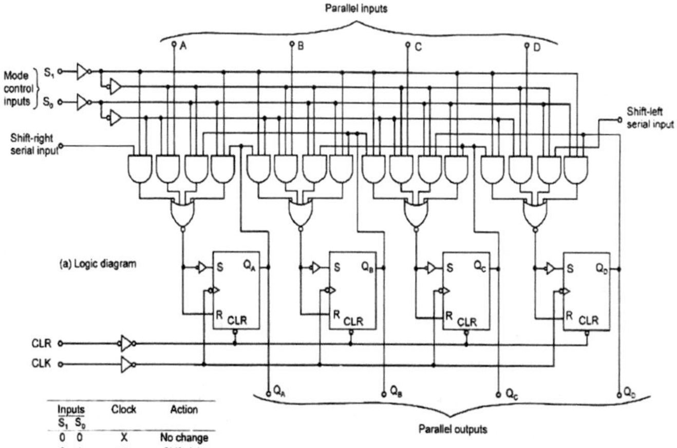

Inputs S_1 S_0		Clock	Action
0	0	X	No change
0	1	m	Shift-right
1	0	m	Shift-left
1	1	m	Parallel load

Truth table

- ## Block Diagram of 4 Types of Shift Registers (n-bit):

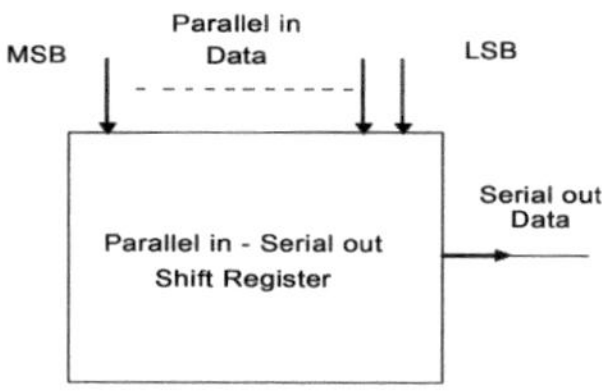

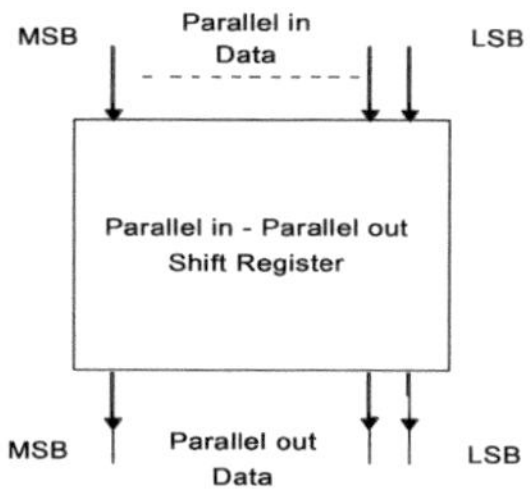

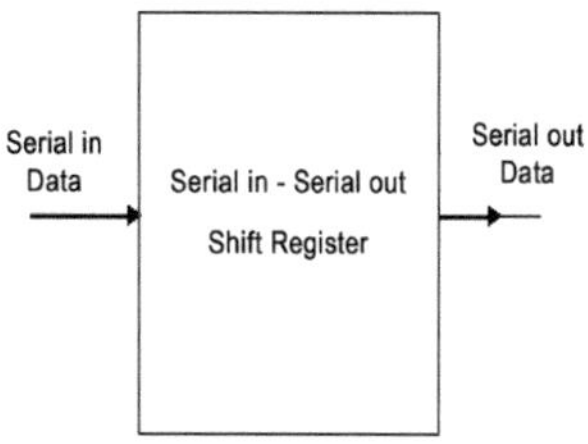

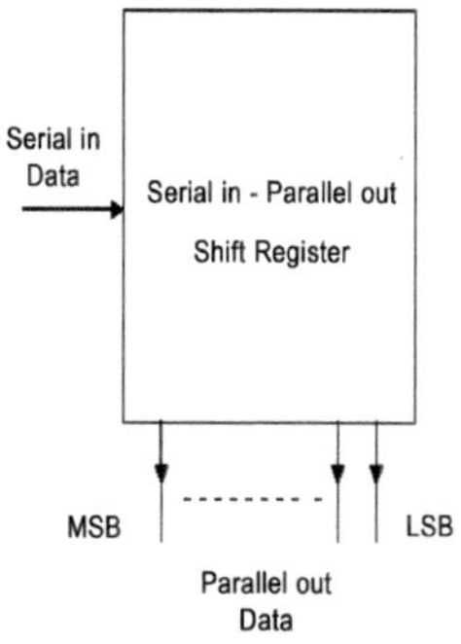

- **Truth Table:**

INPUTS										OUTPUTS			
CLEAR	MODE		CLOCK	SERIAL		PARALLEL				QA	QB	QC	QD
	S1	S0		LEFT	RIGHT	A	B	C	D				
H	X	X	L	X	X	X	X	X	X	QA0	QB0	QC0	QD0
H	H	H	↑	X	X	a	b	c	d	a	b	c	d
H	L	H	↑	X	H	X	X	X	X	H	QAn	QBn	QCn
H	L	H	↑	X	L	X	X	X	X	L	QAn	QBn	QCn
H	H	L	↑	H	X	X	X	X	X	QBn	QCn	QDn	H
H	H	L	↑	L	X	X	X	X	X	QBn	QCn	QDn	L
H	L	L	X	X	X	X	X	X	X	QA0	QB0	QC0	QD0

- **Procedure:**
  - Derive the wiring diagram.
  - Connect Input terminals to the Logic Input Sockets.
  - S1,S0, SERIAL LEFT,SERIAL RIGHT,PARALLEL DATA-A,B,C and D to Logic Input Sockets.
  - Connect CLEAR to VCC.
  - Connect External Clock to the CLOCK Terminal.
  - Connect QA, QB, QC and QD to the Logic Output terminals.
  - Observe output changes at O/P Terminals with given Truth Table.
- **Conclusion:** Verified the Truth Table of Universal Shift Register.

6.9.22. Experiment 20

- **Aim:** To verify the truth table of decade counter.
- Theory: The counters four outputs are design at ed by the letter symbol Q with a numeric sub script equal to the binary weight of the corresponding bit in the BCD counter circuits code. So, for example, QA, QB, QC and QD. The 74LS90 counting sequence is triggered on the negative going edge of the clock signal, that is when the clock signal CLK goes from logic 1 (HIGH) to logic 0 (LOW).

The additional input pins R1 and R2 are counter "reset" pins while inputs S1 and S2 are "set" pins. When connected to logic 1, the Reset inputs R1 and R2 reset the counter back to zero, 0 (0000), and when the Set inputs S1 and S2 are connected to logic 1, they Set the counter to maximum, or 9 (1001) regardless of the actual count number or position.

As we said before, the 74LS90 counter consists of a divide-by-2 counter and a divide-by-5 counter with in the same package. Then we can use counter to produce a divide-by-2 frequency counter only, adivide-by-5 frequency counter only or the two together to produce our desired divide-by-10 BCD counter. With the four flip-flops making up the divide-by-5 counter section disabled, if a clock signal is applied to input pin 14 (CLKA) and the output taken from pin 12(QA), we can produce a standard divide-by-2 binary counter for use in Pin Diagram circuits as shown below.

- **Pin Diagram of 7490IC is as below:**

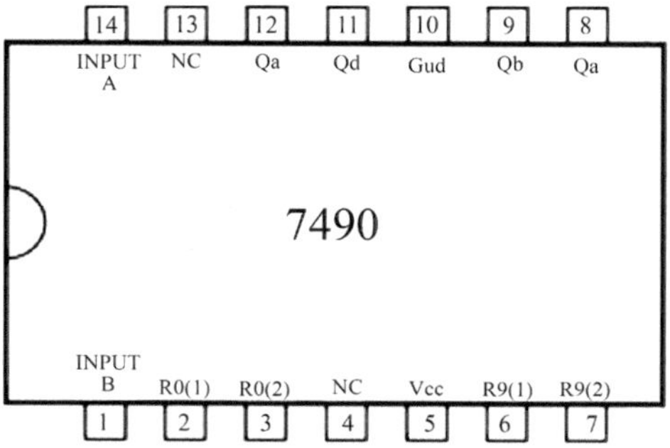

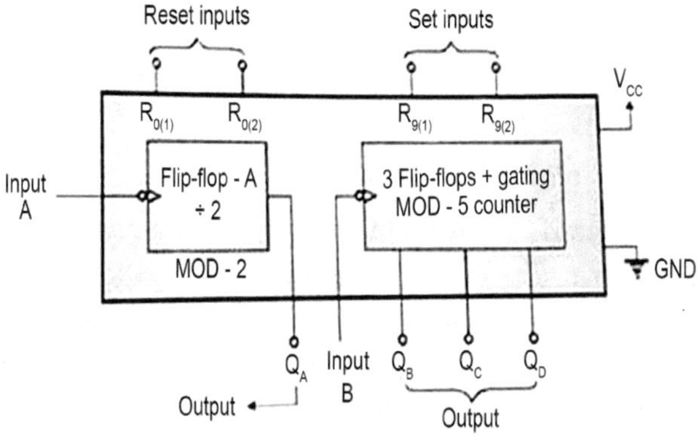

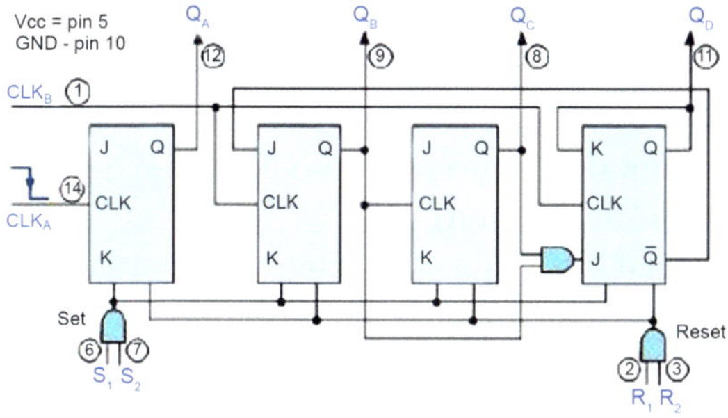

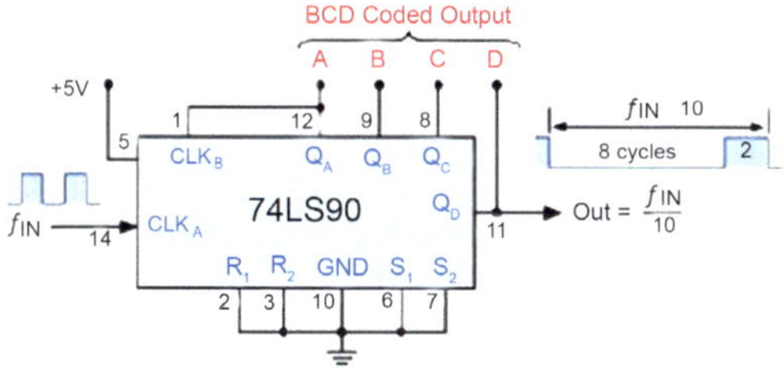

- **Procedure:**
  - Connect inputs RESET0 (pin2), RESET0 (pin3), R3, R2 to the inputs witches and Qa, Qb, Qc, Qd to the outputs witches.
  - Connect Clock A to clock pulse.
  - Connect Clock B to Qa.
  - Feed the logic signal either H/L as shown in the truth table.
  - Monitor the outputs Qa,Qb,Qc,Qd.
  - Verify the truth table.
- **Truth Table:**

ResetI/p				Outputs			
RESET0 (pin2)	RESET0 (pin3)	R3	R2	Qd	Qc	Qb	Qa
H	H	L	X	L	L	L	L
H	H	X	L	L	L	L	L
X	X	H	H	H	L	L	H
X	L	X	L	COUNT			
L	X	L	X	COUNT			
L	X	X	L	COUNT			
X	L	L	X	COUNT			

- **Conclusion:** Hence verified the truth table of Decade Counter.

6.10. PROGRAMMING TECHNIQUES/TASK

- Program 1: Implement a C program to convert a Hexadecimal, octal, and binary number to decimal number vice versa.

```
/*convert decimal to binary*/ #include <stdio.h>
void decimalToBinary(int n) {
        // Size of binary number can be defined as per the expected
range
        int binary[32];
        int index = 0;
        // Handle the case when n is 0
        if (n == 0) {
                printf("Binary representation: 0\n");
                return;
        }
        while (n > 0) {
                binary[index] = n % 2; // Store the remainder
                n = n / 2; // Divide by 2
                index++;
        }
        printf("Binary representation: ");
        // Print the binary number in reverse order
        for (int i = index – 1; i >= 0; i--) {
                printf("%d", binary[i]);
        }
        printf("\n");
}
int main() {
        int number;
        printf("Enter a decimal number: ");
        scanf("%d", &number);
        decimalToBinary(number);
        return 0;
}
```

```
/*convert decimal to octal number*/

#include<stdio.h> #include<conio.h> void main()

{

        long int num,i,j,octnum=0,dnum; clrscr();

        printf("\nEnter a number: "); scanf("%ld",&num); dnum=num;
```

```
        i=1;
        for(j=num;j>0;j=j/8)
        {
                octnum=octnum+(num%8)*i; i=i*10;
                num=num/8;
        }
        printf("\n The Octal of %ld is %ld",dnum,octnum); getch();
}
```

- **Output:**

Enter a number: 79 The Octal of 79 is 117

```
/* convert number from decimal to hexadecimal*/
#include<stdio.h> #include<conio.h> void main()
{
        long int dnum,rem,q,dn=0,i,j,temp; char ch;
        clrscr();
        printf("\nEnter a decimal number: "); scanf("%ld",&dnum);
        q=dnum; for(i=q;i>0;i=i/16)
        {
                temp=i%16; if(temp<10)
                temp=temp+48;
                else
                temp=temp+55;
                dn=dn*100+temp;
        }
        printf("\nThe equivalent hexadecimal number is: ");
for(j=dn;j>0;j=j/100)
        {
                ch=j%100; printf("%c",ch);
        }
        printf("\n");
        getch();
}
```

- **Output:**

Enter a decimal number: 79

The equivalent hexadecimal number is: 4F

Enter a decimal number: 775

The equivalent hexadecimal number is: 307

```
/*convert binary number to decimal*/
#include<stdio.h> #include<conio.h> #include<math.h> void main()
{
        long int bnum;
        long int decnum=0,i=0,d; clrscr();
        printf("\nEnter the binary number: "); scanf("%ld",&bnum);
while(bnum!=0)
        {
                d=bnum%10;          decnum=decnum+d*pow(2,i);
        bnum=bnum/10;
                i++;
        }
        printf("\nThe equivalent decimal number is: %ld",decnum);
getch();
}
```

- **Output:**

Enter the binary number: 1010100 The equivalent decimal number is: 84

```
/*convert octal number to decimal number*/
#include<stdo.h> #include<conio.h>
#include<math.h> void main()
{
        int num,decnum=0,i=0,rem; clrscr();
        printf("\nEnter an octal number(using the digits 0–7): ");
scanf("%d",&num);
        while(num!=0)
```

```
        {
                rem=num%10;        decnum=decnum+rem*pow(8,i);
        num=num/10;
                i++;
        }
        printf("\nThe equivalent decimal number is: %d",decnum);
getch();
}
```

- **Output:**

Enter an octal number(using the digits 0–7): 745 The equivalent decimal number is: 485

Enter an octal number(using the digits 0–7): 25 The equivalent decimal number is: 21

6.10.1. Binary Addition and Subtraction

- **Aim:** To write C program for sum of two binary numbers.
- Source Code:

```
#include <stdio.h>
#include <conio.h>
#include <math.h>
int c = 0,numa[8]={0},numb[8]={0},diff[8]={0},sum[8]={0};
void add();
void sub();
void main()
{
        int ch,i;
        do
        {
                for(i=0; i<8; i++)
                {
                        numa[i] = 0;
                        numb[i] = 0;
                        diff[i] = 0;
```

```
                sum[i] = 0;
            }
            c = 0;
            printf("\tADDITION-SUBTRACTION           USING
        TWO'S COMPLEMENT");
            printf("\n1.ADD\n2.SUBTRACT\nEnter your choice:
        "); scanf("%d",&ch);
            switch(ch){
                case 1: add();
                break;
                case 2: sub();
                break;
                default: printf("\nInvalid Choice: ");
            }
            printf("\nPress 1 to Continue...");
            scanf("%d",&ch);
        }while(ch == 1);
}
void add(){
        int i;
        printf("\nEnter two 8-bit binary numbers\n");
        printf("\nEnter first number: ");
        for(i = 0; i<8; i++)
            {
                scanf("%d",&numa[i]);
            }
            printf("\nEnter second number: ");
            for(i = 0; i<8; i++){
                scanf("%d",&numb[i]);
            }
            for(i = 7; i >= 0; i--){
                sum[i] = numa[i]+ numb[i] + c; if(sum[i]>=2)
            {
```

```
                    c = 1;
            }
            else
            c = 0;
            sum[i] = sum[i]%2;
        }
        printf("\nSum is: ");
        for(i = 0; i<8; i++){
            printf("%d",sum[i]);
        }
}
void sub()
{
        int i;
        printf("\nEnter two 8-bit binary numbers\n");
        printf("\nEnter first number: ");
        for(i = 0; i<8; i++){
            scanf("%d",&numa[i]);
        }
        printf("\nEnter second number: ");
        for(i = 0; i<8; i++){
            scanf("%d",&numb[i]);
        }
        for(i = 7; i >= 0; i--){
            diff[i] = numa[i] - numb[i];
            if(diff[i] < 0){
                numa[i–1] = numa[i–1] – 1;
            }
            diff[i] = fabs(diff[i]%2);
        }
        printf("\nDifference is: ");
        for(i = 0; i<8; i++){
```

```
                printf("%d",diff[i]);
            }
    }
```

Task 6.3. Implement a C Program to Perform Multiplication of Two Binary Numbers

```
#include <stdio.h>
int binaryproduct(int, int);
int main()
{
    long binary1, binary2, multiply = 0;
    int digit, factor = 1;
    printf("Enter the first binary number: ");
    scanf("%ld", &binary1);
    printf("Enter the second binary number: ");
    scanf("%ld", &binary2);
    while (binary2 != 0)
    {
        digit = binary2 % 10;
        if (digit == 1)
        {
            binary1 = binary1 * factor;
            multiply = binaryproduct(binary1, multiply);
        }
        else
        binary1 = binary1 * factor;
        binary2 = binary2 / 10; factor = 10;
    }
    printf("Product of two binary numbers: %ld", multiply); return 0;
}

int binaryproduct(int binary1, int binary2)
{
```

```
    int i = 0, remainder = 0, sum[20];
    int binaryprod = 0;
    while (binary1 != 0 || binary2 != 0)
    {
            sum[i++] =(binary1 % 10 + binary2 % 10 + remainder) % 2;
            remainder =(binary1 % 10 + binary2 % 10 + remainder) / 2;
            binary1 = binary1 / 10;
            binary2 = binary2 / 10;
    }
    if (remainder != 0)
    sum[i++] = remainder;
    --i;
    while (i >= 0)
    binaryprod = binaryprod * 10 + sum[i--];
    return binaryprod;
}
```

- Task 4: Multiplication of two binary numbers (signed) using Booth's Algorithms.

```
#include <stdio.h>
#include <math.h>
int a = 0,b = 0, c = 0, a1 = 0, b1 = 0, com[5] = { 1, 0, 0, 0, 0};
int anum[5] = {0}, anumcp[5] = {0}, bnum[5] = {0};
int acomp[5] = {0}, bcomp[5] = {0}, pro[5] = {0}, res[5] = {0};
void binary(){
        a1 = fabs(a); b1 = fabs(b);
        int r, r2, i, temp;
        for (i = 0; i < 5; i++){
                r = a1 % 2;
                a1 = a1 / 2;
                r2 = b1 % 2;
                b1 = b1 / 2;
                anum[i] = r;
```

```
                anumcp[i] = r;
                bnum[i] = r2;
                if(r2 == 0){
                        bcomp[i] = 1;
        }
        if(r == 0){
                acomp[i] =1;
        }
    }
//part for two's complementing
c = 0;
for (i = 0; i < 5; i++){
    res[i] = com[i]+ bcomp[i] + c;
    if(res[i] >= 2){
        c = 1;
    }
    else
    c = 0;
    res[i] = res[i] % 2;
}
for (i = 4; i >= 0; i--){
    bcomp[i] = res[i];
}
//in case of negative inputs if (a < 0){
    c = 0;
    for (i = 4; i >= 0; i--){
        res[i] = 0;
    }
    for (i = 0; i < 5; i++){
        res[i] = com[i] + acomp[i] + c;
        if (res[i] >= 2){
            c = 1;
```

```
            }
            else
            c = 0;
            res[i] = res[i]%2;
        }
        for (i = 4; i >= 0; i--){
            anum[i] = res[i];
            anumcp[i] = res[i];
        }
}
if(b < 0){
        for (i = 0; i < 5; i++){
            temp = bnum[i];
            bnum[i] = bcomp[i];
            bcomp[i] = temp;
        }
}
}
void add(int num[]){
        int i;
        c = 0;
        for (i = 0; i < 5; i++){
            res[i] = pro[i] + num[i] + c;
            if (res[i] >= 2){
                c = 1;
            }
            else{
                c = 0;
            }
            res[i] = res[i]%2;
        }
        for (i = 4; i >= 0; i--){
```

```
            pro[i] = res[i]; printf("%d",pro[i]);
      }
      printf(":");
      for (i = 4; i >= 0; i--){
            printf("%d", anumcp[i]);
      }
}
void arshift(){//for arithmetic shift right
      int temp = pro[4], temp2 = pro[0], i;
      for (i = 1; i < 5; i++){//shift the MSB of product
            pro[i–1] = pro[i];
      }
      pro[4] = temp;
      for (i = 1; i < 5; i++){//shift the LSB of product
            anumcp[i–1] = anumcp[i];
      }
      anumcp[4] = temp2;
      printf("\nAR-SHIFT: ");//display together
      for (i = 4; i >= 0; i--){
            printf("%d",pro[i]);
      }
      printf(":");
      for(i = 4; i >= 0; i--){
            printf("%d", anumcp[i]);
      }
}

void main(){
      int i, q = 0;
      printf("\t\tBOOTH'S MULTIPLICATION ALGORITHM");
      printf("\nEnter two numbers to multiply: ");
      printf("\nBoth must be less than 16");
```

```
//simulating for two numbers each below 16
do{
        printf("\nEnter A: "); scanf("%d",&a);
        printf("Enter B: ");
        scanf("%d", &b);
}while(a >=16 || b >=16);
printf("\nExpected product = %d", a * b);
binary();
printf("\n\nBinary Equivalents are: ");
printf("\nA = ");
for (i = 4; i >= 0; i--){
        printf("%d", anum[i]);
}
printf("\nB = ");
for (i = 4; i >= 0; i--){
        printf("%d", bnum[i]);
}
printf("\nB'+ 1 = ");
for (i = 4; i >= 0; i--){
        printf("%d", bcomp[i]);
}
printf("\n\n");
for (i = 0;i < 5; i++){
        if (anum[i] == q){//just shift for 00 or 11
                printf("\n-->");
                arshift();
                q = anum[i];
        }
else if(anum[i] == 1 && q == 0){//subtract and shift for 10
        printf("\n-->");
        printf("\nSUB B: ");
        add(bcomp);//add two's complement to implement subtraction
```

```
            arshift();
            q = anum[i];
      }
      else{//add ans shift for 01
            printf("\n-->");
            printf("\nADD B: ");
            add(bnum);
            arshift();
            q = anum[i];
            }
      }
      printf("\nProduct is = ");
      for (i = 4; i >= 0; i--){
            printf("%d", pro[i]);
      }
      for (i = 4; i >= 0; i--){
            printf("%d", anumcp[i]);
      }
}
```

- **Output:**

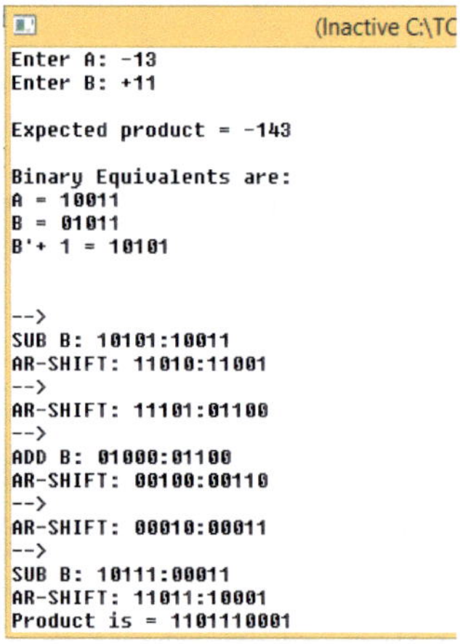

- Task 5: Implement a C Program to Perform Division of Two Binary Numbers (Unsigned) Using Restoring Division Algorithm

```
#include <stdio.h>
#include <conio.h>
#include <math.h>

int a=0,b=0,c=0,com[5]={1,0,0,0,0},s=0;
int anum[5]={0},anumcp[5] ={0},bnum[5]={0};
int acomp[5]={0},bcomp[5]={0},rem[5]={0},quo[5]={0},res[5]={0};

void binary(){
        a = fabs(a);
        b = fabs(b);
        int r, r2, i, temp; for(i = 0; i < 5; i++){
                r = a % 2;
                a = a / 2;
                r2 = b % 2;
        b = b / 2;
        anum[i] = r;
        anumcp[i] = r;
        bnum[i] = r2;
        if(r2 == 0){
                bcomp[i] = 1;
        }
        if(r == 0){
                acomp[i] =1;
        }
}
//part for two's complementing c = 0;
for(i = 0; i < 5; i++){
        res[i] = com[i]+ bcomp[i] + c; if(res[i]>=2){
                c = 1;
        }
```

```
        else
        c = 0;
        res[i] = res[i]%2;
}
for(i = 4; i>= 0; i--){
        bcomp[i] = res[i];
        }
}
void add(int num[]){
        int i;
        c = 0;
        for(i = 0; i < 5; i++){
                res[i] = rem[i]+ num[i] + c;
                if(res[i]>=2){
                        c = 1;
                }
                else
                c = 0;
                res[i] = res[i]%2;
        }
        for(i = 4; i>= 0; i--){
                rem[i] = res[i];
                printf("%d",rem[i]);
        }
        printf(":");
        for(i = 4; i>= 0; i--){
                printf("%d",anumcp[i]);
        }
}
void shl(){//for shift left
        int i;
        for(i = 4; i > 0; i--){//shift the remainder
```

```
            rem[i] = rem[i–1];
        }
        rem[0] = anumcp[4];
        for(i = 4; i > 0; i--){//shift the remtient
            anumcp[i] = anumcp[i–1];
        }
        anumcp[0] = 0;
        printf("\nSHIFT LEFT: ");//display together
        for(i = 4; i>= 0; i--){
            printf("%d",rem[i]);
        }
        printf(":");
            for(i = 4; i>= 0; i--){
                printf("%d",anumcp[i]);
            }
        }

void main(){
        clrscr(); int i;
        printf("\t\tRESTORING DIVISION ALGORITHM");
        printf("\nEnter two numbers to multiply: ");
        printf("\nBoth must be less than 16");
        //simulating for two numbers each below 16
        do{
            printf("\nEnter A: ");
            scanf("%d",&a);
            printf("Enter B: ");
            scanf("%d",&b);
        }while(a>=16 || b>=16);
        printf("\nExpected Quotient = %d", a/b);
        printf("\nExpected Remainder = %d", a%b);
        if(a*b <0){
```

```
            s = 1;
    }
    binary();
    printf("\n\nUnsigned Binary Equivalents are: ");
    printf("\nA = ");
    for(i = 4; i>= 0; i--){
            printf("%d",anum[i]);
    }
    printf("\nB = ");
    for(i = 4; i>= 0; i--){
            printf("%d",bnum[i]);
    }
    printf("\nB'+ 1 = ");
    for(i = 4; i>= 0; i--){
            printf("%d",bcomp[i]);
    }
    printf("\n\n-->");
    //division part shl();
    for(i=0;i<5;i++){
            printf("\n-->"); //start with subtraction
            printf("\nSUB B: ");
            add(bcomp);
            if(rem[4]==1){//simply add for restoring
                    printf("\n-->RESTORE");
                    printf("\nADD B: ");
                    anumcp[0] = 0;
                    add(bnum);
            }
            else{
                    anumcp[0] = 1;
            }
            if(i<4)
```

```
            shl();
        }
        printf("\n");
        printf("\nSign of the result = %d",s);
        printf("\nRemainder is = ");
        for(i = 4; i>= 0; i--){
            printf("%d",rem[i]);
        }
        printf("\nQuotient is = ");
        for(i = 4; i>= 0; i--){
            printf("%d",anumcp[i]);
        }
        getch();
}
```

Task 6. Implement a C Program to Perform Division of Two Binary Numbers (Unsigned) Using Non-Restoring Division Algorithm

```
#include<stdio.h>
void comp();
void nonresdiv();
void shiftleft();
void a_minus_b();
void a_plus_b();
int a[5]={0,0,0,0,0},q[4],b[5],b2c[5];

void comp()
{
        int i=4; do
        {
            b2c[i]=b[i]; i--;
        }while(b[i+1]!−1);
        while(i>=0)
        { b2c[i]=(b[i]+1)%2;
```

```
                i--;
        }
        printf("\n\tB's complement:");
        for(i=0;i< 5;i++)
        printf("%d",b2c[i]);
        printf("\n");
}

void nonresdiv()
{
        shiftleft();
        if(a[0]==0)
        a_minus_b();
        else a_plus_b();
        q[3]=(a[0]+1)%2;
}

void shiftleft()
{
        int i;
        for(i=0;i< 4;i++)
        a[i]=a[i+1];
        a[4]=q[0];
        for(i=0;i< 3;i++)
        q[i]=q[i+1];
}

void a_minus_b()
{
        int i,carry=0,sum=0;
        for(i=4;i>=0;i--)
        {
```

```
            sum=(a[i]+b2c[i]+carry);
            a[i]=sum%2;
            carry=sum/2;
        }
}

void a_plus_b()
{
        int i,carry=0,sum=0;
        for(i=4;i>=0;i--)
        {
            sum=(a[i]+b[i]+carry);
            a[i]=sum%2;
            carry=sum/2;
        }
}

void main()
{
        int i,j,k;
        printf("Enter dividend in binary form\t: ");
        for(i=0;i< 4;i++)
        scanf("%d",&q[i]);
        printf("Enter divisor in binary form\t: ");
        for(i=0;i< 5;i++)
        scanf("%d",&b[i]);
        comp();
        printf("\n\t[A]\t[M]\n");
        for(i=0;i< 4;i++)
        {
            nonresdiv();
            printf("\t");
```

```
        for(j=0;j< 5;j++)
        printf("%d",a[j]);
        printf("\t");
        for(k=0;k< 4;k++)
        printf("%d",q[k]);
        printf("\n");
    } if(a[0]==1)
    a_plus_b();
    printf("\t");
    for(j=0;j< 5;j++)
    printf("%d",a[j]);
    printf("\t");
    for(k=0;k< 4;k++)
    printf("%d",q[k]);
    printf("\n");
    printf("\n\tThe Quotient Is\t: ");
    for(k=0;k< 4;k++)
    printf("%d",q[k]);
    printf("\n\tThe Remainder Is\t: ");
    for(j=0;j< 5;j++)
    printf("%d",a[j]);
    getch();
}
```

INDEX

W